That I May Dwell among Them

*Incarnation and Atonement in
the Tabernacle Narrative*

Gary A. Anderson

WILLIAM B. EERDMANS PUBLISHING COMPANY
GRAND RAPIDS, MICHIGAN

Wm. B. Eerdmans Publishing Co.
4035 Park East Court SE, Grand Rapids, Michigan 49546
www.eerdmans.com

Book design by Leah Luyk

Printed in the United States of America

29 28 27 26 25 24 23   1 2 3 4 5 6 7

ISBN 978-0-8028-8306-3

Library of Congress Cataloging-in-Publication Data

A catalog record for this book is available from the Library of Congress.

Contents

CONTENTS

vi

Preface

Over the course of the past few decades, I have returned to the subject of the Tabernacle Narrative many times in my teaching and writing. Though I have always been thoroughly in love with the material, it is clear to me that most readers are not! It can be a daunting task to introduce students to these texts because most of them find this material to be tedious and difficult to appreciate on literary grounds alone, not to mention theological ones. While one pores over the details of the different fabrics that make up its curtains, or the shapes of the wooden framing pieces and tent pegs, one's attention begins to flag. Many readers think that the closest genre to this set of instructions would be the directions for assemblage that one must consult prior to putting together a piece of furniture purchased at Ikea. So, one concern in writing about these texts is this: What could these mundane and monotonous details have to do with the God who redeemed Israel from painful servitude in Egypt?

One scholarly "solution" to this problem is to propose that the document has grown considerably over time and then attempt to reconstruct what its original, more compact literary form might have looked like. Scholars who engage in this sort of work distinguish between what they would call the original form of the priestly composition (*Grundform* in German, or Pᵍ as it is often represented) and the various supplementary additions (Pˢ) that were tacked on over the course of time. In the hands of an imaginative historical critic, the hundreds of verses that make up the biblical story can be whittled down to a more manageable size, sometimes to just a few dozen. Needless to say, this is far less taxing to read.

The skeptic, however, will wonder whether the biblical scholar can be trusted in this effort to reconstruct a shorter, more original form of the text. For, truth be told, biblical scholars often rely too heavily on their imaginative reconstructions. But in this instance, there is some objective evidence in their favor: the form of these chapters varies considerably in the Greek translation (LXX) of the Bible. Chapters 35–40 of the book of Exodus are so dramatically different from the Hebrew form of the text we now possess (the so-called Masoretic text, or MT) that scholars have rightfully claimed that they represent a different stage in the book's composition.[1] In other words, the evidence of the LXX shows that these materials underwent considerable alteration prior to their final "publication." But it should be added that the Greek version is still a rather long document, and as a result does not furnish support for the radical type of textual surgery practiced by some historical critics. However we reconstruct the process of composition, it is clear that in its final form, attention to detail became one of its defining features, and any competent analysis of the tabernacle narrative must come to terms with it.

An insightful approach to this hermeneutical challenge was suggested to me by Carolyn Walker Bynum's work on the cult of relics in the medieval world. She described the challenge of explaining to her undergraduate students at Columbia University why medieval persons would reverence the clothing, books, and other material objects that a saint had worn or used during the course of his or her lifetime. She illustrated her point through the British movie *Truly, Madly, Deeply*. In this film, a woman suffers the death of her beloved husband, who happened to be a cellist. Soon afterwards a neighbor stops by for a visit and wonders whether she could purchase that cello for her son who is beginning to take lessons. Aghast at the suggestion, the recently widowed woman refuses to part with an object that was so dear to her husband. As the movie progresses, however, it becomes clear that her period of mourning cannot come to a close until she parts with this instrument. It seems that the cello has the power to conjure the presence of her husband even after his passing. At first these ghost-like appearances provide some consolation for her, but in time they begin to become tiresome. Life can only return to normal once she parts with the cello and bids her husband goodbye. As Bynum notes, this curious plot twist—for all of its otherworldly aura—is surprisingly mundane. Anyone who has lost a loved one knows how difficult it is to dispose of their possessions, for these objects retain something of the essence of their original owner. What interested Bynum was the way this film revealed the ability of material objects to convey the presence of the deceased. It is a phenomena I have labeled "ontological leakage," meaning the way the aura of persons overflows their corporal limits and spills onto their personal belongings.

One can observe this principle in even more pedestrian ways. I have always been moved by videos posted on YouTube that show LeBron James or

---

1. My presumption here, shared by nearly all scholars, is that the Greek version goes back to a Hebrew original that varied considerably from our current Hebrew version (MT).

Stefan Curry giving their basketball shoes or jerseys to young, adoring fans. The paroxysms of sheer joy that appear in the faces of those recipients needs no commentary. We're not talking about mere fabric or shoe leather—these items contain something of the person who wore them. Certainly, they will find a place of honor in the homes of the recipients where they'll be prominently displayed, cherished, and revered. But the point to be observed here is that this reverence follows from the intense love these fans have for the player in question. And similarly, I would suggest, for the fabrics that constitute the dwelling of God in the wilderness of Sinai. Because the authors of these texts had such a profound sense that the Maker of heaven and earth had taken up residence in this building, every piece of it was thought to pulse with his presence. Elsewhere in the ancient Near East, the various parts of a temple could be identified as "divine" by the scribes who described them. So thoroughly was this divine power "absorbed" that even these minor architectural features could become the subject of sacrifice and veneration. Biblical writers had another strategy for illustrating such ontological leakage: their fulsome and detailed description of every article of the tabernacle that came into close contact with the divine. Without this profound sense of the deity residing in this building, all those technical details lose their compelling force. Just as the attention lavished on a pair of basketball shoes points to the "real presence" of the one who wore them, so for the attention paid to the furniture of the tabernacle. The detailed descriptions of these items are an index of the sense of presence they possessed in the mind of the author. And so, dear reader, if you wish to relish the narrative that I will offer in this book you must respect the peculiar form of piety that attended its composition. Perhaps a brief turn to YouTube will help clarify the enjoyment the ancient Israelites derived from the architectural detail of the tabernacle!

My second concern pertains to the relationship between the two Testaments of the Christian Bible. As this book moved toward publication, I had some hesitation about the subtitle because I feared it might send the wrong message about my approach. For many Christian readers, the way in which the Tabernacle Narrative is "salvaged" as a readable text is to approach it from the opposite direction. That is, one begins with images of the atonement and incarnation that have been gleaned from the New Testament and then attaches them—often very artificially—to their putative Old Testament antecedents. My approach, however, will come at the question from the reverse direction: Given that the Tabernacle Narrative is focused on how God dwelt among his people Israel and allowed them to serve him at the sacrificial altar, how might the witness of the Old Testament (which could be glossed "Elder Testament"[2] to eliminate any sense that "Old" means "out of date") *on its own terms* inform the way we understand the life of Jesus Christ? In other words, can the Old Testament teach us something more about the identity of Jesus Christ, or does it simply provide us with a set of pegs to which we can attach what we have already learned from the New?

As I will explain at greater length in the final two chapters of this book, my approach is very similar to that of the great biblical scholar from Yale Divinity School, Brevard Childs (1923–2007). For Childs, the Christian Bible is thoroughly dialectical in character: to understand fully who Jesus was and is, we need to correlate how he is understood in both Testaments.

Let us pause for a second on the word *dialectical*. In Christian theology, it is axiomatic that the full and final meaning of the Old Testament is revealed in the New. For some readers, the Old Testament's relationship to the New can be subsumed under the rubric of prophecy and fulfillment. This is nicely illustrated in the Gospel of Matthew, a writer who is quite fond of providing his readers with texts from the Old Testament that point to specific events in the life of Jesus of Nazareth. On this view, Jesus uniquely fulfilled what Israel's prophets had predicted. But there is more to the role of the Old Testament than this particular textual strategy would imply.

Let us consider, for example, the Christian claim that God's nature is fundamentally trinitarian in character. In a brilliant essay, the New Testament scholar C. Kavin Rowe argues that though the New Testament makes a claim for the divinity of Christ and the Holy Spirit, it never articulates in a formal, ontological manner how these various divine figures can constitute one God.[3] The development of a mature expression of God's trinitarian character would unfold over the next several centuries. For some, the turn to ontological concepts ("one-in-being" or "consubstantial" with the Father) to define the Son's divine nature is as artificial as it is unbiblical. But the impetus to frame the

---

2. This locution comes from Christopher Seitz's book *The Elder Testament: Canon, Theology, Trinity* (Waco, TX: Baylor University Press, 2018).

3. C. Kavin Rowe, "Biblical Pressure and Trinitarian Hermeneutics," *Pro Ecclesia* 9 (2002): 295–312. Especially pertinent are these words from his concluding paragraph: "To interpret the Bible in light of the doctrine of the Trinity does not, therefore, distort its basic content but penetrates to its core with respect to the reality of the divine identity, the living God outside of the text known truly by Israel and fully in Jesus Christ. Such interpretative liberty does not entail a dismissal of the original sense of the text but instead seeks to illuminate the full breadth of ontological reality about which the biblical text, Old and New Testament together, speaks in its entirety."

character of God in ontological terms, Rowe contends, derives from the Old Testament's indisputable assertion that there is only one God. It is the "pressure" exerted by this strong claim that compelled the church to ponder more deeply the nature of the divine sonship of Jesus Christ.

In the case of my book, the act of listening carefully to what the Old Testament has to say about the tabernacle, priesthood, and sacrifice will help the Christian theologian to dive deeper into what Scripture has to say about their Christian correlates. The unstated assumption in this hermeneutical approach is the continuity of God's character. To be sure there is a momentous shift when we move from a tent and altar that Moses set up in the desert beside Mount Sinai to the person of Jesus Christ. But the theological reader will not be satisfied with simply articulating the difference. His or her work will not be complete until the witness of the Old Testament has been allowed to broaden and deepen what the New has disclosed. As Pope Benedict XVI wrote in one of his last essays, the challenge the church has faced in articulating the character of its priestly offices has been due to the loss of an ability to read the Old Testament on precisely these questions![4] A reading of Jesus's life and work will not be complete without taking a full conspectus of what God has revealed across the entirety of his sacred word.[5]

---

4. Benedict XVI and Robert Cardinal Sarah, *From the Depths of Our Hearts: Priesthood, Celibacy, and the Crisis of the Catholic Church* (San Francisco: Ignatius, 2019), 25–60.

5. I should mention three books that I have not utilized in the writing of this book: Matthias Ederer, *Identitätsstiftende Begegnung*, FAT 121 (Tübingen: Mohr Siebeck, 2018); Liane Feldman, *The Story of Sacrifice: Ritual and Narrative in the Priestly Source*, FAT 141 (Tübingen: Mohr Siebeck, 2020); and Meike J. Röhrig, *Innerbiblische Auslegung und priesterliche Fortschreibungen in Lev 8–10*, FAT II/128 (Tübingen: Mohr Siebeck, 2021). The books of Feldman and Röhrig were published after I had completed my manuscript. The book by Ederer I simply overlooked.

Acknowledgments

This book has been in the works for a long time. I have worked on the subject of the Tabernacle Narrative, off and on, over the course of my whole career, though truth be told, most of the concentrated work has been done over the past decade. Hence it would be impossible for me to list all the institutions and individuals who have aided and supported me along the way.

But I must mention a few. First, I'd like to thank my dear friend and colleague Markus Bockmuehl of Oxford University for his gracious act of serving as my host when I delivered the Speaker's Lectures at Oxford in 2014. Second, I should mention Menahem Kister of Hebrew University and Esti Eshel of Bar-Ilan University, who organized a yearlong seminar at the Israel Institute for Advanced Studies on the Givat Ram campus of the Hebrew University of Jerusalem in 2016–2017. It was an extraordinary experience to be a part of that small group of outstanding scholars and to have the opportunity to present my work at the leading universities in Israel. My time in Jerusalem was generously funded by the European Institutes for Advanced Studies Fellowship Programme (EURIAS).

Numerous scholars have read portions of my manuscript and given me invaluable feedback. These include Edward Greenstein, Jon Levenson, Shimon Gesundheit, Nathan MacDonald, and Benjamin Sommer. I should also thank my doctoral student Kacie Klamm as well as Claude Hanley for reading the entire manuscript in its penultimate form. Finally, I owe a word of thanks to James Ernest of Eerdmans Publishing for reading through the manuscript and helping me reshape chapter 1 in a way that would be more felicitous for the potential reader. Needless to say, the comments of all these persons have aided me immeasurably in crafting the final form of this book.

Because I have been at this project for some time, elements of this book have already appeared in a wide variety of publications. If you read through all my articles that I have listed in the bibliography, you will be able to spot a number of ideas that appear in fuller and more mature form in this book. But three previous publications were drawn on extensively, and I gratefully acknowledge permission to reuse this material. For chapter 1, I drew on "Literary Artistry and Divine Presence," in *Contextualizing Jewish Temples*, edited by Tova Ganzel and Shalom Holtz (Boston: Brill, 2020), 85–102; for chapter 6: "'Through Those Who Are Near to Me, I Will Show Myself Holy': Nadab and Abihu and Apophatic Theology," *Catholic Biblical Quarterly* 77 (2015): 1–19; and for chapter 9: "Mary in the Old Testament," *Pro Ecclesia* 16 (2007): 33–55.

All quotations from the Bible are taken from the NRSV unless otherwise noted.

Abbreviations

Ancient Sources

ALD	Aramaic Levi Document
Athanasius, *Ep.*	Athanasius, *Letters*
4 Bar.	4 Baruch
Josephus, *Ant.*	Josephus, *Jewish Antiquities*
Jub.	Jubilees
LAB	Biblical Antiquities (Pseudo-Philo)
Lev. Rab.	Leviticus Rabbah
LXX	Septuagint
Pesiq. Rab.	Pesiqta Rabbati
Prot. Jas.	Protevangelium of James
Shabb.	Shabbat
Sir.	Ben Sira

Secondary Sources

AB	Anchor Bible
AJSR	*Association for Jewish Studies Review*
BEATAJ	Beiträge zur Erforschung des Alten Testaments und des antiken Judentum
BKAT	Biblischer Kommentar, Altes Testament
BRLA	Brill Reference Library of Judaism
BZAW	Beihefte zur Zeitschrift für die alttestamentliche Wissenschaft
CAT	Commentaire de l'Ancien Testament

CBQ	*Catholic Biblical Quarterly*
CBR	*Currents in Biblical Research*
FAT	Forschungen zum Alten Testament
HAT	Handbuch zum Alten Testament
HBS	Herders biblische Studien
HCOT	Historical Commentary on the Old Testament
HThKAT	Herders Theologischer Kommentar zum Alten Testament
JAOS	*Journal of the American Oriental Society*
JBL	*Journal of Biblical Literature*
JNSL	*Journal of Northwest Semitic Languages*
JSJ	*Journal for the Study of Judaism*
JSNTSup	Journal for the Study of the New Testament Supplement Series
JSOT	*Journal for the Study of the Old Testament*
JSOTSup	Journal for the Study of the Old Testament Supplement Series
JSQ	*Jewish Studies Quarterly*
NCBC	New Century Bible Commentary
NEA	*Near Eastern Archaeology*
NICOT	New International Commentary on the Old Testament
NovT	*Novum Testamentum*
NPNF²	*The Nicene and Post-Nicene Fathers*. Series 2. Edited by Philip Schaff. 1886–1889. 14 vols. Repr., Peabody, MA: Hendrickson, 1994
OTL	Old Testament Library
OTP	*Old Testament Pseudepigrapha*. Edited by James H. Charlesworth. 2 vols. New York: Doubleday, 1983, 1985
RHR	*Revue de l'histôire des religions*
SC	Sources chrétiennes. Paris: Cerf, 1943–
STDJ	Studies on the Texts of the Desert of Judah
SVTP	Studia in Veteris Testamenti Pseudepigraphica
VT	*Vetus Testamentum*
VTSup	Vetus Testamentum Supplement
ZAW	*Zeitschrift für die alttestamentliche Wissenschaft*

CHAPTER 1

The Place of the Tabernacle Narrative in the Christian Bible

At the heart of the problem of Biblical Theology lies the issue of doing full justice to the subtle canonical relationship of the two testaments within the one Christian Bible. On the one hand, the Christian canon asserts the continuing integrity of the OT witness. . . . On the other hand, the NT makes its own witness. It tells its own story of the new redemptive intervention of God in Jesus Christ. The NT is not just an extension of the Old, nor a last chapter in an epic tale. Something totally new has entered in the gospel. . . . As a result, a major task of Biblical Theology is to reflect on the whole Christian Bible with its two very different voices, both of which the church confesses bear witness to Jesus Christ.

Brevard Childs[1]

Why study the Tabernacle Narrative? Next to the genealogies, it is regarded by most readers as the most tedious portion of the entire Bible. Yet embedded within this story are two supremely important theological ideas—God's decision to dwell among the people Israel and be served by them at his altar. Both of these ideas are central to Israelite religion, but they also inform the core doctrines of the early church. In fact, one of the surprising features of my own research has been how productive these chapters were in shaping how Christians have thought about the incarnation and the atonement.

The Prologue to John's Gospel

Perhaps the best evidence for the influence of the Tabernacle Narrative on the idea of the incarnation is found in the Prologue to John's Gospel: "And

---

1. Brevard Childs, *Biblical Theology of the Old and New Testaments: Theological Reflection on the Christian Bible* (Minneapolis: Fortress, 1992), 78.

the Word became flesh and lived among us, and we have seen his glory, the glory as of a father's only son, full of grace and truth" (1:14).[2] The expression "to live among us" comes from the Greek verb *skēnoō*, which literally means "to pitch a tent." As Raymond Brown, author of perhaps the most important modern commentary on the Gospel of John, observes:

> The theme of "tenting" is found in Exod 25:8-9 where Israel is told to make a tent (the Tabernacle—*skēnē*) so that God can dwell among His people; the Tabernacle became the site of God's localized presence on earth. . . . When the Prologue proclaims that the Word made his dwelling among men, we are being told that the flesh of Jesus Christ is the new localization of God's presence on earth, and that Jesus is the replacement of the ancient Tabernacle.[3]

But it is not just the act of indwelling that links the prologue to the Tabernacle Narrative. The Gospel adds that its purpose is to make the glory of God visible ("the Word became flesh . . . and we have seen his glory"). This notion of visibility is derived from the appearance (or "theophany") of the God of Israel at the close of Exodus when the construction of the tabernacle was finished.

> Then the cloud covered the tent of meeting, and the glory of the Lord filled the tabernacle. Moses was not able to enter the tent of meeting because the cloud settled upon it, and the glory of the Lord filled the tabernacle. (Exod. 40:34-35)

The importance of the glory becoming visible is emphasized at several other key moments in the history of Israel. The dedication of the temple by King Solomon is accompanied by a visible display of divine glory (1 Kings 8:10-11). And just prior to the Babylonian invasion of Jerusalem and destruction of the temple, that same glory exits the city (Ezek. 11:23). Afterward, when Ezekiel sees the vision of a new Jerusalem, the account of its construction concludes with the glory of God entering the complex and filling the temple (44:4). "Thus, it is quite appropriate," Brown concludes, "that, after the description of how the Word set up a Tabernacle among men in the flesh of Jesus, the Prologue should mention that his *glory* became visible."[4]

---

2. All translations from the Bible are from the NRSV unless otherwise noted.

3. Raymond Brown, *The Gospel according to John I–XII*, AB 29 (Garden City, NY: Doubleday, 1966), 32.

4. Brown, *John I–XII*, 34.

The New Testament in Light of the Old

In making these observations about the influence of the Tabernacle Narrative on the Gospel of John, I am repeating what numerous New Testament scholars have already written. Biblical scholarship, like much of modern literary inquiry, is deeply influenced by the historical method. No writer works in a vacuum; all literary products have been influenced by earlier documents. It is the task of critical scholarship to trace the literary sources at a writer's disposal. A theological reading of the biblical text cannot bypass questions of historical formation. But neither can it be wholly defined by them. The danger here is the tendency of the reader to presume that once a historical source for a writer has been identified, the role played by that source has been exhausted. The way those ideas are employed by the subsequent writer becomes the focus of attention.

Let me illustrate by way of a metaphor. Reading a text according to the process of its historical development is a bit like a relay race. With each leg of the race, a runner hands the baton off to the next person in the sequence. Once a runner has completed her task, her role is finished. All attention is focused on the person who currently holds the baton. We could describe the relationship between the Tabernacle Narrative and John, as many modern persons read them, in a similar fashion. Once an interpreter has identified the Old Testament background to the Prologue, the formative role of that Old Testament material comes to its conclusion. One's focus turns to the ways in which the Gospel writer develops what he has inherited. As we move forward to the christological debates of the third and fourth centuries, if the baton analogy holds true, the role played by the Old Testament would disappear from view.

Strikingly, however, this is not what happens in the history of Christian interpretation. The voice of the Tabernacle Narrative does not lessen in volume. Quite the contrary, it continues to sound its notes throughout the patristic and medieval periods. Its own unique voice—not just its refraction in John 1:14!—continues to be registered and applied to the problem of understanding the character of the incarnation. Because the Old Testament has an integrity of its own, one can probe its distinctive witness to the incarnation in a deeper and deeper fashion. To appreciate this sort of exegetical work, we need to take a short detour and consider how the two Testaments function in Christian theology.

No biblical scholar over the past generation has given more thoughtful consideration to the relationship between the Old and New Testaments than has Brevard Childs. The shape of the Christian scriptures, he has argued, requires a dialectical approach to do justice to its form. On the one hand,

3

no matter how deep our sympathies for the Jewish scriptures go, we have to concede that "the New Testament is not just an extension of the Old, nor a last chapter in an epic tale. . . . Something totally new began with the resurrection, and this sharp discontinuity in Israel's tradition is rightly reflected in the formation of two separate and distinct testaments. The old came to an end; the new began."[5] Raymond Brown nicely illustrates this side of the equation when he notes that after the Babylonian exile several prophets appeared who proclaimed that a new temple would be built that would assume many of the tasks laid out for the tabernacle in the book of Exodus. Prayers for the building of that temple remain a staple of traditional Jewish prayer life. The incarnation, however, mandates that the Christian take a very different stance toward these prophecies. As John's Gospel makes clear, Jesus becomes the new localization of God's presence on earth. Or, as Brown summarizes the matter, "Jesus is the replacement of the ancient Tabernacle."[6] Nothing in the Old Testament would have prepared us for this remarkable turn of events in salvation history (see fig. 1.1). In one sense, the old has come to an end and the new has begun.

But one would make a terrible error if one elevated this last sentence to the position of a governing principle for the entire Christian Bible. Such a conclusion, Childs argues, would be

highly misleading and one-sided in the extreme. Although it is obviously true that the Old Testament was interpreted in the light of the gospel, it is equally important to recognize that the New Testament tradition was fundamentally shaped from the side of the Old. The Old Testament was not simply a collage of texts to be manipulated, but the Jewish scriptures were held as the authoritative voice of God, exerting a major coercion on the early church's understanding of Jesus' mission. In fact, the Jewish scriptures were the church's only scripture well into the second century. As H. von Campenhausen has forcefully stated, the problem of the early church was not what to do with the Old Testament in the light of the gospel, which was Luther's concern, but rather the reverse. In the light of the Jewish scriptures which were acknowledged to be the true oracles of God, how were Christians to understand the good news of Jesus Christ?[7]

5. Childs, *Biblical Theology*, 78.

6. Brown, *John I–XII*, 34.

7. Childs, *Biblical Theology*, 225–26. Childs here cites von Campenhausen, *The Formation of the Christian Bible*, trans. John Austin Baker (London: A&C Black, 1972), 69–70.

Figure 1.1 Portrayal of Ezekiel on the Sistine Chapel, by Michelangelo, ca. 1512; photo © Governorate of the Vatican City State—Directorate of the Vatican Museums

Note that the angel to the left of the prophet Ezekiel points upward. Above the prophet is the image of Eve being born from the rib of a recumbent Adam. In traditional Christian exegesis this was a figure for the birth of the church from the side of Christ on the cross.

Ezekiel is one of Israel's prophets who predicted the coming of a glorious second temple. In traditional Christian exegesis, influenced by John 1:14, Ezekiel's prophecy was redirected—its fulfillment was not the pristine and holy temple he expected but the church born from the rib of the Second Adam.

Michelangelo is aware that this redirection of the vision would have shocked Ezekiel. This is registered by having Ezekiel turn sharply to his right (note that his shawl is still hanging in the air from this movement) and appear astonished. This nicely illustrates Childs's contention that the incarnation of God in the flesh of Christ was in "sharp discontinuity [with] Israel's tradition." The old had come to an end; something new and unexpected had arrived.

Let's begin by slightly reformulating the last sentence of Childs—in light of the account of the tabernacle (and temple to be), how are we to understand the person of Jesus Christ? For those who approach this from a purely historical vantage point, the imagery of the relay race returns. During the exchange of our first two runners, the concept of a tabernacle was passed on to John who applies it to the figure of Jesus. But once John hands the baton to the early church, the significance of the Tabernacle Narrative as a source of "hard data" about the incarnation begins to wane. For these theologians, one might reason, the exegesis of the Old Testament gives way to a different task: that of relating the concept of the *Logos* (Word) to Greek philosophical categories such as *ousia* (being), *prosōpon* (person), and *hypostasis* (substance). In this strictly developmental account, the Old Testament no longer played a formative role in guiding Christian theology. "[It] functioned as normative scripture for Christians only in so far as it was read from the perspective of the message of Jesus. The Old Testament provided a depository of imagery which could be freely construed to function as a prophetic warrant for the Christ event."[8] But such an assessment does not accord with how the Old Testament was used by the earliest Christian theologians.

How the Old Testament Continues to Shape
Our Understanding of the New

One excellent example of this can be seen in the role played by the temple in Athanasius's letter to Adelphius. Athanasius lived in Alexandria, Egypt during the fourth century and was one of the chief figures in the christological debates leading up to the council of Nicea in 325. The creed that emerged from that council was a strenuous critique of the Arian heresy, which questioned the full divinity of Christ. One of Athanasius's arguments against the supporters of Arius was that insofar as they worshipped Jesus Christ but continued to assert that the Word is a creature, they were committing idolatry for they were offering worship to a creature. The Arians countered, however, by claiming that their worship was rendered to the Father alone. Even though "we reverence [*veneramur*] the Son," they explained, "we are certain that his glory ascends to the Father."[9] But the Arians did not stop here. They made the counter-accusation that Athanasius and his circle worshipped a creature since they

---

8. Childs, *Biblical Theology*, 225.
9. Khaled Anatolios, *Athanasius* (New York: Routledge, 2004), 235.

did not "qualify their worship of Christ even while acknowledging that the humanity [or flesh] of Christ was created."

For Athanasius, this accusation was a sacrilege. "We do not worship a creature. Never!" he replied. Though Athanasius does concede that the human flesh, when taken on its own, is a part of creation, nevertheless when it is assumed by the Son, it becomes part of the body of God. But proving this solely on the basis of John 1:14 was difficult. Sensing this problem, Athanasius directs his readers back to the Old Testament paradigm from which John 1:14 arose:

> Moreover, we would like your Reverence to pose to them the following question: When Israel was commanded to go up to Jerusalem to worship in the temple of the Lord, where there was the ark and above it the cherubim of glory overshadowing the mercy-seat, was this a good deed or a bad one? If they were doing a bad deed, why is it that those who did not heed this law were consigned to punishment? For it is written that the one who disregards it and does not go up is to be cut off from among the people. But if they were doing a good deed, through which in fact they were pleasing to God, must not these defiled Arians, whose heresy is the most shameful of all, be utterly deserving of destruction? For in that case, they commend the ancient people for the honor rendered by them to the temple but do not wish to worship the Lord who is in his flesh, as in a temple. And yet the old temple was fashioned from rocks and gold and was merely a shadow, but when the reality arrived the image was henceforth annulled, according to the words of the Lord, and there did not remain a stone upon another stone, that was not thrown down.
>
> Although they saw that the temple was made of stones, the [ancient people] did not think that the Lord speaking in the temple was a creature, nor did they scorn the temple and go far off from it to worship. But, in accordance with the law, they went into the temple and served the Lord who spoke from the temple. This being so, how can one not worship the all-holy and all-sacred body of the Lord, which was announced by the angel Gabriel and fashioned by the Holy Spirit and became a garment for the Word? . . . Therefore, the one who dishonors the temple dishonors the Lord who is in the temple and the one who separates the Word from the body rejects the grace that was granted to us in the Word. (Athanasius, *Letter 40: To Adelphius Bishop and Confessor, Against the Arians* 7–8)[10]

---

10. Anatolios, *Athanasius*, 240–41. There is no critical edition of the text; for the Greek see Migne's Patrologia Graeca 1080D–1081C.

The striking feature of Athanasius's argument is the close alignment between the identity of God and the building that he inhabits. Athanasius realizes that Israel is required by divine law to go to the temple to worship their God. Though they knew God was not limited to that building, at the same time they did not use that limitation as license for not going up to Jerusalem. Worshipping God entailed going to that holy city and prostrating oneself before the temple. Just as the Israelites of old had complete justification in venerating a building of stone and not "dividing" their God from the house in which he dwelt, so Christians have complete justification in prostrating themselves before Jesus and not dividing God from the flesh that contains him.

I believe that the arguments used in this passage provide an excellent illustration of what Childs means when he asserts that the Old Testament is not simply a collage of texts to be manipulated in whatever direction an interpreter might see fit, as if the authority of the New Testament was so all-encompassing that the only purpose of the Old was to be a one-dimensional "arrow" pointing toward it. Or, to revert to our image of the relay race, the role of the Old Testament was exhausted once the New Testament authors had grabbed the baton. Von Campenhausen's formulation of the issue offers far more clarity: Christians turned to the Old Testament to learn things about the divine Son that the New Testament passed over too quickly. When God descends into the tabernacle, we learn something essential about the relationship of God to the material world he created (see fig. 1.2).

The high valuation put on the Tabernacle Narrative comes from the perception that, in coming to dwell in the tabernacle, Scripture tells us something eternally true about the relationship of God to the material world. This includes (1) what happens to the building itself when God chose to inhabit it, (2) the protocol subsequently established that will allow ordinary persons to draw near to God (for the inherent challenge involved, consider the rhetorical question from the psalmist, "Who shall ascend the hill of the Lord? And who shall stand in his holy place?"), and (3) the type of sacrificial service that will accord due honor to the God who has so graciously made himself available to humanity. In the chapters that follow we will explore how these questions are addressed in the Old Testament before turning, at the end of our volume, to the way they were subsequently applied to the incarnation and sacrifice of Christ.

Structure of This Book

In the first three chapters of this book, I will consider how the stories of the founding of the tabernacle reveal crucial information about its theological

Figure 1.2 *Madonna del Parto*, by Piero della Francesco, ca. 1460; photo courtesy of the Municipality of Monterchi

This is an image of the Holy of Holies within the tabernacle. The two angelic cherubim who sat upon the ark of the covenant—marking the place where the God of Israel had "tabernacled"—are pulling apart the inner veil to mark an epiphany of the God who resided within. But instead of seeing the ark, the viewer contemplates Mary, the Mother of God, who discreetly splits the front of her dress to reveal her womb, which holds the Son of God. It is similar to a set of Russian dolls: God is nested within the womb of the woman nested within the tabernacle.

The declarations of the Councils of Nicea and Chalcedon that the flesh of Jesus participated in his divinity deepened the church's understanding of Mary as a receptacle for God. She assumes an identity that owes more to the Old Testament than the New. This nicely illustrates Childs's contention that the Old Testament "exerted a major coercion" on how the church understood the mystery of the incarnation. The way in which Israel honored the building that "contained the uncontainable" was extended in the new dispensation to the Mother who sheltered the Second Person of the Trinity.

meaning. In the first chapter we will consider the problem of chronology. According to the order of events as presented in Exodus and Leviticus, the tabernacle is completed on the first of Nisan and then, on the eighth day, the altar is dedicated and put into operation. Both events are marked by impressive appearances of Israel's God.

Rabbinic readers understood these two theophanies as a single historical event. In other words, the theophany reported at the end of Exodus 40 flashes forward to that of Leviticus 9. On closer inspection, it is clear why the rabbis have read the narrative in this fashion. The Exodus story of the tabernacle's founding is written in such a way as to fold the dedication of the altar into the rite of erecting the tabernacle.

The question then becomes why has the narrative been written in this cumbersome fashion? William Propp offers one good suggestion. Because the onset of the cult points back to the creation of the universe, the nonlinear character of time at creation reappears here as well. Beginning in Exodus 25 the restless advance of chronological time slows to a halt and even, in some places, flows backward. Sacred time is, as Mircea Eliade has argued, "indefinitely recoverable, indefinitely repeatable. From one point of view, it could be said that [sacred time] does not 'pass,' that it does not constitute an irreversible direction."[11]

But that is not the only way to explain the problem. We should also attend to the principles that guide the presentation of the material. The presentation of the tabernacle across Exodus, Leviticus, and Numbers is ordered just as much by theme as it is chronology. Exodus is devoted to the structure of the tabernacle, Leviticus 1–10 to the service of the altar, and Numbers 1–10 to the role played by the tabernacle in guiding the Israelites to the land of Canaan. Sometimes events that occurred in a single moment are separated from one another to fit into their proper thematic section. This is made explicit in Numbers 7 when our writer introduces the story of the tribal chieftains' gifts of wagons and draught animals to transport the tabernacle. Though the unit belongs in the "guidance" section of our narrative (thus its placement in the book of Numbers), the gifts themselves were given on the day the tabernacle was erected (Num. 7:1). Had chronological time been the strict principle of organization, this narrative should have been located at the close of the book of Exodus.

In my second and third chapters I will explore the theological significance of the structure of the tabernacle and the function of its altar. The latter prob-

---

11. Mircea Eliade, *The Sacred and the Profane: The Nature of Religion*, trans. Willard R. Trask (New York: Harcourt, 1959), 69.

ably needs little explanation—most readers will readily concede the centrality of the priesthood and sacrifice to biblical religion. (Though a big challenge for Christian readers is that sacrifice in the Tabernacle Narrative is not principally ordered toward atonement. We will address this challenge in the last chapter of our book.) The building, however, provides a challenge. What is the theological significance to hundreds of verses describing over and over again each piece of the tabernacle? I will argue that the presence of God within the building did not leave its physical structure unchanged. Rather, something of God's being was thought to adhere to the building such that reverence toward its structure was thought to be an act of worship directed toward the God who dwelt there. For some, this proposal will seem like a commendation of idolatry, the worst possible theological error. But such a worry misses one of the most profound themes of these chapters.

The chief theme of chapters 4 and 5 will be what I call the doctrine of "immediate" sin (as opposed to "original" sin). As scholars have noted, ancient Near Eastern accounts of temple-founding invariably describe the event in euphoric and near utopian terms. The erection or refurbishment of a shrine is understood to be a crucial action in securing the blessing of the gods upon human affairs. Because this act of devotion always redounds to the favor of the king, all these narratives take a special interest in foregrounding his meticulous care in preparing for and attending to all the details of the shrine. The Tabernacle Narrative constitutes an enormous variation on this pattern for at the climax of the story we do not find a beatific experience but gross priestly errors (Lev. 10) that will require spiritual repair (Lev. 16). In these chapters, I will lay out the nature of those errors and, at least for Leviticus 10, why it is so difficult to explain their cause.

Up to this point, following scholarly convention my book treats the writings of the Priestly source in isolation (Exod. 25–31; 35–40, Lev. 1–10). But those editors who were responsible for assembling the Bible in its final form dropped the story of the golden calf in the middle of the tabernacle account. In chapters six and seven I will consider the significance of this editorial decision. Chapter 6 will examine the verses that were inserted in order to provide a linkage between the Priestly and non-Priestly accounts, thereby providing the reader with some general pointers as to how to read the narrative as a whole. Chapter 7 will go one step further and explore the linkages that are established between the story of the calf and the sacrifice of Isaac. This will, in turn, prompt a return to the subject of sacrifice (chapter 3) and suggest new ways of understanding the place of the sacrificial cult in biblical theology.

The last two chapters will venture into the New Testament and consider how the Tabernacle Narrative might function in the Christian scriptures. They will operate on the principle that Jesus's life must be understood in a way consistent with the Old Testament (in the words of the creed: "in accordance with the scriptures"). Chapter 8 will return to the role of John 1:14, which states that "the Word became flesh and dwelt among us." I will examine how this text functioned in early christological debates and in the church's exploration of the figure of Mary, the Mother of God. The last chapter will take the logical next step and ask how the sacrificial material we have examined with respect to the tabernacle can be employed to understand the passion of the Christ. As I noted briefly above, sacrifice in the Old Testament does not focus on atonement. In this last chapter I will show—somewhat improbably(!)—how this datum will deepen rather than problematize our reading of the passion.

The Literary Character of the Tabernacle Narrative

When I introduce students to this portion of the Bible, one of the biggest challenges is getting them to see the *literary* character of the material. Like genealogies, most readers presume that the long architectural descriptions serve a purely utilitarian purpose: how to build and assemble the tabernacle. These texts would seem to have more in common with a set of assemblage instructions included in an Ikea package than any form of high literature. But one thing we will discover over the course of this book is how inaccurate such a characterization is.

Let me illustrate by way of an example. Exodus 26 presents us with a description of the fabrics that will make up the tabernacle. Exodus 27 presents us with the fabrics that will line the outer barrier of the courtyard, blocking access to all but those deemed fitting to enter this holy site. The sacredness of the former is marked by both the quality of the material that is employed for its construction as well as the higher register of the literary description. I have divided the text into three rubrics following the presentation of chapter 26: a description of the inner curtains (perhaps better understood as wall tapestries), the wooden framework that those curtains will rest upon, and the curtains or "veils" that will constitute the entrances to holy and holy of holies rooms.

Exodus 26:1–14 | Curtains of Tabernacle
[1] Moreover you shall *make* the tabernacle with ten CURTAINS of fine twined linen and blue and purple and scarlet stuff; with cherubim skil-

fully worked shall you *make* them. ² The length of each CURTAIN shall be twenty-eight cubits, and the breadth of each CURTAIN four cubits; all the CURTAINS shall have one measure. ³ Five CURTAINS shall be coupled to one another; and the other five CURTAINS shall be coupled to one another. ⁴ And you shall *make* loops of blue on the edge of the outmost CURTAIN in the first set; and likewise you shall *make* loops on the edge of the outmost CURTAIN in the second set. ⁵ Fifty loops you shall *make* on the one CURTAIN, and fifty loops you shall *make* on the edge of the CURTAIN that is in the second set; the loops shall be opposite one another. ⁶ And you shall *make* fifty clasps of gold, and couple the CURTAINS one to the other with the clasps, that the tabernacle may be one whole.

⁷ You shall also *make* CURTAINS of goats' hair for a tent over the tabernacle; eleven CURTAINS shall you *make*. ⁸ The length of each CURTAIN shall be thirty cubits, and the breadth of each CURTAIN four cubits; the eleven CURTAINS shall have the same measure. ⁹ And you shall couple five CURTAINS by themselves, and six CURTAINS by themselves, and the sixth CURTAIN you shall double over at the front of the tent. ¹⁰ And you shall *make* fifty loops on the edge of the CURTAIN that is outmost in one set, and fifty loops on the edge of the CURTAIN which is outmost in the second set. ¹¹ And you shall *make* fifty clasps of bronze, and put the clasps into the loops, and couple the tent together that it may be one whole. ¹² And the part that remains of the CURTAINS of the tent, the half CURTAIN that remains, shall hang over the back of the tabernacle. ¹³ And the cubit on the one side, and the cubit on the other side, of what remains in the length of the CURTAINS of the tent shall hang over the sides of the tabernacle, on this side and that side, to cover it. ¹⁴ And you shall *make* for the tent a covering of tanned rams' skins and goatskins.

26:15–30 | Wooden Framework
(I will not include the text here)

26:31–37 | Entrances to the Tabernacle
³¹ You shall make a curtain [*parokhet*] of blue, purple, and crimson yarns, and of fine twisted linen; it shall be made with cherubim skillfully worked into it. ³² You shall hang it on four pillars of acacia overlaid with gold, which have hooks of gold and rest on four bases of silver. ³³ You shall hang the curtain [*parokhet*] under the clasps, and bring the ark of the covenant in there, within the curtain; and the curtain shall separate for you the holy place from the most holy. ³⁴ You shall put the mercy seat on the ark of

the covenant in the most holy place. [35] You shall set the table outside the curtain, and the lampstand on the south side of the tabernacle opposite the table; and you shall put the table on the north side.

[36] You shall make a screen for the entrance of the tent, of blue, purple, and crimson yarns, and of fine twisted linen, embroidered with needlework. [37] You shall make for the screen five pillars of acacia, and overlay them with gold; their hooks shall be of gold, and you shall cast five bases of bronze for them.

No such division is made with respect to the construction of the courtyard.

Exodus 27:9–19 | The Courtyard

[9] You shall *make* the court of the tabernacle. On the south side the court shall have hangings of fine twisted linen one hundred cubits long for that side; [10] its twenty pillars and their twenty bases shall be of bronze, but the hooks of the pillars and their bands shall be of silver. [11] Likewise for its length on the north side there shall be hangings one hundred cubits long, their pillars twenty and their bases twenty, of bronze, but the hooks of the pillars and their bands shall be of silver. [12] For the width of the court on the west side there shall be fifty cubits of hangings, with ten pillars and ten bases. [13] The width of the court on the front to the east shall be fifty cubits. [14] There shall be fifteen cubits of hangings on the one side, with three pillars and three bases. [15] There shall be fifteen cubits of hangings on the other side, with three pillars and three bases. [16] *For the gate of the court there shall be a screen twenty cubits long, of blue, purple, and crimson yarns, and of fine twisted linen, embroidered with needlework; it shall have four pillars and with them four bases.* [17] All the pillars around the court shall be banded with silver; their hooks shall be of silver, and their bases of bronze. [18] The length of the court shall be one hundred cubits, the width fifty, and the height five cubits, with hangings of fine twisted linen and bases of bronze. [19] All the utensils of the tabernacle for every use, and all its pegs and all the pegs of the court, shall be of bronze.

The first thing to note is that the tabernacle proper is made up of four layers of fabrics (26:1–14). The inner two layers closest to the sacred furniture are made from a number of "curtains" and are described in considerable detail (vv. 1–6 and 7–13). The outer two layers are described in a single verse (v. 14) and serve as "coverings."

The inner layer is made of the finest materials: "fine twined linen and blue and purple and scarlet stuff; with cherubim skillfully worked [into them]." Only after describing these fabrics does the text address the wooden frame upon which they will sit (27:15–30). Portions of this frame will be adorned with gold and silver. The "hangings" that surround the courtyard, on the other hand, are constructed of twisted linen, a far less precious material (vv. 9–15). The pillars and hooks, which will give them their shape, are made of silver and bronze (v. 10). And unlike the tabernacle proper, these supporting structures are described in conjunction with their respective fabrics. The literary effect is far more economical and functional in character.

So far we have considered the more obvious differences: the greater holiness of the fabrics of the tabernacle is marked by the higher value of the fabrics and metals used to make them. But there are other, more subtle, distinctions that are worth noting. Exodus 26:1-14, for example, treats the word "curtain" with a high degree of reverence. It is used twenty-four times over the first fourteen verses (units of twelve being an important symbolic number) and is only rarely replaced by a personal pronoun. It seems that any time our author can use this word, he will. Exodus 27, by contrast, uses the correlative word "hangings" just five times, once for each of three sides and twice when the hangings flank both sides of the entranceway. And it is replaced by the requisite pronoun at every opportunity (see v. 11: "hangings one hundred cubits long, *their* pillars . . . *their* bases").

Exodus 26 is also profligate in its use of the verb "to make," repeating it twice in the very first sentence to create a poetic effect: "you shall *make* the tabernacle with ten curtains of fine twined linen and blue and purple and scarlet stuff; with cherubim skilfully worked shall you *make* them." In total, this verb is used twelve times across these fourteen verses. Exodus 27 is far more restrained, using the verb just once at the very beginning (v. 9) and making that single usage govern all the actions recounted over the next ten verses. Finally, the description of the courtyard weaves into its account a description of the screen, which will serve as its entrance point (see 27:16; I have put it in italics for emphasis.) This varies from the curtains of the tabernacle building proper where the entrance points are described in a separate location to emphasize their unique and holy character (Exod. 26:31–37). The inner screen is given a unique technical term (*parokhet*) and is described in conjunction with the location of the sacred furniture (26:33–35).

In sum, we can see that the description of the tabernacle parts is hardly utilitarian in character. The way in which the story is told is meant to tell us something about the way God's presence structures the character of the building. Because the curtains of the inner space of the tabernacle are so close to the God who dwells therein, they are treated with a literary reverence very different from the fabrics that make up the walls that surround the tabernacle compound. *How* something is said is just as important as *what* is said.

PART ONE

The Priestly Narrative

CHAPTER 2

Inauguration of the Tabernacle

Then the cloud covered the tent of meeting, and the glory of the LORD filled the tabernacle.

Exodus 40:34

Fire came out from the LORD and consumed the burnt offering and the fat on the altar; and when all the people saw it, they shouted and fell on their faces.

Leviticus 9:24

Sacred time is indefinitely recoverable, indefinitely repeatable. From one point of view it could be said that it does not "pass," that it does not constitute an irreversible duration.

Mircea Eliade[1]

This chapter has both a major and minor goal. The major goal concerns the surprising fact that the Tabernacle Narrative is marked by two separate visible appearances ("theophanies") of Israel's God. The first in Exodus 40:34 marks the completion of the tabernacle structure while the second in Leviticus 9:23–24 heralds the successful offering of the first public sacrifices. The minor goal concerns the larger theological frame in which the Tabernacle Narrative has been placed. An initial reading of the book of Exodus would suggest that

1. Mircea Eliade, *The Sacred and the Profane: The Nature of Religion*, trans. Willard R. Trask (New York: Harcourt, 1959), 69.

the tabernacle is related to the founding of Israel's religious life shortly after their exodus from Egypt. Though that is obviously true, the authors of this account have taken special care to relate the construction of the tabernacle to the creation of the world. It will be the task of this chapter to explain why the narrative has two apogees and how both of these apogees are related to a theology of creation.

Narrative and Historical Order

Most readers presume that the order in which events unfold in a story reflects how they would have occurred as well. But this is not always the case. Consider, for example, Steven Spielberg's movie *Saving Private Ryan*. The film opens with Private Ryan visiting a cemetery in Normandy sometime in the 1980s and then cuts back to the events of D-day. Only by the end of the film is it clear what has happened. The man at the beginning of the film is visiting the grave of the man with whom he fought. In order to gather fully the significance of the opening scene, one would need to stay in the theatre for a second viewing. Something similar happens in the Epic of Gilgamesh. That story boils down to Gilgamesh's search for the meaning of life in light of his mortal condition. He only comes upon the answer to his plight at the end of that long tale. Yet the first eighteen lines of the story describe the solution that Gilgamesh ultimately reached. They are an anticipation or "flash forward" to where Gilgamesh will eventually arrive. But to the first-time reader of the epic, they are inscrutable until the end of the story. In both the movie and epic, the unfolding of narrative (or cinematic) time does not always reflect the actual sequence of events.

For most readers, the order of events as narrated appears to be logical. Moses receives instructions to assemble the tabernacle (Exod. 40:1-16), which he subsequently carries out (vv. 17-33). God honors the newly built shrine by appearing in a cloud and filling the inside of the tabernacle (vv. 34-35). Thereupon Moses is invited forward (Lev. 1:1) to receive a set of laws governing sacrificial practice (1:2-7:38). Afterward, he brings Aaron forward to initiate the seven-day ordination service (8:1-36). On the eighth day, the routine daily liturgy begins (9:1-24). To mark the successful inauguration of Aaron's service at the altar, a divine fire consumes the first public sacrifice (vv. 23-24). Because the date on which Moses is to assemble the tabernacle is given as the first of the year (i.e., the first of Nisan), it would stand to reason that the priests underwent their ordination during the first seven days of that month and that the appearance of God ("theophany") at the altar took place on the eighth of Nisan.

But for rabbinic readers, who had a deep sense for the warp and woof of biblical narrative, the chronological character of the story is more complex. Consider this tradition about all the events that took place on the first of Nisan in the Babylonian Talmud.

> [The first of Nisan] had ten crowns. It was the first day of creation, the first day for the tribal chieftains, the first for the priesthood, the first for public sacrifices, the first for the *descent of the altar fire* (Lev. 9:24), the first for eating sacrificial food, the first for the *indwelling of the Shekinah* (Exod. 40:34–35), the first for the priestly blessing, the first for the forbidding of high places, and the first of the firsts of the month. (b. Shabb. 87a)

Note that the descent of the altar fire and the indwelling of the tabernacle occur on the same day, the first of Nisan.[2] On this view, Exodus 40:34–35 flashes forward to the events of Leviticus 9:23–24. It is also important to note that the day of creation has been coordinated with the erection of the tabernacle. They do not occur at the same moment to be sure, but by placing them on the same day, this talmudic tradition wants to correlate these events. Before we can understand what is going on in Exodus 40 and Leviticus 9, we need to see how they both are related to the creation of the world.

Creation and Tabernacle

Scholars have long noted an arc drawn from the story of creation to the building of the tabernacle (and eventually to the temple). In his commentary on Exodus 40:2 ("On the first day of the first month you shall set up the tabernacle of the tent of meeting"), the great medieval Jewish exegete Abraham Ibn Ezra writes, "This is the beginning of the world, and it is a great mystery."[3] But what might this correlation between creation and tabernacle/temple mean?

---

2. This idea was the majority view not only among the rabbis but the medieval interpreters as well. See the succinct summary in Abraham Shama, "Two Thematic Tendencies in the Dedication of the Tabernacle and Their Reflection in the Laws of Sacrifice" (Hebrew), *Megadim* 1–2 (1986): 132–44. For clarity of presentation, I have chosen to illustrate this idea with this talmudic example. Earlier Rabbinic attestations to this idea can be found in Sifre Numbers §44 and Seder Olam, ch. 7.

3. The commentary of Ibn Ezra can be found in any rabbinic Bible (*Miqraot Gedolot*). For an English translation, see Michael Carasik, *The JPS Miqraot Gedolot: Exodus* (Philadelphia: Jewish Publication Society, 2005), 332.

To answer this question, let us consider the way the rabbis interpreted the verse: "Thus *all* the work that King Solomon did on the house of the LORD was finished" (1 Kings 7:51):

> Only when Solomon came and built the Temple would the Holy One, blessed be He, say that the work of creating heaven and earth was now finished: "Thus *all* the work . . . was finished." Indeed, he was called Solomon (Hebrew: *Shlomo*, from the root *sh-l-m* meaning "to bring to completion, finish") because it was through the work of his hands that the Holy One, blessed be He, completed the work of the six days of creation. (Pesiq. Rab. 6:6)[4]

As is typical in midrash, we see that a tendency to overread the significance of individual words can yield a profound theological insight. In this instance, our rabbinic reader notices the text could just as easily have said that Solomon finished "the work" he was charged to do. Why would the text extend his accomplishment to "*all* the work?" Because, the rabbis reasoned, the work begun in Genesis 1 had not yet been completed. It awaited the actions of King Solomon (whose name could mean "to complete") to be brought to closure.

In drawing this linkage between creation and temple, the rabbis were following a theological pattern that stretches back millennia to ancient Mesopotamia. The purpose of creation myths in the ancient world was to establish a point of connection between the divine and human realms. Human beings were created to love and serve their maker and the ancient writers underscored that idea by incorporating the act of founding a temple into their creation story. For example, the Babylonian creation myth, Enuma Elish, finishes its account of the origins of the universe with the building of a temple in the capital city of Babylon.[5] It is only fitting that the biblical author would do the same. And so, according to the rabbis, the work of creation that God began in Genesis only reached its appointed end when the tabernacle was finished and Israel could draw near to her God.[6]

---

4. William Braude, *Pesikta Rabbati* (New Haven: Yale University Press, 1968), 126.

5. Moshe Weinfeld, "Sabbath, Temple and the Enthronement of the Lord," in *Mélanges bibliques et orientaux en l'honneur de M. H. Cazelles*, ed. A. Caquot and M. Delcor (Neukirchen-Vluyn: Neukirchener, 1981), 501–12.

6. See Jon Levenson, *Sinai and Zion* (Minneapolis: Harper & Row, 1985), 117–37, and more recently, Bernd Janowski, "Tempel und Schöpfung: Schöpfungstheologische Aspekte der Priesterschriftlichen Heiligtumskonzeption," in *Gottes Gegenwart in Israel:*

But this was not an insight of the rabbis alone. The connection between creation and temple was already articulated in the Bible. One way to see this is through the vocabulary that the creation account shares with the building of the tabernacle.[7] The author of the Tabernacle Narrative describes the erection of that building using a vocabulary borrowed from the story of creation.[8] In the chart below one will notice that it does not take much editorial work to convert many of the sentences describing the creation of the world into descriptions of the making of the tabernacle. It is also significant that the parallelism is not simply formal but also material: Exodus 39–40 employs a number of technical terms specific to the creation story in his account of the tabernacle.

Genesis 1:1–2:3	Exodus 39–40
A. God saw all that he had made, and indeed, it was very good. (1:31)	A'. Moses saw that they had done all the work just as the LORD had commanded. (39:43)
B. Thus the heavens and the earth were *finished*, and all their multitude. (2:1)	B'. In this way *all the work* of the tabernacle of the tent of meeting was *finished*. (39:32)
C. God *finished* the *work* that he had done. (2:2)	C'. So Moses *finished* the *work*. (40:33)
D. God *blessed* the seventh day (2:3)	D'. Moses *blessed* them. (39:43)
E. and *sanctified* it (2:3)	E'. [A]nd *sanctified* it and all its furniture (40:9)

In brief, the tabernacle is a microcosm of the universe; it is the world in miniature. This is the reason why that talmudic text we cited earlier said that the day of creation was the same day that the tabernacle was dedicated. When God indwells the tabernacle, the goal of the created order has been reached.

This important principle of Old Testament theology was extended in the New Testament. Consider the opening verses of John's Gospel:

Beiträge zur Theologie des Alten Testaments, ed. B. Janowski (Neukirchen-Vluyn: Neukirchener, 1993), 214–46.

7. Joseph Blenkinsopp, "The Structure of P," *CBQ* 38 (1976): 280–81.

8. I am speaking here in terms of how the final form of the biblical narrative unfolds. The historical order of composition may be the reverse. That is, the tabernacle account might have been written first and the creation account was shaped in light of it.

¹˸¹ *In the beginning was the Word*, and the Word was with God, and the Word was God. ² He was in the beginning with God. ³ All things came into being through him, and without him not one thing came into being. What has come into being ⁴ in him was life, and the life was the light of all people. ⁵ The light shines in the darkness, and the darkness did not overcome it.

¹˸¹⁴ *And the Word became flesh and lived among us*, and we have seen his glory, the glory as of a father's only son, full of grace and truth. ¹⁵ (John testified to him and cried out, "This was he of whom I said, 'He who comes after me ranks ahead of me because he was before me.'") ¹⁶ From his fullness we have all received, grace upon grace. ¹⁷ The law indeed was given through Moses; grace and truth came through Jesus Christ. ¹⁸ No one has ever seen God. It is God the only Son, who is close to the Father's heart, who has made him known.

The Prologue of John's Gospel begins with the creation of the world. The phrase "In the beginning was the Word" is patterned on the first verse of the book of Genesis ("In the beginning, when God created the heavens and the earth") and is meant not only to recall that text but to deepen our understanding of it. It is not the case that God "created the heavens and the earth" just by himself, as one might conclude if all we had was the text of Genesis. God fashioned the world, John now informs us, with the assistance of the Word. But just as we saw in the Bible and rabbinic tradition, the agent of creation (in this case, the Word) not only plays a role in creating the universe, but seeks intimate relations with the human race it has fashioned: "And the Word became flesh and lived among us, and we have seen his glory" (1:14). The world was created (v. 1), we can conclude, for the purpose of revealing the glory of the Word (v. 14).

It is important to note that the phrase translated, "and *lived* among us," could be more literally rendered: "and *tabernacled* among us." As Raymond Brown has noted, the Greek verb *skēnoō* has very important associations with the Old Testament.

The theme of "tenting" is found in Exodus 25:8–9 where Israel is told to make a tent (the tabernacle; *skēnē*) so that God can dwell among God's people. The tabernacle became the site of God's localized presence on earth. It was promised that in the ideal days to come this tenting among humanity would be especially impressive. The Septuagint version (LXX) of Joel 3:17 says, "You will know that I am the LORD your God who makes his dwelling [*kataskēnōn*] in Zion." At the time of the return from the Babylonian exile, Zechariah 2:10 LXX proclaims: "Sing and rejoice, O daughter of Zion, for look, I come and will make my dwelling [*kataskēnōsō*] in your midst."[9]

Just as the Tabernacle Narrative drives home the point that creation reaches completion with the indwelling of the deity so for the Prologue of John's Gospel: creation (1:1: "In the beginning was the word") points to that very same word "tabernacling among us" (1:14).

Patterns of Seven in the Creation Account

Let us pursue the connections between Genesis 1 and Exodus 40 more deeply. A striking feature of the two chapters is the way they are structured by a patterned usage of the number seven. In the ancient Near East, the number seven had a symbolic value of perfection or completion. Mesopotamian lexical lists—"dictionaries" of sorts—defined the number seven by the term *kiššatu* meaning "wholeness," or "completion."[10]

Let us take a closer look at the way this number structures Genesis 1. The words that are underlined and in italics occur in units of seven.

1:1 In the beginning when <u>God</u> created the heavens and the earth, 2 the earth was a formless void and darkness covered the face of the deep, while a wind from <u>God</u> swept over the face of the waters. 3 Then <u>God</u> said, "Let there be light"; and there was light. 4 (#1) *And <u>God</u> saw that the light was good*; and <u>God</u> separated the light from the darkness. 5 <u>God</u> called the light

---

9. Raymond Brown, *The Gospel according to John I–XII*, AB 29 (Garden City, NY: Doubleday, 1966), 32–33. For the recent state of the discussion, see Jörg Frey, "The Incarnation of the Logos and the Dwelling of God in Jesus Christ," in *The Glory of the Crucified One* (Waco, TX: Baylor University Press, 2018), 261–84.

10. For *kiššatu*, see B. E. Schafer, "Sabbath," in *The Interpreter's Dictionary of the Bible, Supplementary Volume* (Nashville: Abingdon, 1976), 760, and Laurie Pearce, *Cuneiform Cryptography: Numeric Substitutions for Syllabic and Logographic Signs* (PhD diss., Yale University, 1982), 106–8. For the significance of seven, see Jon Levenson, *Creation and the Persistence of Evil* (Princeton: Princeton University Press, 1994). It should be noted that the number seven plays such an important role in Genesis 1 because of its association with the sabbath. Though the sabbatical week has become part of the natural order of things, it is important to recognize that it arrived relatively late in the day in the Old Testament. As a result, the author of Genesis 1 took special care to inscribe this number deeply into the fabric of the text. It was as if he wished to say that the seven-day sabbatical week provided the backbone of the entire cosmos.

Day, and the darkness he called Night. And there was evening and there was morning, the first day.

⁶ And God said, "Let there be a dome in the midst of the waters, and let it separate the waters from the waters." ⁷ So God made the dome and separated the waters that were under the dome from the waters that were above the dome. And it was so. ⁸ God called the dome Sky. And there was evening and there was morning, the second day.

⁹ And God said, "Let the waters under the sky be gathered together into one place, and let the dry land appear." And it was so. ¹⁰ God called the dry land Earth, and the waters that were gathered together he called Seas. (#2) *And God saw that it was good.* ¹¹ Then God said, "Let the earth put forth vegetation: plants yielding seed, and fruit trees of every kind on earth that bear fruit with the seed in it." And it was so. ¹² The earth brought forth vegetation: plants yielding seed of every kind, and trees of every kind bearing fruit with the seed in it. (#3) *And God saw that it was good.* ¹³ And there was evening and there was morning, the third day.

¹⁴ And God said, "Let there be lights in the dome of the sky to separate the day from the night; and let them be for signs and for seasons and for days and years, ¹⁵ and let them be lights in the dome of the sky to give light upon the earth." And it was so. ¹⁶ God made the two great lights—the greater light to rule the day and the lesser light to rule the night—and the stars. ¹⁷ God set them in the dome of the sky to give light upon the earth, ¹⁸ to rule over the day and over the night, and to separate the light from the darkness. (#4) *And God saw that it was good.* ¹⁹ And there was evening and there was morning, the fourth day.

²⁰ And God said, "Let the waters bring forth swarms of living creatures, and let birds fly above the earth across the dome of the sky." ²¹ So God created the great sea monsters and every living creature that moves, of every kind, with which the waters swarm, and every winged bird of every kind. (#5) *And God saw that it was good.* ²² God blessed them, saying, "Be fruitful and multiply and fill the waters in the seas, and let birds multiply on the earth." ²³ And there was evening and there was morning, the fifth day.

²⁴ And God said, "Let the earth bring forth living creatures of every kind: cattle and creeping things and wild animals of the earth of every kind." And it was so. ²⁵ God made the wild animals of the earth of every kind, and the cattle of every kind, and everything that creeps upon the ground of every kind. (#6) *And God saw that it was good.*

²⁶ Then God said, "Let us make humankind in our image, according to our likeness; and let them have dominion over the fish of the sea, and

over the birds of the air, and over the cattle, and over all the wild animals of the earth, and over every creeping thing that creeps upon the earth."

²⁷ So <u>God</u> created humankind in his image,
    in the image of <u>God</u> he created them;
    male and female he created them.

²⁸ <u>God</u> blessed them, and <u>God</u> said to them, "Be fruitful and multiply, and fill the earth and subdue it; and have dominion over the fish of the sea and over the birds of the air and over every living thing that moves upon the earth." ²⁹ <u>God</u> said, "See, I have given you every plant yielding seed that is upon the face of all the earth, and every tree with seed in its fruit; you shall have them for food. ³⁰ And to every beast of the earth, and to every bird of the air, and to everything that creeps on the earth, everything that has the breath of life, I have given every green plant for food." And it was so. ³¹ (#7) *God saw everything that he had made, and indeed, it was very good.* And there was evening and there was morning, the sixth day.

²:¹ Thus the heavens and the earth were finished, and all their multitude. ² And on the seventh day <u>God</u> finished the work that he had done, and he rested on the seventh day from all the work that he had done. ³ So <u>God</u> blessed the seventh day and hallowed it, because on it <u>God</u> rested from all the work that he had done in creation.

The first feature, which hardly needs to be stated, is the division of the work of creation over six days, culminating in the seventh day of rest (Gen. 2:1–3). But if we go a little deeper we will see that the approbatory phrase, "God saw that it was good" is also used seven times (I have put this phrase in italics) and that the last usage is expressed in a more emphatic form that befits its role marking the conclusion of creation: "God saw *everything that he had made, and indeed, it was very* good" (1:31).

And there is more. Having finished the seven acts of creation over the first six days, God concludes the act of creation with a description of the seventh day that includes five clauses made up of thirty-five words (five times seven) of which the inner three clauses consist of seven words apiece, each including a reference to the seventh day (Gen. 2:1–3):[11]

---

11. For the usage of seven in general, see Umberto Cassuto, *A Commentary on the Book of Genesis* (Jerusalem: Magnes, 1961), 1:12–15. For Genesis 2:1–3, see Aryeh Toeg, "Genesis 1 and the Sabbath" (Hebrew), *Beit Miqra* 50 (1972): 291.

Thus the heavens and the earth were finished, and all their multitude.
(5 Hebrew words)
[2] And on the *seventh day* God finished the work that he had done, (7)
and he rested on the *seventh day* from all the work that he had done. (7)
[3] So God blessed the *seventh day* and hallowed it, (7)
because on it God rested from all the work that he had done in creation. (9)

Finally, Umberto Cassuto noted that several key words occur in units of seven. If we take the very first sentence to establish our bearings ("In the beginning, when God created the heavens and the earth . . ."), we'll note that the nominal subject (God) and the objects (heaven and earth) each occur in units of thirty-five, twenty-one, and twenty-one respectively. I have marked the thirty-five usages of the term "God" by underlining each occurrence above. In sum, the "sevenness" of the sabbatical week was a key structural feature to the story of creation. The Mesopotamian definition of the number seven as "wholeness, completion" is aptly borne out in the way it structures the first chapter of Genesis.

Constructing the Tabernacle in Exodus 25–39

A prelude to the story of the tabernacle begins at the close of Exodus 24. Moses, having received the Ten Commandments and formalized the covenant between God and the people Israel, ascends Mount Sinai once again.

> [24:15b] And the cloud covered the mountain. [16] The glory of the LORD settled on Mount Sinai, and the cloud covered it for *six days*; on the *seventh day* he called to Moses out of the cloud. [17] Now the appearance of the glory of the LORD was like a devouring fire on the top of the mountain in the sight of the people of Israel. [18] Moses entered the cloud, and went up on the mountain. Moses was on the mountain for forty days and forty nights.

The first pattern to notice is that Moses must wait six days before he completes his ascent to God on the seventh. As Edward Greenstein observes, this is double the time that Israel has to wait (19:11) in order to prepare for the revelation of the Ten Commandments (20:1–21). The increase in time is proportional to the greater intimacy that Moses will enjoy with God.[12] But, more

---

12. *The HarperCollins Study Bible*, ed. H. Attridge (San Francisco: HarperCollins,

importantly, the sequence of six days of preparation followed by a seventh day of intimacy with the deity imitates the pattern of creation.

This imitation does not stop here. On the seventh day, when Moses is called forward into the presence of God, he will hear seven addresses each beginning with the phrase, "God spoke to Moses, saying . . ."[13] The first six addresses deal with various aspects of the building program, the seventh (hardly an accident!) concerns the celebration of the sabbath. As important as the construction of the tabernacle is, the workers must take care, as God did when God fashioned the world in Genesis 1, to hallow the seventh day by refraining from work.

^{25:1} (#1) The Lord spoke to Moses, saying: ² Tell the Israelites to take for me an *offering*; from all whose hearts prompt them to give you shall receive the offering for me.

^{30:11} (#2) The Lord spoke to Moses, saying: ¹² When you take a *census* of the Israelites to register them, at registration all of them shall give a ransom for their lives to the Lord, so that no plague may come upon them for being registered.

^{30:17} (#3) The Lord spoke to Moses, saying: ¹⁸ You shall make a *bronze basin* with a bronze stand for washing.

^{30:22} (#4) The Lord spoke to Moses, saying: ²³ Take the finest spices: of liquid myrrh five hundred shekels, and of sweet-smelling cinnamon half as much . . . ²⁵ and you shall make of these a sacred *anointing oil* . . . it shall be a holy anointing oil.

^{30:34} (#5) The Lord said to Moses: Take sweet spices, stacte, and onycha, and galbanum . . . ³⁵ and make an *incense* . . . pure and holy.

^{31:1} (#6) The Lord spoke to Moses, saying: ² See, I have called by name *Bezalel* son of Uri son of Hur, of the tribe of Judah: ³ and I have filled him with divine spirit, with ability, intelligence, and knowledge in every kind

---

2006), 126. One should note that this observation cuts across traditional source critical observations. The author of Exodus 19:11 was the not the same as that of 24:16.

13. Peter Kearney, "Creation and Liturgy: The P Redaction of Exodus 25–40," *ZAW* 89 (1977): 375–87.

of craft, ⁴ to devise artistic designs, to work in gold, silver, and bronze, ⁵ in cutting stones for setting, and in carving wood, in every kind of craft.

³¹:¹² (#7) <u>The LORD spoke to Moses, saying</u>: ¹³ You yourself are to speak to the Israelites: "Nevertheless, you shall *keep my sabbaths*, for this is a sign between me and you throughout your generations, given in order that you may know that I, the LORD, sanctify you.

The first address is the longest by far, stretching across six chapters and consisting of nearly two hundred verses. The other six, in contrast, are limited to a chapter and a half, taking up just thirty-nine verses. The initial address begins with a command to bring the required materials (25:1–9), continues with instructions concerning the construction of tabernacle proper (25:10–27:19), and concludes with the priestly vestments, ordination, and laws regarding the celebration of the daily liturgy (27:20–31:10). What follows are five additional instructions regarding other materials necessary for the tabernacle or its operation, concluding with the seventh and final set of instructions about the sabbath.

The next section of the Tabernacle Narrative (Exod. 35–39) documents the successful execution of all the commands given in chapters 25–31. The unit concludes with this observation: "In this way all the work of the tabernacle of the tent of meeting was finished; the Israelites had done everything just as the Lord had commanded Moses" (39:32).

This leads naturally to the climax of the first part of the story: the erection of the tabernacle (40:1–33) and the entrance of the deity into the building (40:34–35).

Erecting the Tabernacle in Exodus 40

The structure of Exodus 40 mirrors both the preceding section of the Tabernacle Narrative and Genesis 1. In the text below, notice that the command (vv. 1–16) and execution sections (vv. 17–33) begin and end with the use of the personal name Moses (underlined) and that the execution section is punctuated by a seven-fold repetition of the formula: *"as the Lord had commanded Moses."*

Commands to (A) Assemble the Tabernacle
⁴⁰:¹ The LORD spoke to <u>Moses</u>: ² On the first day of the first month you shall set up the tabernacle of the tent of meeting. ³ You shall put in it the ark of the covenant, and you shall screen the ark with the curtain. ⁴ You

shall bring in the table, and arrange its setting; and you shall bring in the lampstand, and set up its lamps. ⁵ You shall put the golden altar for incense before the ark of the covenant, and set up the screen for the entrance of the tabernacle. ⁶ You shall set the altar of burnt offering before the entrance of the tabernacle of the tent of meeting, ⁷ and place the basin between the tent of meeting and the altar, and put water in it. ⁸ You shall set up the court all around, and hang up the screen for the gate of the court.

(B) Anoint the Tabernacle and the Priests

⁹ Then you shall take the anointing oil, and anoint the tabernacle and all that is in it, and consecrate it and all its furniture, so that it shall become holy. ¹⁰ You shall also anoint the altar of burnt offering and all its utensils, and consecrate the altar, so that the altar shall be most holy. ¹¹ You shall also anoint the basin with its stand, and consecrate it.

¹² Then you shall bring Aaron and his sons to the entrance of the tent of meeting, and shall wash them with water, ¹³ and put on Aaron the sacred vestments, and you shall anoint him and consecrate him, so that he may serve me as priest. ¹⁴ You shall bring his sons also and put tunics on them, ¹⁵ and anoint them, as you anointed their father, that they may serve me as priests: and their anointing shall admit them to a perpetual priesthood throughout all generations to come.

¹⁶ <u>Moses</u> did everything just as the Lord had commanded him.

Execution of Those Commands

¹⁷ In the first month in the second year, on the first day of the month, the tabernacle was set up.

¹⁸ <u>Moses</u> set up the tabernacle; he laid its bases, and set up its frames, and put in its poles, and raised up its pillars; ¹⁹ and he spread the tent over the tabernacle, and put the covering of the tent over it; (#1) *as the Lord had commanded Moses.*

²⁰ He took the covenant and put it into the ark, and put the poles on the ark, and set the mercy seat above the ark; ²¹ and he brought the ark into the tabernacle, and set up the curtain for screening, and screened the ark of the covenant; (#2) *as the Lord had commanded Moses.*

²² He put the table in the tent of meeting, on the north side of the tabernacle, outside the curtain, ²³ and set the bread in order on it before the Lord; (#3) *as the Lord had commanded Moses.* ²⁴ He put the lampstand in the tent of meeting, opposite the table on the south side of the tabernacle, ²⁵ and set up the lamps before the Lord; (#4) *as the Lord had commanded Moses.* ²⁶ He put the golden altar in the tent of meeting before the curtain,

²⁷ and offered fragrant incense on it; (#5) *as the* Lord *had commanded Moses.* ²⁸ He also put in place the screen for the entrance of the tabernacle.

²⁹ He set the altar of burnt offering at the entrance of the tabernacle of the tent of meeting, and offered on it the burnt offering and the grain offering (#6) *as the* Lord *had commanded Moses.* ³⁰ He set the basin between the tent of meeting and the altar, and put water in it for washing, ³¹ with which Moses and Aaron and his sons washed their hands and their feet. ³² When they went into the tent of meeting, and when they approached the altar, they washed; (#7) *as the* Lord *had commanded Moses.* ³³ He set up the court around the tabernacle and the altar, and put up the screen at the gate of the court. So <u>Moses</u> finished the work.

Climax of the Narrative: God Enters the Tabernacle

³⁴ Then the cloud covered the tent of meeting, and the glory of the Lord filled the tabernacle. ³⁵ Moses was not able to enter the tent of meeting because the cloud settled upon it, and the glory of the Lord filled the tabernacle.

Like the preceding narrative—the command to build in Exodus 25–31, and the execution of those commands in chapters 35–39—this chapter is divided into two sections: the commands that Moses receives about how to assemble the tabernacle (40:1–16, compare chs. 25–31) and an account of the execution of those commands (40:17–33, compare chs. 35–39). Like Genesis 1, the chapter shows an extraordinary affection for the number seven and in so doing reaffirms that the building of a house for God is a microcosm of the entire created order. Just as Genesis 1 was characterized by seven repetitions of the formula of approbation ("God saw that it was good"), so the erection of the tabernacle is marked by seven repetitions of the fact that Moses had acted just "as the Lord had commanded [him]."¹⁴ Just as Genesis 1 ends by sanctifying a moment in time by describing the deity at rest, so Exodus 40 ends with God sanctifying a place through anointing (vv. 9–11) and indwelling (vv. 34–35).

---

14. As commentators have long noted, three prominent texts in the Tabernacle Narrative are structured by sevenfold approbation formulas: Exodus 39, 40, and Leviticus 8. Yet it is important to note that this sevenfold pattern is not mindlessly repeated; in each deployment there are significant variations that conform to the needs of the specific narrative environment. Attention to these variations will reveal a sophisticated literary design that governs these chapters. For a detailed analysis of this phenomenon, see my article "The Inauguration of the Tabernacle Service at Sinai," in *The Temple of Jerusalem: From Moses to the Messiah*, ed. S. Fine, BRLA 29 (Leiden: Brill, 2010), 1–15.

But perhaps the most striking similarity between Genesis 1 and Exodus 40 is the repetition of key terms in units of seven. Let's begin with the execution section. This unit marks its beginning and end by citing the name of Moses as the subject of the first verb (the name is underlined, see vv. 16, 18, and 33) whereas the sentences in between employ the third-person pronoun, "he," to indicate the subject of the remaining verbs. In between these two termini we have twenty-eight (four units of seven) active-transitive verbs that mark each of the actions required to erect the tabernacle. These verbs are, in turn, divided into four paragraphs of seven verbs each devoted to the various sections of the tabernacle, beginning with the fabrics and wooden frame that make up the tent proper (vv. 17–19), the ark and mercy seat that reside within the holy of holies (vv. 20–21), the furniture contained in the holy chamber (vv. 22–28), and, last, the makeup of the courtyard that surrounds the tent (vv. 29–33).

The command section (vv. 1–15) also consists of twenty-eight active-transitive verbs.[15] It can be divided into two units of fourteen, the first dealing with the tabernacle building, the second with the rites of anointing that would pertain to the building and the priests who serve it. This second part is evenly weighted: seven verbs for the building and seven for the priests.

Ordaining the Priests in Leviticus 8–9

Genesis 1 and Exodus 40 are not the only chapters that include a sevenfold approbatory formula. There are two additional examples in the Tabernacle Narrative: the account of the construction of the priestly vestments (Exod. 39:1–31) and the ordination of Aaron and his sons (Lev. 8).[16] The latter is of more interest to us because it, like the story of the tabernacle (Exod. 40:17–35), ends in a theophany. If we scan the chapter as it is presented below, we will note that the ordination service can be broken down into seven discrete activities, each of which ends with the exact same formula that we saw in Exodus 40: "[Moses did so-and-so] as the LORD commanded [him]."

15. I did not mark the clause "you shall bring his sons also" in Exodus 40:14 because that identical action had been commanded in v. 12.

16. J. W. Watts, *Ritual and Rhetoric in Leviticus: From Sacrifice to Scripture* (Cambridge: Cambridge University Press, 2007), 103–4, has argued that there are actually nine usages of the formula in the chapter. But the two additional usages that he proposes (8:5 and 34) are not approbatory formulae marking the completion of a command given in Exodus 29. Watts does not understand the importance of the approbatory gesture in these lists.

Ordination of the Priesthood (Leviticus 8)

1. Gathering

8:1 The LORD spoke to Moses, saying: 2 Take Aaron and his sons with him, the vestments, the anointing oil, the bull of sin offering, the two rams, and the basket of unleavened bread; 3 and assemble the whole congregation at the entrance of the tent of meeting. 4 *And Moses did as the LORD commanded him.* When the congregation was assembled at the entrance of the tent of meeting, 5 Moses said to the congregation, "This is what the LORD has commanded to be done."

2. Vesting

6 Then Moses brought Aaron and his sons forward, and washed them with water. 7 He put the tunic on him, fastened the sash around him, clothed him with the robe, and put the ephod on him. He then put the decorated band of the ephod around him, tying the ephod to him with it. 8 He placed the breastpiece on him, and in the breastpiece he put the Urim and the Thummim. 9 And he set the turban on his head, and on the turban, in front, he set the golden ornament, the holy crown, *as the LORD commanded Moses.*

3. Anointing

10 Then Moses took the anointing oil and anointed the tabernacle and all that was in it, and consecrated them. 11 He sprinkled some of it on the altar seven times, and anointed the altar and all its utensils, and the basin and its base, to consecrate them. 12 He poured some of the anointing oil on Aaron's head and anointed him, to consecrate him. 13 And Moses brought forward Aaron's sons, and clothed them with tunics, and fastened sashes around them, and tied headdresses on them, *as the LORD commanded Moses.*

4. Bull for Sin Offering

14 He led forward the bull of sin offering; and Aaron and his sons laid their hands upon the head of the bull of sin offering, 15 and it was slaughtered. Moses took the blood and with his finger put some on each of the horns of the altar, purifying the altar; then he poured out the blood at the base of the altar. Thus he consecrated it, to make atonement for it. 16 Moses took all the fat that was around the entrails, and the appendage of the liver, and

the two kidneys with their fat, and turned them into smoke on the altar. ¹⁷ But the bull itself, its skin and flesh and its dung, he burned with fire outside the camp, *as the Lord commanded Moses.*

5. Ram for Burnt Offering

¹⁸ Then he brought forward the ram of burnt offering. Aaron and his sons laid their hands on the head of the ram, ¹⁹ and it was slaughtered. Moses dashed the blood against all sides of the altar. ²⁰ The ram was cut into its parts, and Moses turned into smoke the head and the parts and the suet. ²¹ And after the entrails and the legs were washed with water, Moses turned into smoke the whole ram on the altar; it was a burnt offering for a pleasing odor, an offering by fire to the Lord, *as the Lord commanded Moses.*

6. Ram for Ordination Offering

²² Then he brought forward the second ram, the ram of ordination. Aaron and his sons laid their hands on the head of the ram, ²³ and it was slaughtered. Moses took some of its blood and put it on the lobe of Aaron's right ear and on the thumb of his right hand and on the big toe of his right foot . . . ²⁹ Moses took the breast and raised it as an elevation offering before the Lord; it was Moses' portion of the ram of ordination, *as the Lord commanded Moses.* ³⁰ Then Moses took some of the anointing oil and some of the blood that was on the altar and sprinkled them on Aaron and his vestments, and also on his sons and their vestments. Thus he consecrated Aaron and his vestments, and also his sons and their vestments.

7. Sacrificial Feasting

³¹ And Moses said to Aaron and his sons, "Boil the flesh at the entrance of the tent of meeting, and eat it there with the bread that is in the basket of ordination offerings, as I was commanded, 'Aaron and his sons shall eat it'; ³² and what remains of the flesh and the bread you shall burn with fire. ³³ You shall not go outside the entrance of the tent of meeting for seven days, until the day when your period of ordination is completed. For it will take seven days to ordain you; ³⁴ as has been done today, the Lord has commanded to be done to make atonement for you. ³⁵ You shall remain at the entrance of the tent of meeting day and night for seven days, keeping the Lord's charge so that you do not die; for so I am commanded." ³⁶ *Aaron and his sons did all the things that the Lord commanded through Moses.*

Rites of the Eighth Day (Leviticus 9)

[9:1] On the eighth day Moses summoned Aaron and his sons and the elders of Israel. [2] He said to Aaron, "Take a bull calf for a sin offering and a ram for a burnt offering, without blemish, and offer them before the LORD. [3] And say to the people of Israel, 'Take a male goat for a sin offering; a calf and a lamb, yearlings without blemish, for a burnt offering; [4] and an ox and a ram for an offering of well-being to sacrifice before the LORD; and a grain offering mixed with oil. For today the LORD will appear to you.'"

[22] Aaron lifted his hands toward the people and blessed them; and he came down after sacrificing the sin offering, the burnt offering, and the offering of well-being. [23] Moses and Aaron entered the tent of meeting, and then came out and blessed the people; *and the glory of the LORD appeared to all the people.* [24] *Fire came out from the LORD and consumed the burnt offering and the fat on the altar*; and when all the people saw it, they shouted and fell on their faces.

It is important to bear in mind that Leviticus 8 constitutes the execution of a set of commands that were given earlier in Exodus 29:1–37. In other words, just as Exodus 40 consisted of commands and their fulfillment, so for Leviticus 8, though the commands were delivered many chapters earlier. Leviticus 9 documents the onset of the public liturgy and the ceremonial lighting of the altar. It is an unexpected and dramatic expansion of the commands given for the daily sacrifice in Exodus 29:38–42a.

A Chronological Puzzle

As we saw at the beginning of this chapter, many readers have presumed that the order of events follows the way the story unfolds. If the tabernacle was erected on the first of Nisan (Exod. 40:17) and several chapters later the altar is ignited on the eighth day, then that event must have occurred on the eighth of Nisan. Nothing would seem more logical: first, erect the tabernacle, then ordain the priests, and finally, light the sacrificial hearth.

Yet if we look more closely at the literary structure of these chapters, we will see that the sequence of events is not so clear. For example, in our initial reading of Exodus 40 we observed that vv. 1–16 outlined the commands that Moses received for assembling the tabernacle, while vv. 17–33 described their execution. But there is a wrinkle in this fabric. The first half of this chapter divides into two parts: Exodus 40:1–8 describes the instructions about constructing the tabernacle, while Exodus 40:9–15 provides instructions for anointing that structure as well as the priests who will serve it (see pp. 30–31). The second half of the chapter (vv. 17–33) provides an account of the assemblage of the tabernacle—in other words only the execution of those instructions found in vv. 1–8. The commands to anoint the tabernacle and the priests (vv. 9–15) will not be executed until we reach the rite of ordination in Leviticus 8.[17]

It is important to note that the author of Exodus 40 is quite conscious of the chronological problem embedded in this chapter. This becomes clear when we compare the sevenfold approbatory formula of the chapter with similar deployments of this formula in Leviticus 8 and Genesis 1.

Leviticus 8	Genesis 1	Exodus 40
1. [He did] as the LORD commanded him.	1. God saw that it was good.	1. As the LORD commanded Moses.
2. [He did] as the LORD commanded him.	2. God saw that it was good.	2. As the LORD commanded Moses.
3. [He did] as the LORD commanded him.	3. God saw that it was good.	3. As the LORD commanded Moses.
4. [He did] as the LORD commanded him.	4. God saw that it was good.	4. As the LORD commanded Moses.

---

17. As we have noted, the ordination service in Leviticus 8 is, for the most part, built upon the commands given in Exodus 29. But one set of commands is missing:

Exodus 29:7–9
You shall take the anointing oil, and pour it on his head and anoint him.

Leviticus 8:10–13
Then Moses took the anointing oil <u>and anointed the tabernacle and all that was in it, and consecrated them.</u> [11] He <u>sprinkled some of it on the altar seven times, and anointed the altar and all its utensils, and the basin and its base, to consecrate them.</u> [12] He poured some of the anointing oil on Aaron's head and anointed him, to consecrate him . . . as the Lord commanded Moses.

In Exodus 29 Moses is commanded to anoint the priests but not the tabernacle or altar. For those commands we must wait for Exodus 40:9–15. The ordination service in Leviticus 8 has a double focus. It is made up of both Exodus 29 and 40.

5. [He did] as the LORD commanded him.	5. God saw that it was good.	5. As the LORD commanded Moses.
6. [He did] as the LORD commanded him.	6. God saw that it was good.	6. As the LORD commanded Moses.
7. Aaron and his sons did *everything* that the LORD commanded through Moses.	7. God saw *everything* that he had made, and indeed, it was very good	7. As the LORD commanded Moses.

As we noted earlier the sevenfold formula in both Genesis 1 and Leviticus 8 concludes with a pronounced rhetorical flourish: the seventh and final repetition is written in a fuller, more baroque form than the previous six. Exodus 40 differs from this pattern by repeating the approbatory phrase ("[Moses did] as God had commanded him") seven times in *identical* terms; there is no variation for the seventh and last usage.

But Exodus 40 is not a complete outlier. A longer, summarizing expression of the formula can be found, but in a very unusual position. In v. 16, at the conclusion of the command section, but before Moses has completed a single action, our writer observes: "Moses did *everything* just as the LORD had commanded him." This is very odd. Everywhere else in the Priestly writings, this type of concluding formula comes *after* the completion of what is commanded, not before.[18] But an explanation is close at hand. Because the commands found in vv. 1–15 are not executed in toto in the following narrative (vv. 17–33), the summarizing completion formula ("Moses did *everything* . . .") could not be placed at the end of that narrative. By placing this particular completion formula in v. 16, it assumes a new function: it *anticipates* what will be the case once the reader has reached Leviticus 8 and 9. This makes it possible that the theophany at the close of Exodus 40 flashes forward to the rites of the eighth day that close the ordination sequence (Lev. 9:23–24).[19]

18. See Blenkinsopp, "Structure of P," 275–76.

19. There is one additional feature of this text that supports reading the theophany as an anticipation of Leviticus 9. As we have seen above, the final approbatory formulas found in Genesis 1:31 and Leviticus 8:37 close their respective chapters; *no* additional actions take place beyond the seventh and concluding formula. But this is not the case in Exodus 40. In this instance, the seventh and final formula is followed by additional actions on the part of Moses:

What Happened on the First of Nisan?

We have already noted the rabbinic notion that both Exodus 40 and Leviticus 9 describe a single event. But this interpretive judgment can be found a few centuries earlier in Pseudo-Philo's Biblical Antiquities (Latin title: *Liber Antiquitatum Biblicarum*), a text dating sometime in the first or second centuries CE that retells the biblical story while introducing important interpretive modifications:

> [13.1a] And Moses hastened and did everything that God had commanded him. [1b] And he went down and made the tent of meeting and its vessels and the ark and the lamp and the table and the altar of holocausts and the altar of incense and the ephod and the breastplate and the precious stones and the laver and the basins and everything that was shown to him. [1c] And he arranged all the vestments of the priests, the belt and the robe and the headdress and the golden plate and the holy crown (Exod. 35–39). [1d] *And the oil for anointing priests as well as the priests themselves he consecrated* (Lev. 8). [1e] And when all this was done, the cloud covered them all (Exod. 40:34–35).
>
> [14.1] Then Moses called to the LORD, and God spoke to him from the tent of meeting, saying, "This is the law of the altar . . ." (Lev. 1:1–17). (LAB 13.1a–e; 14.1)[20]

This text opens with a description of Moses's descent from Mount Sinai (13.1a) and the construction of the various pieces that made up the tabernacle

---

[32] When they went into the tent of meeting, and when they approached the altar, they washed; *as the* LORD *had commanded Moses.* [33] He set up the court around the tabernacle and the altar, and put up the screen at the gate of the court. So Moses finished the work.

As several scholars have noted, this is hardly problematic, for the final sign of divine approval is the entrance of the glory of the Lord into the tabernacle in the very next verse. But if that is the case, then we must revise our account of how the chapter is structured. It is not the case that the execution section of the tabernacle is solely defined by a sevenfold approbatory structure. We could also describe it as a seven plus one structure where the eighth item is the theophany. But if that is the case, then the outline of the execution section is strikingly similar to Leviticus 8–9, which is also made up of a sevenfold approbatory sequence (ch. 8) that culminates in a theophany on the eighth day (the conclusion of ch. 9). For a longer discussion of this particular feature see my article "The Inauguration of the Tabernacle Service at Sinai."

20. The translation is that of Daniel Harrington in *OTP* 2:321.

and the vestments with which the priests would adorn themselves (13.1b and c). All of these actions can be found in Exodus 35–39. The text closes with a reference to the cloud covering the tent (13.1e), an obvious reference to the theophany at the close of Exodus 40—and the revelation of the sacrificial laws that mark the beginning of the book of Leviticus (14:1). But in the middle of this sequence we find a reference to the consecration of the priests (13:1d). This is an obvious reference to the actions described in Leviticus 8. As a result, when the paragraph closes with a description of the theophany (13:1e), it presumes the actions described in both Exodus 40 and Leviticus 8. In other words, the erection of the tabernacle and the consecration of the priesthood are understood as a single, uninterrupted ritual sequence.

It is important to observe that for this narrative sequencing to work, the seven days of ordination must begin on the twenty-third of Adar so that the eighth day can fall on the first of Nisan. Strikingly, this sequence can be found in the book of Ezra when the exiles return, rebuild, and rededicate the temple.

> [14] So the elders of the Jews built and prospered, through the prophesying of the prophet Haggai and Zechariah son of Iddo. They finished their building by command of the God of Israel and by decree of Cyrus, Darius, and King Artaxerxes of Persia; [15] and this house was finished on the [twenty-]third day of the month of Adar, in the sixth year of King Darius. [16] The people of Israel, the priests and the Levites, and the rest of the returned exiles, celebrated the dedication of this house of God with joy. [17] They offered at the dedication of this house of God one hundred bulls, two hundred rams, four hundred lambs, and as a sin offering for all Israel, twelve male goats, according to the number of the tribes of Israel. [18] Then they set the priests in their divisions and the Levites in their courses for the service of God at Jerusalem, as it is written in the book of Moses. (Ezra 6:14–18)

Once the Persians had conquered the Babylonians (mid-sixth century BCE) and taken control of the vast majority of the ancient Near East, they permitted the Judean exiles in Babylon to return home and rebuild their temple (Ezra 1:2–4). In the spring of 515 BCE, the temple was completed and liturgical life was reinstated. As Hugh Williamson has noted, it is almost certain that the Aramaic text of Ezra 6:15 needs to be corrected from the third to the twenty-third of Adar. Such is the reading found in the Greek 1 Esdras, which was based on an earlier and more accurate form of the

Aramaic original. Williamson explains: "Since Adar was the last month of the year, a week's dedication celebration would then lead neatly to the new year festivities as the start of the resumed temple services."[21] Since it is a commonplace that temple building and creation are strongly correlated in the ancient world, it stands to reason that the date given in 1 Esdras is original.

It is important to note that Williamson articulates the ritual pattern found in the book of Ezra without knowledge or recourse to the chronological problem of Leviticus 9. His arguments are of a history of religions nature—the resumption of cultic activity in Jerusalem follows a well-known pattern from the ancient Near East. Julian Morgenstern, however, makes a similar observation but ties it back to the chronology of the Tabernacle Narrative. "[The text of] Ezra 6:15," he argues,

> undoubtedly employed a calendar which set the New Year's Day upon [1 Nisan]. For certainly the 3rd of Adar here, a day without any significance whatsoever, we should read, with 1 Esdras 7:5 . . . the 23rd. This would imply that the rejoicing of the Jewish community of Palestine and its celebration of the dedication of the Temple, rebuilt during the reign, and with the permission and support, of Darius, the Persian king, began upon the 23rd of Adar, continued for the traditional seven festal days, Adar 23–29, the last seven days of the month and likewise the last seven days of the year, and reached its climax upon the eighth day, the first of Nisan. . . . Plainly, the pattern for this dating of the Temple dedication was the account of the dedication of the tabernacle in the wilderness of Exod 40:1ff.[22]

21. H. G. Williamson, "1 Esdras," in *Eerdmans Commentary on the Bible*, ed. James D. G. Dunn and John Rogerson (Grand Rapids: Eerdmans, 2003), 857.

22. Julian Morgenstern, "The Calendar of the Book of Jubilees," *VT* 5 (1955): 63 n. 3. It is important to clarify that we have two different arguments for coordinating the theophanies of Exodus 40 and Leviticus 9. First is the history of religions argument of Williamson. He argues that because it was standard in the ancient Near East to coordinate the dedication of a temple with the first day of the year (1 Nisan), any preparatory ritual would have to have taken place at the end of the previous month (Adar). Williamson makes this argument independent of the chronological problems we have been tracing in the Tabernacle Narrative. I assume he is unaware of them. Morgenstern's argument, on the other hand, is grounded in the peculiar form of Exodus 40, which correlates the command to erect the tabernacle (40:17–33) with the command to ordain (specifically, anoint) the priesthood. Morgenstern has been seconded by an unpublished essay by Victor Hurowitz, "The Vessels of YHWH and the Debate over Divine Presence in the Second

Perhaps the most striking piece of evidence for the correlation of Exodus 40 and Leviticus 9 is to be found in the book of Chronicles. Dating from the Second Temple period, Chronicles is a learned reflection on and periodic rewriting of the history of Israel as found in Samuel-Kings. One of its striking innovations is the way it weaves into its narrative the priestly laws of the Torah, laws that were strikingly ignored in the book of Kings. In Kings, the introduction of the ark of the covenant into the temple (8:1–13) and the offering of the first sacrifices (8:62–64) are presented as two completely separate moments in time. The former is clearly patterned on the events of Exodus 40 and most scholars would attribute this to the influence of the Tabernacle Narrative.[23] But the offering of the first sacrifices shows no sign of the influence of Leviticus 9. Things are quite different when we turn to Chronicles. The conclusion of the first sacrificial liturgy is described in terms drawn from Exodus 40 and Leviticus 9. In fact, the text is really nothing other than a pastiche of those antecedent verses. To illustrate this, I have set the material that comes from Exodus in roman font and Leviticus in italics.

> When Solomon had ended his prayer, *fire came down from heaven and consumed the burnt offering and the sacrifices;* and the glory of the LORD filled the temple. ² The priests could not enter the house of the LORD, because the glory of the LORD filled the LORD's house. ³ *When all the people of Israel saw the fire come down* and the glory of the LORD on the temple, *they bowed down on the pavement with their faces to the ground, and worshiped and gave thanks to the LORD.* (2 Chron. 7:1–3)

It is striking that this liturgical moment is described in terms drawn directly from Exodus 40 and Leviticus 9.[24] The minor differences that remain were necessary to make these citations fit their new context. Already in the fifth or

Temple—Downgrading a Divine Symbol" (presented at the SBL annual meeting in 2006), which argues that the two arguments belong together, each supporting the other ("the pattern . . .").

23. See Thomas Römer, "Redaction Criticism: 1 Kings 8 and the Deuteronomists," in *Method Matters, Essays on the Interpretation of the Hebrew Bible in Honor of David L. Peterson*, ed. J. LeMon and K. Richards (Atlanta: Society of Biblical Literature, 2009), 63–76.

24. See the commentaries of H. G. Williamson, *1 and 2 Chronicles*, New Century Bible Commentary (Grand Rapids: Eerdmans, 1982), 221–22; and Sara Japhet, *I and II Chronicles*, OTL (Louisville: Westminster John Knox, 1993), 609–10. Christophe Nihan, "Cult Centralization and the Torah Traditions in Chronicles," in *The Fall of Jerusalem and the Rise of the Torah*, ed. P. Dubovsky, D. Markl, and J. P. Sonnet, FAT 107 (Tübingen: Mohr Siebeck, 2015), 268–69, has noted the importance of Chronicles for understanding the Priestly

fourth century (accepted dates for the Chronicler), just a hundred years or so after the completion of the Tabernacle Narrative, we see a reader presuming the chronological overlap of Exodus 40 and Leviticus 9, a reading that would be repeated in Ezra 6 and several other postbiblical Jewish writings.[25]

One Story, Two Foci

The literary structure of the Tabernacle Narrative is more complex than an initial reading might have suggested. What had appeared to be two successive theophanies could be collapsed into one. But it is important to note that whatever solution to this conundrum we adopt, problems will remain.[26] Absolute certainty about the order of events will never be realized. The question then becomes why introduce such a chronological puzzle into the text?[27] William

---

source. But neither he nor anyone else to my knowledge has recognized its importance for the chronological challenge the final form of the Torah has bequeathed to its readers.

25. I should add that Chronicles describes two successive theophanies to mark the completion of the temple. The first is in 2 Chronicles 5:11-14 and is based on 1 Kings 8:10-11 (which is itself based on Exod. 40:34-35) and marks the introduction of the ark of the covenant into the temple. The second in 2 Chronicles 7:1-3 has no antecedent in the book of Kings and is based on a combination of Leviticus 9:23-24 and Exodus 40:34-35. Clearly our writer could have followed the strict narrative order of the Pentateuch and used Exodus 40 for the consecration of the temple building in 2 Chronicles 5 and Leviticus 9 for the first sacrifices in 2 Chronicles 7:1-3. His choice to combine the two in 2 Chronicles 7:1-3 reflects his understanding of the peculiar narrative arrangement of the Pentateuch. S. Japhet describes 2 Chronicles 7:1-3 as a "resumptive repetition" of 2 Chronicles 5:11-14 whose purpose is "to express simultaneity of events"; see *I & II Chronicles*, 222.

26. There are good grounds for reading the appearance of the glory of the LORD as a flash forward to the theophany of the eighth day. But there are also good grounds for rejecting this view. The problems begin when we go a little deeper and try to coordinate all the textual details. If we let the chronology of Ezra 6 be our guide, then the seven days of ordination begin on the twenty-third of Adar and conclude on the thirtieth, and the dedication of the tabernacle and the altar occurs on 1 Nisan. The problem with this timeline is that the seven days of ordination require that the tabernacle be set up, yet Exodus explicitly states this occurred on 1 Nisan. The rabbis and most medieval Jewish interpreters worked out a solution to this, but it is extremely implausible. In their mind, Moses set up and took down the tabernacle during each of the days of ordination (according to some, multiple times per day!) and then set it up permanently on the eighth day (= 1 Nisan). It is that last act that concerns the text of Exodus 40. For more on this problem, see n. 34 below.

27. William Propp, *Exodus 19-40: A New Translation with Introduction and Commentary*, AB 2A (New York: Doubleday, 2006), 673, observes that the logical place to

Propp has suggested that the biblical author has deliberately slurred time, collapsing all these foundational events into an atemporal *illud tempus*, that is, a moment in sacred time that interrupts the restless advance of ordinary, historical time.[28] A useful comparison could be found in the Protevangelium of James. This apocryphal text from the second century CE tells the story of the birth of Christ from the vantage point of the Virgin Mary. Following the order of Luke's Gospel, it recounts the events leading up to the birth of Christ in a matter-of-fact way. Then, while Joseph is out looking for a midwife to help with the birth (not realizing that this is not necessary), the narrator abruptly switches from a third-person account to Joseph's own experience. When Christ is born, time stops:

> I, Joseph, was walking and yet I was not walking. I lifted my gaze toward the vault of heaven and saw it standing still; then at the air and I saw it seized with dread; and the birds of the heaven, motionless. Then I looked upon the earth and saw a cooking-pot placed there and workmen reclining with their hands in the pot. Those who were chewing did not chew; those who were in the midst of serving themselves did not take; and those who were raising food toward their mouths did not raise it. But the face of all were turned upwards. Then I saw sheep being driven and sheep were stopped. The shepherd raised his hand to smite them, but his raised hand was immobilized. Then I looked upon the flow of the river and I saw kidgoats with their mouths posed over the water, but they did not drink.

---

have the story of the consecration of the tabernacle and priesthood (Lev. 8) would have been after the description of the lustration rites in Exodus 40:30–32. Had the story been written this way the commands given regarding the consecration (vv. 9–15) would have been completed in the same chapter.

28. It is important to note, in support of this thesis, that there are a number of other details that reflect the slurring of time. At the conclusion of Exodus 40 there is a reference to the role the tabernacle will have in guiding Israel through the desert. Its placement here is premature; it points forward to Numbers 9:15–23, the story of that guidance once the people of Israel are on the march. Similarly, in Numbers 7 the story of the offerings of the tribal chiefs is said to have coordinated with the erection of the tabernacle but is retold many chapters later. There is no need to give a complete tally of such details. The point should be clear: the events of the Sinai period do not unfold in a strict chronological fashion. In the case of the erection of the tabernacle and the beginning of altar service—because they were actions grounded in creation itself—it is fitting that they would be narrated in a mode that was outside the restless advance of quotidian time.

Then all things, in one instant, were being driven on again by their own impetus. (Prot. Jas. 18)[29]

As Mircea Eliade, the great scholar of comparative religion, has observed, sacred time has a Parmenidean character.[30] It does not pass like ordinary time. The restless advance of this world is momentarily put on hold to mark the intrusion of God into space and time. Propp's suggestion is certainly apt. The difficulty the reader has in coordinating the theophanies of Exodus 40 and Leviticus 9 parallels, in its own way, the stoppage of time we see in the Protevangelium of James.

But this explanation is not the whole story. Menahem Haran and Baruch Katz have suggested that the presentation of events in the Pentateuch is driven just as much by literary theme as it is by chronological order. The book of Exodus emphasizes the *structure* of the tabernacle building (Exod. 25–31, 35–40);[31] Leviticus, on the other hand, focuses on the altar and its *service* (Lev. 1–10). The book of Numbers turns its attention to the mustering of the tribes around the tabernacle and its role in the *guidance* of Israel through the wilderness to the promised land (Num. 1–9). In broadest array, this thematic presentation of the material respects the chronological unfolding of the story. In order for there to be an altar where God can be served, there must be a tabernacle wherein God can dwell. And in order for the deity to guide Israel in wilderness, there must be priestly and Levitical hands to oversee and carry out the porterage of the tabernacle.

Yet elements within these three thematic categories can also upset the strict rules that govern chronological progression. Let us look at the story about the sacrificial materials and draught animals that the tribal elders brought to the tabernacle in Numbers 7. These elders were first mentioned in the census of Numbers 1:5–15 and the need for draught animals was explained in the rules governing the transport of the tabernacle in Numbers 4. In this respect Numbers 7 fits the context. Yet the chronological notice that opens the chapter

29. Translation is taken from François Bovon, "The Suspension of Time in Chapter 18 of *Proevangelium Jacobi*," in *The Future of Early Christianity*, ed. B. Pearson (Minneapolis: Fortress, 1991), 394.

30. Mircea Eliade, *The Sacred and the Profane: The Nature of Religion*, trans. Willard R. Trask (New York: Harcourt, 1959), 69.

31. Menahem Haran, "Book-Size and Thematic Cycles in the Pentateuch," in *Die Hebräische Bibel und ihre zweifache Nachgeschichte*, ed. E. Blum, C. Macholz, and E. Stegemann (Neukirchen-Vluyn: Neukirchener, 1990), 165–76; Baruch Katz, "Make Me a Sanctuary That I Might Dwell among You" (Hebrew), *Megadim* 6 (1998): 17–21.

breaks this chronological frame and takes us back to the events of Exodus 40: "On the day when Moses had finished setting up the tabernacle (= 1 Nisan), and had anointed and consecrated it with all its furnishings, the leaders of Israel . . . made offerings" (7:1–2).[32] Clearly the subject matter of the chapter (the draught animals offered by the tribal elders) has governed its literary placement rather than chronology.[33]

The thematic manner of presentation also allows our author to give the several dimensions of the tabernacle the independent development due to them.[34]

---

32. The Hebrew literally reads: "On the *day* (*be-yom*) that Moses finished setting up the tabernacle. "If so, the narrative about the offerings made by the chieftains would have begun on the first of Nisan. But this Hebrew phrase could also be translated: "*When* Moses finished . . .*"; so, Milgrom, *The JPS Torah Commentary: Numbers* (Philadelphia: Jewish Publication Society, 1989), 53 and 362–63. In this case, the offerings would have been sometime after the first of Nisan. Contra Milgrom, Liane Feldman, *The Story of Sacrifice: Ritual and Narrative in the Priestly Source*, FAT 141 (Tübingen: Mohr Siebeck, 2020), 121–34, argues that this unit is a flashback to Exodus 40, making many of the same arguments that I do (see the following note).

33. If we presume that Numbers 7 is a flashback to events of Exodus 40, then the curious reference to the manner in which Moses received the revelation of the law within the tabernacle at the close of the chapter (7:89) makes more sense. It is not a mysterious non sequitur. Rather, it recalls (and parallels) the chronological placement of its double, Leviticus 1:1. Just as Leviticus 1:1 comes after the building and consecration of the tabernacle on 1 Nisan, so Numbers 7:89 follows immediately after the tabernacle was erected and consecrated. A single event is narrated in two different places. In any event, it is worth noting that some ancient Jewish readers placed the giving of the laws that began in Leviticus 1:1 after the lighting of the sacrificial pyre in Leviticus 9:23.

And just as the end of Exodus (40:36–38) proleptically anticipates the journey of the tabernacle in the book of Numbers (9:15–23), so Leviticus 1:1 anticipates the revelation of the law to Moses in Numbers 7:89. We should also note the unusual placement of the priestly blessing in Numbers 6:22–27 as well as the doublet regarding the lighting of the lamps of the menorah (Num. 8:1–4; compare Exod. 27:20–21). The blessing has often been linked to consecration of the tabernacle (Lev. 9:22) and the lighting of the lamps is also associated with the beginning of the tamid rites of the tabernacle (see Exod. 40:4 and 24). All told, three different texts in this portion of Numbers can be read as flashbacks to the events of the first of Nisan (Num. 6:22–27; 7:89; and 8:1–4).

See Pseudo-Philo, LAB 14.1 for some significant parallels. The revelation of the sacrificial law (Lev. 1:1) follows the ordination of the priesthood (LAB 13.1d [= Leviticus 8–10]). Similarly, Josephus in his *Jewish Antiquities* (*Ant.* 3.224) recounts the giving of the sacrificial laws (Lev. 1:1) just after concluding the narrative about the consecration of the priesthood and the error of Nadab and Abihu (Lev. 8–10).

34. See Shama, "Two Thematic Tendencies." Building on Katz, "Make Me a Sanctuary," he argues that the chronological problems are not resolvable but represent the two thematic centers of the narrative. The irresolvable nature of the problem should be

The tabernacle structure, as a result, is neither a vehicle for enacting cultic law nor a spot that provides the platform for sacrifice. No, the building and the theology of divine presence that it represents constitute a good unto itself. Bringing the tabernacle erection to a full stop long before the priests are ordained, Jeffrey Tigay suggests, "allow[s] the reader to contemplate the phenomenon of God dwelling on earth with a symbol of his presence in full view of the Israelites."[35]

I cannot unpack at this point the full ramifications of this thesis. In part, that will be the task of the next two chapters. But in order to illustrate the importance of this thematic thread let me point to two images of the tabernacle from the Second Temple period. Both images have important eschatological dimensions. They describe what the Jewish people looked forward to when they prayed for the rebuilding of the temple. The first image is a coin from the second Jewish revolt, otherwise known as the Bar Kokhba revolt (ca. 132–135 CE) (see fig. 3.2 in the next chapter). A substantial hope during this period was the rebuilding of the temple. We will look at the coin in greater depth in our next chapter, but it is important to point out that the coin depicts the façade of the temple with the table of presence (Exod. 25:23–30) moved forward to the central opening for viewing. The temple, according to the theology of this coin, is the home in which God *dwells*. The other image is from a synagogue floor mosaic found in the Galilean city of Sepphoris dating to the fifth century (see panel 3 of the mosaic, fig. 4.1 below). The panel that I have excerpted depicts the events of the daily sacrificial (tamid) rite described at the end of Exodus 29 once Aaron had been ordained to the priesthood. The mosaic directs our attention to the altar where God is *served*.

These two images depict the central themes of the Tabernacle Narrative we have been tracing in this chapter. By writing the story the way he did, the Priestly author accords an independent significance to each of these two themes and prevents the reader from reducing the significance of the building

---

emphasized. Though the rabbinic reading would seem to solve the problem of how to orient the commands given in Exodus 40:1–16 with the fulfillment of those commands in 40:17–33 and Leviticus 8–9, it must be stated this rabbinic solution creates some rather unwieldy problems of its own. On their reckoning Moses must put up and take down the tabernacle for the last seven days of Adar. The final moment of assemblage would take place on the eighth day (i.e., 1 Nisan), which is the moment of construction narrated in the second half of Exodus 40. For a glimpse at how complicated the Rabbinic solutions could become, consult the summary of Nachmanides (also known as the Ramban) in his commentary on Exodus 40. See the edition of Charles Ber Chavel, *Ramban: Commentary on the Torah*, 5 vols. (New York: Shilo, 1971–1976), 2:616–20.

35. Adele Berlin and Marc Zvi Brettler, eds., *The Jewish Study Bible* (Oxford: Oxford University Press, 2004), 202.

to simply the site for liturgical activity. The building, as the house of God, participates in and reflects something of the very being of God.

Conclusion

In the opening pages of this chapter, I noted that it would have a major and a minor goal. The major burden of the chapter has been to lay out why the Tabernacle Narrative was composed with two climaxes, one focusing on indwelling, the other on altar service. The independence of these two themes was visually illustrated in the rabbinic period by two different ways of conceptualizing the hopes for a rebuilt temple. One image put the furniture of the temple front and center and so stressed the temple as God's dwelling place; the other image set its focal point on the altar and the restoration of temple sacrifice. As our discussion has drawn to a close we have seen, however, that our chapter's minor theme—the tabernacle as the completion of creation—was not actually so minor. As William Propp has shown, drawing on the work of Mircea Eliade, the temporal confusion that characterizes the way these two themes are laid out owes much to their linkage back to creation itself. Time, in that primordial moment, does not participate in the restless advance of historical progress. Creation is characterized by an atemporal *illud tempus* that "overcomes the limits of linear, profane time." By deliberately confusing the reader as to the relationship between the first of Nisan (Exod. 40) and the eighth day (Lev. 8–9), the chronological advance of the Sinaitic revelation seemingly grinds to a halt and, in certain texts, appears to flow backwards (Num. 7).[36] There has been an understandable tendency among interpreters to try to find the solution to this textual puzzle. It has been my contention, however, that the creation of this puzzle was the intention of our author. Any sort of final certainty will never be attained.

---

36. Over the course of this chapter I have examined three chapters that are structured around a sevenfold approbation formula (Gen. 1, Exod. 40, and Lev. 8). There is one more chapter we could include in this genre—Exodus 39, which documents the making of the priestly vestments. For a more thorough examination of how this formula structures each of these chapters and how each chapter utilizes this formula in its own unique way (ordered to the unique literary needs of each chapter) see my article "The Inauguration of the Tabernacle Service at Sinai," 1–15.

CHAPTER 3

Seeing God

Walk about Zion, go all around about it, count its towers, consider well its ramparts, go through its citadels, that you may tell the next generation that *this is God*, our God forever and ever.

Psalm 48:12–14

It is not for nothing that the blessed Moses is commanded to submit first to purification and then to be separated from those who have not undergone this. When every purification is complete (his forty days of fasting) he hears the many-voiced trumpets. He sees the many lights, pure and with rays streaming abundantly. Then, standing apart from the crowds and accompanied by chosen priests, he pushes ahead to the summit of the divine ascents. *And yet he does not meet God Himself, but contemplates, not Him Who is invisible, but rather where He stands.*

St. Denys the Areopagite[1]

One of the best places in the Bible to see how the structure of the tabernacle is related to the divine presence is Numbers 4. This chapter describes how the tabernacle is to be dismantled to prepare for its journey to the land of Israel. The chapter is, in many respects, a reversal of Exodus 40, the story of its erection. But because the Levites play such a central role in this chapter, we will need to digress for a moment and provide some background knowledge about them.

1. The text is from Paul Rorem, "Moses as Paradigm for the Liturgical Spirituality of Pseudo-Dionysius," in *Studia Patristica* 18:2, ed. Elizabeth A. Livingstone (Kalamazoo, MI: Cistercian Publications, 1989), 275–79, here 276. In most modern treatments St. Denys is referred to as Pseudo-Dionysius since the figure in question is certainly not the person named in Acts 17:34. I have followed traditional church practice and have dropped the title "pseudo" from his name. All modern scholars believe that the author of the "Mystical Theology" lived in the fifth or sixth century.

49

The Levitical Family

The term "Levite" poses something of a challenge for the ordinary reader of the Bible. On the one hand, the term refers to the offspring of the patriarch Levi, the third son of Jacob's wife Leah. Because Levi is the father of Israel's priestly line the third biblical book bears his name. The book of Leviticus thus deals with the laws that govern service of the altar.

But in the priestly writings of the Pentateuch, the term Levite has a narrower meaning. It refers to those individuals who served as assistants to the priests. All of this can be gleaned from the genealogy of the priestly line preserved in Exodus. I have highlighted the individuals in Levi's offspring that will lead to the priestly family proper:

> [16] The following are the names of the sons of Levi according to their genealogies: Gershon, *Kohath*, and Merari, and the length of Levi's life was one hundred thirty-seven years. [17] The sons of Gershon: Libni and Shimei, by their families. [18] The sons of Kohath: *Amram*, Izhar, Hebron, and Uzziel, and the length of Kohath's life was one hundred thirty-three years . . . [20] Amram married *Jochebed* his father's sister and she bore him *Aaron* and Moses, and the length of Amram's life was one hundred thirty-seven years. (Exod. 6:16–20)

The story begins with Levi begetting three sons: Gershon, Kohath, and Merari, each of whom will become the name of a major Levitical clan. Kohath sires Amram who marries Jochebed. She gives birth to Aaron, the man through whom the office of priest will descend. The remaining sons who descend from Gershon, Kohath, and Merari will serve in a subordinate role. Aaron and his sons will tend the tabernacle proper and its altar; the Levitical clans will assist from a safe distance away.

The first four chapters of the book of Numbers are devoted to the preparations Israel must undertake to continue their journey to the promised land. The first order of business is to take a census—hence the name of the book, the *numbering* of the tribes of Israel—of the twelve tribes and to station the respective tribes around the tabernacle as they embark on their journey (Num. 1:1–45; see fig. 3.1). The tribe of Levi, however, is exempted from this initial census because of their sacral responsibilities:

> Only the tribe of Levi you shall not enroll, and you shall not take a census of them with the other Israelites. [50] Rather you shall appoint the Levites

over the tabernacle of the covenant, and over all its equipment, and over all that belongs to it; they are to carry the tabernacle and all its equipment, and they shall tend it, and shall camp around the tabernacle. [51] When the tabernacle is to set out, the Levites shall take it down; and when the tabernacle is to be pitched, the Levites shall set it up. And any outsider who comes near shall be put to death. [52] The other Israelites shall camp in their respective regimental camps, by companies; [53] but the Levites shall camp around the tabernacle of the covenant, that there may be no wrath on the congregation of the Israelites; and the Levites shall perform the guard duty of the tabernacle of the covenant. (Num. 1:49–53)

Dismantling the Tabernacle: Numbers 4

One of the principal tasks of the Levitical families is to assist Aaron in the dismantling of the tabernacle and preparing it for its journey to the promised land. Numbers 4 describes the actions that will be incumbent on each of the three families, beginning with Kohath and then Gershon and Merari.

Kohath	Gershon	Merari
[4:1] The LORD spoke to Moses and Aaron, saying:	[4:21] Then the LORD spoke to Moses, saying:	
[2] Take a census of the *Kohathites* separate from the other Levites,	[22] Take a census of the *Gershonites* also,	[4:29] As for the *Merarites*, you shall enroll them
by their clans and their ancestral houses,	by their ancestral houses and their clans;	by their clans and their ancestral houses;
[3] from thirty years old up to fifty years old, all who qualify to do work relating to the tent of meeting.	[23] from thirty years old up to fifty years old you shall enroll them, all who qualify to do work in the tent of meeting.	[30] from thirty years old up to fifty years old you shall enroll them, everyone who qualifies to do the work of the tent of meeting.
[4] This is the service of the Kohathites relating to the tent of meeting: the most holy things.	[24] This is the service of the clans of the Gershonites, in dismantling and carrying.	[31] This is what they are charged to carry, as the whole of their service in the tent of meeting:

51

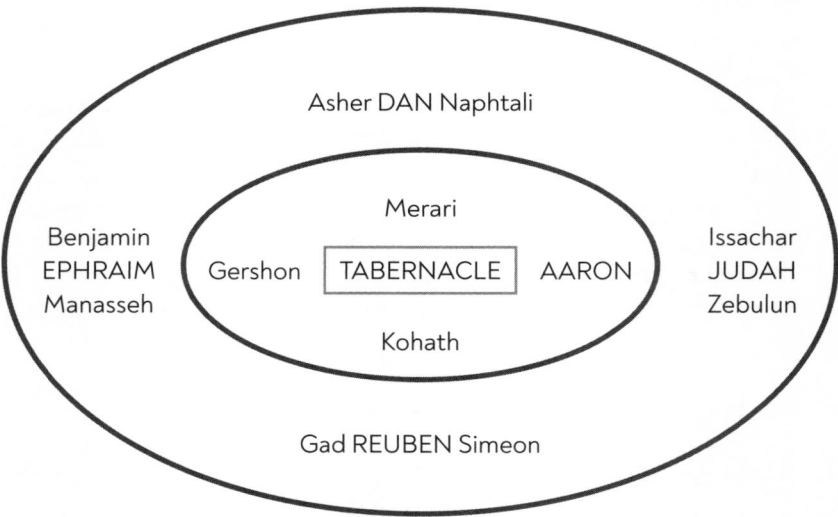

Figure 3.1 Israel's encampment in the wilderness of Sinai with twelve tribes around the outer perimeter and three Levitical clans and Aaron around the inner perimeter

There are a number of similarities between the lists. Each (a) singles out the Levitical family in question (vv. 2, 22, and 29), (b) limits the men to be counted to those between the ages of thirty and fifty (vv. 3, 23, and 30), and (c) introduces the items each clan will dismantle and carry (vv. 4, 24, and 31).

The last item will be the focus of our interest. After the opening sentences, the author lists the pieces of the tabernacle that each Levitical family must carry. The specific responsibilities of the latter two families, Gershon and Merari, are presented in a very similar fashion.

Gershon	Merari
⁴:²⁴ This is the service of the clans of the Gershonites, in serving and bearing burdens: ²⁵ They shall carry:	⁴:³¹ This is what they are charged to carry, as the whole of their service in the tent of meeting:

the curtains of the tabernacle, and the tent of meeting with its covering, and the outer covering of fine leather that is on top of it, and the screen for the entrance of the tent of meeting, [26] and the hangings of the court, and the screen for the entrance of the gate of the court that is around the tabernacle and the altar.

the frames of the tabernacle, with its bars, pillars, and bases, [32] and the pillars of the court all around with their bases, pegs, and cords, with all their equipment and all their related service; and you shall assign by name the objects that they are required to carry.

In the case of the Kohathites, the presentation is quite different.

[4] This is the service of the Kohathites relating to the tent of meeting: the most holy things.
   [5] When the camp is to set out, Aaron and his sons shall go in and take down the screening curtain, and cover the ark of the covenant with it; [6] then they shall put on it a covering of fine leather, and spread over that a cloth all of blue, and shall put its poles in place. [7] Over the table of the bread of the Presence they shall spread a blue cloth, and put on it the plates, the dishes for incense, the bowls, and the flagons for the drink offering; the regular bread also shall be on it; [8] then they shall spread over them a crimson cloth, and cover it with a covering of fine leather, and shall put its poles in place. [9] They shall take a blue cloth, and cover the lampstand for the light, with its lamps, its snuffers, its trays, and all the vessels for oil with which it is supplied; [10] and they shall put it with all its utensils in a covering of fine leather, and put it on the carrying frame. [11] Over the golden altar they shall spread a blue cloth, and cover it with a covering of fine leather, and shall put its poles in place; [12] and they shall take all the utensils of the service that are used in the sanctuary, and put them in a blue cloth, and cover them with a covering of fine leather, and put them on the carrying frame. [13] They shall take away the ashes from the [bronze] altar, and spread a purple cloth over it; [14] and they shall put on it all the utensils of the altar, which are used for the service there, the firepans, the forks, the shovels, and the basins, all the utensils of the altar; and they shall spread on it a covering of fine leather, and shall put its poles in place.
   [15] When Aaron and his sons have finished covering the sanctuary and all the furnishings of the sanctuary, as the camp sets out, after that the Kohathites shall come to carry these, but they must not touch the holy things, or they will die. These are the things of the tent of meeting that the Kohathites are to carry. (Num. 4:5–15)

Unlike the cases of the Gershonites and the Merarites, the responsibilities of the Kohathites do not follow directly from the introductory words: "This is the service of the Kohathites . . ." (v. 4). A long digression (vv. 5–14) regarding *Aaron's* responsibilities stands in its place. Only in v. 15 does the text return to the responsibilities for the Kohathites. Why this lengthy digression? The answer is given at the end of the paragraph: "[the Kohathites] must not touch the holy things, or they will die" (v. 15).

Clearly the furniture is of a much higher order of sanctity than either the curtains of the tabernacle or its wooden framework. The significance of the furniture is marked in two ways: how it is to be dismantled and its manner of transportation. The fabrics as well as the beams and boards are to be loaded onto carts and hauled by oxen. The inner furniture, however, is to be "appareled" in expensive fabrics and borne on the shoulders of the sons of Kohath.[2] The sanctity of the various items of furniture is graded according to the number, color, and quality of the materials used to cover them. The ark is clearly the most sacred. This is marked by the fact that Aaron must first take down the inner veil, the most sacred of all the fabrics of the tabernacle, and walk in such a way that he will not see the ark as he places the veil over it. The standard rule in the tabernacle was no one could lay their eyes directly on this most sacred item. The ark was then adorned with a piece of fine leather. A purple fabric was put on top so that all the Israelites who had a view of the Kohathites in procession would know which piece of furniture was the ark. The remainder of the items, including the table, the lampstand, and the golden and bronze altars, were similarly adorned but with fabrics that became increasingly less valuable, reflecting the lower grade of sanctity that attended them.

There is another detail worth pondering in this chapter. The Priestly narrator punctuates significant moments in his story by introducing them with the formula: "The LORD spoke to Moses, saying . . ." We saw this formula used seven times in Exodus 25–31 to mark the discrete commands needed to erect and initiate the use of the tabernacle. In Numbers 3, the beginning of the laws governing the Levitical clans, it is used five times to mark major themes within the chapter: the initial command to bring Levi forward (v. 5); the statement that the Levites constitute a replacement for the firstborn of the womb (v. 11);

---

2. Jacob Milgrom, *The JPS Torah Commentary: Numbers* (Philadelphia: Jewish Publication Society, 1990), 26, where he notes that the Hebrew word *beged*, translated as "cloth" (used seven times), "usually covers only human beings; it is no accident that a conspicuous exception is made with all the sancta in that they too are initially covered by a *beged*. They are treated with the same respect as human beings, indeed, like royalty since they are dressed in regal clothing made of violet or purple."

and the commands to record all the male Levites (v. 14), record all the firstborn males among the Israelites (v. 40) and subtract the number of Levites from the firstborn of Israel and make up the difference by means of a five shekel redemption fee (v. 44).

Numbers 4 constitutes a second, more focused census; all the Levites from the ages of thirty to fifty must be conscripted for transporting the tabernacle. As expected, the chapter begins with the formula, "The LORD spoke to Moses and Aaron saying: take a census of the Kohathites" (v. 1), and the formula is repeated for the Gershonites (v. 21). What is unexpected is the repetition of the formula of address within the commands given to the Kohathites (v. 17). What is so significant about this particular paragraph that it must be introduced in this solemn fashion?

> [17] Then the LORD spoke to Moses and Aaron, saying: [18] You must not let the tribe of the clans of the Kohathites be destroyed from among the Levites. [19] This is how you must deal with them in order that they may live and not die when they come near to the most holy things: Aaron and his sons shall go in and assign each to a particular task or burden. [20] But the Kohathites must not go in to look on the holy things even for a moment; otherwise, they will die.[3]

The first couple of admonitions reinforce what had already been stated in v. 15: touching the holy furniture will be fatal. It is uncharacteristic of the laws in Numbers to engage in repetition of this sort; our author clearly wants to underscore the dangers involved. But the last sentence of this paragraph goes further. Not only is touching dangerous; even *seeing* these sacred objects could be lethal (v. 20).

The idea that even seeing the furniture constitutes a mortal danger calls to mind an obvious parallel: the danger of seeing God directly. For example, when Moses asks to see God's glory, God responds: "You cannot see my face; for no one shall see me and live" (Exod. 33:20). Or when Manoah, the father of Samson, sees the angel of the Lord ascend in the flames around his sacrificial offering, he exclaims to his wife: "We shall surely die, for we have seen God" (Judg. 13:22).[4] By comparing the danger of seeing the furniture to

---

3. The phrase "even for a moment" is uncertain (v. 20) and disputed. On various solutions, see Milgrom, *Numbers*, 29. But none of the different explanations will affect the point we are making.

4. Milgrom astutely observes that the lethal danger that attends viewing the sacred

that of seeing God Almighty, the author of Numbers 4:20 has drawn a strong parallel between the being of God and the furniture that adorns his house. In some undefined fashion, the furniture participates in the being of God. In what follows, I would like to suggest some other biblical texts that share this high estimation of the tabernacle furniture.

The Ark and the Presence of God

As scholars have long noted, the ark is regularly identified with the LORD's presence and at one time in its history was the subject of ceremonial processions. This is certainly implied by the liturgical refrain of Num. 10:35–36:

> When the ark was to set out, Moses would say:
> Advance, O LORD!
> May your enemies be scattered,
> And may your foes flee before you!
> And when it halted, he would say:
> Return, O LORD,
> Unto the ten thousands of Israel!

The feature to be noted here is the inseparable connection between the ark and the being of God. As the ark ventures forth in battle, Moses can confidently assert: "Advance, O Lord!" A similar identification of the ark with the being of God is presumed by the entrance liturgy of Psalm 24:7–10, "Lift up your heads, O gates! And be lifted up, O ancient doors! That the King of glory may come in." According to Frank M. Cross this portion of Psalm 24 was used as an antiphonal liturgy in the autumn festival and "had its origin in the procession of the Ark to the sanctuary at its founding, celebrated annually in the cult of Solomon and perhaps even of David."[5]

The close nexus between God and this piece of cultic furniture is nicely illustrated in the story of the battle with the Philistines that would eventually

---

furniture stems from ancient Near Eastern notions about the relationship between a god (or goddess) and the temple that he or she inhabits. In one text, for example, the city of Agade is cursed because "the Akkadians saw the holy vessels of the gods." In another text, the city of Ur is destroyed because "the holy kettles that no one (was permitted) to look upon, the enemy looked upon." See *Numbers*, 29.

5. Frank M. Cross, *Canaanite Myth and Hebrew Epic* (Cambridge: Harvard University Press, 1973), 93.

lead to its capture. Having been routed badly in an initial exchange of hostilities, the Israelite militia regroup to prepare a new strategy. "Let us bring the ark of the covenant of the LORD here from Shiloh," they decide, "so that he may come among us and save us from the power of our enemies" (1 Sam. 4:3). The response to the ark's entry into the Israelite war camp reveals the closeness of the attachment of God's being to this piece of furniture.

> When the ark of the covenant of the LORD came into the camp, all Israel gave a mighty shout, so that the earth resounded. ⁶ When the Philistines heard the noise of the shouting, they said, "What does this great shouting in the camp of the Hebrews mean?" When they learned that the ark of the LORD had come to the camp, ⁷ the Philistines were afraid; for they said, "Gods have come into the camp." They also said, "Woe to us! For nothing like this has happened before. ⁸ Woe to us! Who can deliver us from the power of these mighty gods? These are the gods who struck the Egyptians with every sort of plague in the wilderness. (1 Sam. 4:5-8)

To the surprise of the Israelites, the Philistines emerge as victors, capturing the ark and returning home with it as a symbol of the supreme power of their god. As the story unfolds, the Philistines learn the devastating price of possessing this piece of furniture; after taking counsel, they decide to return it to Beth Shemesh in order to be rid of the troubles it causes. Initially, the response of the Israelites is jubilation at its return: "Now the people of Beth Shemesh were reaping their wheat harvest in the valley. When they looked up and saw the ark, they went with rejoicing to meet it" (1 Sam. 6:13). Next, the proper Levitical authorities come forward, as the law required, to remove the ark from the cart on which it had traveled (6:15).⁶ Then sacrifices are made in honor of its return. The Israelites, however, did not fully learn their lesson about the power of God that resides in the ark. When it arrives in Beth Shemesh, some of the residents die "when they looked into the ark of the LORD" (1 Sam. 6:19). As P. Kyle McCarter notes, this punishment follows directly from the logic of Numbers 4:20.⁷ Laypersons were not qualified to look at the ark; only the proper sacerdotal authorities could attend it. The

---

6. Outside of the books of Leviticus and Deuteronomy, the distinction between priest and Levite is not consistently observed. P. K. McCarter, *I Samuel*, AB 8 (Garden City, NY: Doubleday, 1980), 136, regards the reference to the Levites as secondary and "inserted late in the literary history of the passage by a fastidious scribe, who insisted that the ark must have been handled by the Levites, members of the official priestly tribe of Israel."

7. McCarter, *I Samuel*, 131.

close linkage of the being of God to the furniture of the sanctuary could not be clearer. As Stephen Chapman observes, the ark's relationship to the deity cannot be "merely symbolic, the narrative depicts the ark as representing the 'real presence' of God precisely by personifying it."[8] This becomes clear from the reaction of the people of Beth Shemesh to the deaths of those who looked improperly at the ark. "Who is able to stand before the LORD, this holy God?" (1 Sam. 6:20). These words—echoed in two entrance liturgies to the temple (Pss. 15:1 and 24:3)—identify standing before the LORD with standing before the ark. A similar thought is expressed by the prophet Jeremiah, who follows up his words of praise for the ark, "O glorious throne [=ark], exalted from the beginning. Shrine of our sanctuary!" with the exclamation: "O hope of Israel! O LORD!" Though God is not reducible to the ark, his presence is nevertheless so closely interwoven with it that one can point to the ark as it approaches in processions and say, "Here comes God."[9]

There can be no denying the significance of the ark as a marker of divine presence in Israelite religion. But as we learn from Numbers 4, it is not only the ark that carries such significance, but the other sacred pieces of tabernacle furniture as well. The point to be noted is that the very real, palpable presence of the invisible God within his shrine is linked in some way to the attending furniture. In other texts, however, the sanctity of the shrine could extend even further. Consider Psalm 48, a text that describes the circumambulation of the city of Jerusalem after the destruction of enemy forces that foolishly attempted to overtake it. Having exhorted the inhabitants of Zion and the surrounding province of Judah to stream forth in pilgrimage to celebrate this event, the

---

8. Stephen Chapman, *1 Samuel as Christian Scripture* (Grand Rapids: Eerdmans, 2016), 93.

9. It may be worth pointing out that in the *Chicago Assyrian Dictionary* the entry *ilu* or "god" has as its seventh meaning: "image of the deity." For the way this works itself out in Second Temple Judaism one might note the important and widespread theme that the most valuable temple furniture (notably the ark) was hidden prior to the Babylonian destruction and will be revealed at the eschaton. There will not be time in this essay to go into any of the details, but clearly implied here is the notion that just as God himself was not as fully present in the Second Temple neither was his full array of furniture. Like a summer beach house, the provisions of that reconstructed building were of a lower grade than the furniture of one's true home. Strikingly the Temple Scroll from Qumran includes instructions for assembling almost all the furniture and in the glory of its original condition. See the essay by Lawrence Schiffman, "The Furnishings of the Temple according to the Temple Scroll," in *The Madrid Qumran Congress: Proceedings of the International Congress on the Dead Sea Scrolls*, ed. Luis Vegas Montaner and Julio Trebolle Barrera, STDJ 11 (Leiden: Brill, 1992), 2:621–34. He does not discuss the relationship of the instructions to build this furniture with parallel traditions that await their revelation at the end of time.

psalmist urges them to make a close visual inspection of the architecture of the city. "Walk about Zion, go all around about it," he urges, "count its towers, consider well its ramparts, go through its citadels, that you may tell the next generation that this is God, our God forever and ever" (48:12–14). It is the last line that should occasion some surprise. For here our author seems to take his paean of praise to unimaginable heights. It is these buildings, he claims, that testify to the very being of God. As even the very traditional Jewish commentator Amos Hacham puts it, "[Regarding the phrase] 'this is God,' the word 'this' [*zeh*] is similar in meaning to 'look here.' It is an expression of palpable excitement and its point is that the one who sees the Temple in its splendor and glory feels within himself as if he saw, face to face, the glory (*kavod*) of the Lord. He cries, 'this [building] is God, our God.'"[10]

What I would like to suggest is that this language is not solely a result of the excess or superfluity that characterizes the genre of praise (though obviously this is a factor). Rather, these materials give witness to a deeply held view that God really dwells in the temple and that all the pieces of that building share in some fashion in his tangible and visible presence. To use a modern metaphor, one might imagine the temple as a giant electrical plant powering the land of Israel. In its core was a nuclear reactor in which the radioactive rods emitted divine energy absorbed by the entire infrastructure of the building. Though the glow was brightest at the center, even the periphery had to be entered and handled with caution. Not even the thickest cement wall or lead surface could prevent these divine energies from overwhelming their boundaries and radiating their divine powers upon whatever stood in its vicinity.

Mesopotamian texts provide a very close parallel. "The aura of a god in his temple," W. G. Lambert writes, "could so attach itself to the temple, or architectural parts of it in particular, also to the implements he used, and to the city which housed the temple, in such a way that these various things also became gods and received offerings as a mark of the fact."[11] Certainly it should occasion no surprise to learn that the statue of the god was imbued with the veritable presence of the deity in question, but most remarkable is that even the furniture and other appurtenances dedicated to the temple would come to share in this divine aura.[12] The whole building pulsated with the veritable

10. Amos Hacham, *Sefer Tehillim*, Da'at Miqra (Jerusalem: Mossad Harav Kook, 1990), 278 (Hebrew). The translation is my own.

11. W. G. Lambert, "Ancient Mesopotamian Gods: Superstition, Philosophy, Theology," *RHR* 207 (1990): 129.

12. Note the concluding observations of Gebhard Selz's remarkable essay, "The Holy Drum, the Spear, and the Harp: Towards an Understanding of the Problems of Deification

presence of the god. Mesopotamian texts had a decisive grammatical advantage over their biblical brethren; they could mark the overflow of the divine energies by attaching a DINGIR sign (the cuneiform sign that marks an object as divine or divine-like) to lists of temple furniture.[13] The physical structure of the temple itself literally shared in the presence of the invisible deity who dwelled therein.

Some readers will, no doubt, get nervous at the suggestion that the tabernacle building somehow shared in the presence of God. Israel's religion was famously aniconic in the sense that any representation of the deity in the form of a statue was strictly forbidden. Taken to an extreme, one would have to deny any ontological connection between the structure of the tabernacle and the deity that dwelled within. But I think that this would be a difficult position to maintain. What Numbers 4, the Ark Narrative in Samuel, and Psalm 48 share is the sense that gazing on the sacred artifacts is akin to seeing some aspect of God himself. These artifacts should not be confused with God, but neither are they completely separate from him. In this sense, Lambert's observation that the aura of a god in his temple could attach itself to anything close at hand remains relevant. Though Israel did not place a statue of her God in the tabernacle, she fervently asserted that the deity resided in the tabernacle or temple just the same. And the objects in his near vicinity were not unaffected by that presence.

Surprisingly, ancient readers of the Bible did not share the nervousness many moderns feel about linking the divine to material reality. Instead, it is precisely these sorts of media that render the invisible, ineffable God approachable and knowable. The Byzantine theologian John of Damascus grounds this type of spiritual experience in our creaturely nature. "Because we are twofold, fashioned of soul and body, and because our soul is not naked, but covered as if by a veil, it is impossible for us to attain to spiritual things apart from corporeal realities."[14] Certainly this is the reason that St. Denys, the father of Christian

---

in the Third Millennium Mesopotamia," in *Sumerian Gods and Their Representations*, ed. Irving L. Finkel and Markham J. Geller (Grönigen: Styx, 1997), 184: "A statue of a god was an independent entity, because it stood on a holy place, and had the name of a god, the appearance of a god, and so on. It was these qualities of a statue, including its partaking in certain rituals, which left no doubt that it was the god himself. *The same holds true for the "cultic objects"; it is their function and their special attributes, including their participation in holy rites, which made them god-like*" (emphasis mine). Compare also the essay of Karel van der Toorn, "Worshipping Stones: On the Deification of Cult Symbols," *JNSL* 23 (1997): 1–14.

13. Selz, "Holy Drum," 176–79.

14. Cited in Nicholas Constas, "Symeon of Thessalonike and the Theology of the Icon Screen," *Thresholds of the Sacred*, ed. Sharon E. J. Gerstel (Washington, DC: Dumbarton Oaks, 2006), 168 n. 21.

mysticism, wrote that we cannot "meet God himself," but we can "contemplate
. . . where he stands." Michael Wyschogrod makes a similar point when he observes that many Jews "have this sense of the indwelling of God before the western wall. There are all kinds of stories about extremely assimilated, secular Jews
arriving in Jerusalem and showing up at the western wall and being overcome
by a deep emotional experience." For this reason, the Rav Kook, the great religious Zionist of the first half of the twentieth century, said that the stones of the
Western Wall were not mute and lifeless but in possession of a heart. Though
care should be taken not to overdraw the linkage between God and tabernacle,
one should recognize the correlative danger of ignoring any linkage at all.

Divinized Temple Furniture in Postbiblical Judaism

This deeply rooted ancient Near Eastern and biblical tradition of linking the
appurtenances of the shrine to the indwelling god had a vibrant afterlife in
postbiblical Judaism. In the Songs of Sabbath Sacrifice (4Q400–407, 11Q17)
from Qumran there is regularly some confusion as to whether a particular
title identifies the God of Israel or the building in which God resides.[15] Such
syntactic difficulties are regular enough that one has a hard time imagining
that it is the gulf of many centuries between composition and commentary
creating the problem. The text itself seems to enjoy the confusion it creates between the two categories. As Carol Newsom has argued, these thirteen Songs
are organized around the seventh and central composition. This song opens
with seven highly ornate exhortations to the angelic priesthood to commence
their praise. Having done this, we move from voices of the angelic host to the
sanctuary itself bursting into song.

> Let all the foundations of the holy of holies offer praise,
> the uplifting pillars of the supremely exalted abode,
> and all the corners of its structure. (4Q403 1 I 41)

By having the building break into song in this fashion, the difference between
the angelic host and the building in which they serve has been dramatically
eclipsed.

---

15. See Carol Newsom, *Songs of the Sabbath Sacrifice: A Critical Edition* (Atlanta:
Scholars Press, 1985), 224: "Many occurrences of *elohim* in the [*Songs*] are ambiguous
and might refer to God or to the angels."

But even more striking is the vacillation the text demonstrates over just what is the object of praise. Whereas with the angels it is clear that they must offer praise, it is occasionally the case that the temple not only offers praise but becomes itself the object of praise. After calling on the heavenly host to praise "the firmament of the uppermost heavens," the text goes on to describe this supernal sphere as though it were a temple:

> All its beams and its walls,
> all its structure, the workmanship of its construction—
> Most holy spirits (or: spirits of the holy of holies), living gods,
> Eternally holy spirits above all the holy ones. (4Q403 1 I 43–45)[16]

Though the translation of the phrase "most holy spirits" is not completely clear, its function is. It is meant to gloss or explain the list of architectural features that precedes it. Newsom's commentary on the third line is revealing:

> The expression *ruhey qodesh qodashim* may mean either "most holy spirits" . . . or "spirits of the holy of holies." However the title is construed, these angelic spirits are in some way associated with the heavenly sanctuary which has just been described, either as attendants or as *the animate spiritual substance of the heavenly temple itself.*[17]

No matter which way we go with these two options we reach the same destination. Either the temple is such an overpoweringly holy structure that angelic spirits literally ooze from its surfaces or those surfaces themselves merge with divinity itself. The phrase *elohim hayyim* ("living gods") becomes an attribute of the supernal temple: "a living pulsating godlike [building]."

The fact that these sabbath songs feel no embarrassment about ascribing divine qualities to the temple provides a striking piece of data against which we can contextualize how the Samaritan and Septuagint versions of the Pentateuch handle several texts that speak of seeing God. The Hebrew original of Exodus 23:17 reads: "Three times a year (during the pilgrimage festivals) all your males shall see the face of the Lord, YHWH."[18] The Samaritan version

---

16. Translated with the assistance of Noam Mizrahi.

17. Newsom, *Songs*, 233 (emphasis added).

18. For a good discussion of this problem see S. Chavel, "The Face of God and the Etiquette of Eye-Contact: Visitation, Pilgrimage, and Prophetic Vision in Ancient Israelite and Early Jewish Imagination," *JSQ* 19 (2012): 17 n. 57. It should be noted that several different Hebrew versions were in circulation in the few centuries before the Common Era.

possesses a slight modification of the original. Instead of seeing "the Lord" (*ha-adon*), the text reads "the ark" (*ha-aron*). The scribe, clearly bothered by the overly anthropomorphic sense of the original, made a tiny alteration—the letter *dalet* (*adon*) was almost indistinguishable from *resh* (*aron*)—in order to get a less troublesome reading. Instead of a command to see God, the pilgrim was to view the ark.[19]

Israel Knohl has compared this tradition of identifying an aspect of God's essence with the temple furniture with similar traditions in rabbinic literature. According to the Jerusalem Talmud, it was customary on festival days to bring the sacred furniture out of the temple into the courtyard so that the pilgrims could view it. As Knohl observes, this ritual is at variance with scriptural law. Even the Levitical priests, who had greater privileges than the laity, put their lives at risk when they gazed upon the sacred furniture (Num. 4:20). In Knohl's view, the laity were not subject to this danger because during the pilgrimage festivals they were temporarily elevated to the status of priests. But more important for our purposes is the theological motivation for this elevation:

> It seems to me that the sages departed from convention and permitted the display of the temple furniture before the pilgrims so as to allow them to fulfill their obligation "to see the face of God." Or to put it another way, the presentation of these holy items before the large assembly created the experience of a public theophany. The Israelites who had longed for the temple courts and asked "when may I come to see the face of God" (Ps 42:2) went up to the temple at the pilgrimage feast and gazed upon the vessels of the temple service that were brought out of hiding. In this way their spiritual thirst was slaked and they fulfilled the commandment

---

When I say "Hebrew original," I am referring to what will become the standard rabbinic text (the so-called Masoretic version), which should be contrasted with other text types such as those found at Qumran or transmitted by the Samaritans.

19. The importance of this textual variant for the practices of Second Temple Judaism has already been noted by I. Knohl, "Postbiblical Sectarianism and the Priestly Schools" (Hebrew), *Tarbiz* 60 (1991): 140–41. The Greek translation of the Bible displays a similar affection for the physical structure of the tabernacle. In the Hebrew, for example, God informs us that the entire purpose of building the tabernacle is "so that I may *dwell* among [the people Israel]" (Exod. 25:8). The Septuagint replaces the idiom of dwelling in favor of that of vision; build the sanctuary, Israel is exhorted, "so that I may be *visible* among you." And when the Hebrew declares that Moses and a few others ascended to the top of Mount Sinai and "saw the God of Israel" (Exod. 24:9–11), the Septuagint translates: "they saw *the place where* the God of Israel stood."

of the Torah that "three times a year each male must see the face of the Sovereign LORD, the God of Israel" (Exod. 34:23).[20]

There is some dispute among Talmud scholars as to whether such a ritual really happened or whether the tradition reflects how the rabbis imagined the feast days were celebrated. But for our purposes, this question is of little consequence. For whatever the answer, there is no doubt that the rabbis thought the furniture contained the energies of the divine.

Daniel Schwartz has argued that the rabbinic tradition is confirmed by an apocryphal story about a conflict between Jesus and a priest found in a papyrus from Egypt dated to the fourth or fifth century CE (Oxyrhynchus 840). In this story, Jesus brings his disciples to a place of purification prior to entering the courts of the temple. There he is confronted by "a certain Pharisee, a chief priest, whose name was Levi" who says to him: "Who gave you permission to enter this place of purification and *to see these holy vessels,* when you have not washed yourself, nor have your disciples surely bathed their feet?"[21] As Schwartz observes, the key point is the claim that only persons of sufficient purity may enter the temple precincts to view the sacred vessels. "On this background," Schwartz argues, "it is not unreasonable to assume that [the] practice associated with festive celebrations in the Temple, the exhibition of Temple utensils before the crowds of pilgrims, should be understood in [this] way: it was an attempt [by the Pharisees] to let the public share in what priests had claimed as their own prerogatives."[22]

The most interesting part of Schwartz's article derives from his discussion of the first-century Jewish historian Josephus. When writing about the entrance of the Roman general Pompey into the temple in 63 BCE, Schwartz observes that Josephus

20. Knohl, "Postbiblical Sectarianism," 140–41. The divine name at the close of Exodus 34:23 is somewhat cumbersome to translate into English. I have utilized the Jewish Publication Society version.

21. The translation is from François Bovon, "*Fragment Oxyrhynchus* 840, Fragment of a Lost Gospel, Witness of an Early Christianity Controversy over Purity," *JBL* 119 (2000): 705–28.

22. Daniel Schwartz, "Viewing the Holy Utensils (P. Ox V,840)," *NTS* 32 (1986): 156. But François Bovon, "Fragment," is probably on surer ground when he situates this text within the liturgical practices of the early church. In his view, the issue at stake is the viewing of the sacred vessels related to the celebration of the Eucharist. Because the Eucharist was viewed as a sacrifice, the concepts embedded in the priestly laws of Leviticus and Numbers could be extended to cover this Christian ritual.

lays special emphasis on the fact that he saw the Temple utensils; indeed, he states that "of all the calamities of that time none so deeply affected the nation as the exposure to alien eyes of the Holy Place, hitherto screened from view" (*Jewish War* 1.7.6 §152). Here, indeed, he is speaking of the Sanctuary or the Holy of Holies; nevertheless, the emphasis on sight rather than entry is remarkable. This point is further developed with specific reference to the holy utensils, in the parallel account in *Jewish Antiquities* 14.4.4 §§71–72 (although this development is counterbalanced by some new compliments for Pompey): "And not light was the sin committed against the sanctuary, which before that time had never been entered or seen. For Pompey and not a few of his men went into it and saw what it was unlawful for any but the high priests to see."[23]

Nor indeed is this the only occurrence of this remarkable emphasis on sight. In some half-dozen examples one finds a similar interest in gazing upon the temple and its furniture as opposed to physical entry or touch.

This emphasis on "seeing" is also attested in Jewish coinage from the early second century CE (fig. 3.2). In a recent article on the typology of the coins that hail from the revolt of Bar Kokhba (ca. 132 CE), Dan Barag writes:

> The Temple that appears on these coins . . . has four pillars. In the middle of the façade is [the Table of Presence]. It is obvious that this object or symbol possessed tremendous significance, for in contemporary coins of this period we frequently find images of the Temple in whose center is stationed a god or goddess.[24]

We can be even a bit more emphatic here. The god or goddess so depicted is the patron of the temple in question and as such was represented in those temples by his or her statue. As Martin Price and Bluma Trell remark in their book on the subject, the statue of the god was normally out of view of the worshippers and so the coins do not reflect what one would have seen if one went to the respective cities and compared the image on the face of the coin to the temple façade itself. Indeed, the artist often has to widen "the space between the central columns . . . to accommodate the image which usually identifies the shrine with no possible ambiguity." So, one purpose of bringing

---

23. Schwartz, "Viewing the Holy Utensils," 154.
24. Dan Barag, "The Table of the Bread of Presence and the Façade of the Temple upon the Coins of the Bar Kokhba War" (Hebrew), *Qadmoniot* 20 (1987): 22.

Figure 3.2 Coin from the Bar Kokhba revolt, ca. 134 CE. Note the four pillars of the temple.

the statue forward was to signify just whose town this coin hailed from and under which divine auspices it drew its authority. But equally important, as Price and Trell observe, is the manner by which this identification of god and temple takes place; the presentation of the god at the door of the temple "would suggest the age-old custom of [an] epiphany, a god appearing in person before his worshipers."[25]

Inspired by Barag, Asher Grossberg suggests that this coin reflects the talmudic ritual of displaying the temple furniture before pilgrims. Barag replied that the talmudic evidence is purely imaginative in character and cannot bear this sort of historical weight.[26] But at the end of the day—however we sort out the problem of historicity—I think it is fair to say that the image of the table of presence at the door of the temple indicates that this piece of furniture bore some resemblance to the identity of the God who dwelled therein. If we set this coin next to the rabbinic evidence, we can understand better why some rabbinic texts would understand viewing the furniture as a means of "seeing God."[27]

25. Martin Price and Bluma Trell, *Coins and Their Cities: Architecture on the Ancient Coins of Greece, Rome, and Palestine* (Detroit: Wayne State University Press, 1977) 19.
26. Grossberg's letter and Barag's response can be found in *Qadmoniot* 21 (1988): 56–57.
27. It is worth noting as well that Josephus, in his description of the tabernacle, remarks that the veils could be pulled aside on festival days so that they would not obstruct the view. As the biblical text itself offers no reason to suggest such things, many historians have cited this passage as an indication that viewing the temple furniture was a well-known custom of the Second Temple period. The text in question (*Ant.* 3.124–125,

I have spent the last few pages addressing these postbiblical texts because I believe they build upon a foundation that is deeply biblical. Jon Levenson employs a fair number of rabbinic traditions in his exposition of the Bible's theology of Zion because, he contends, these imaginative traditions "render explicit and prosaic what is implicit and poetic in the Hebrew Bible."[28] And so I would say that these postbiblical traditions imagine the sacred furniture being carried out to the temple courts to be viewed by the assembled pilgrims so that they could, in the words of Israel Knohl, "see the face of the God." I should emphasize that I am not claiming that this rabbinic tradition reflects a historical fact the rabbis remembered, nor do I believe that in biblical times the command "to see God" during the pilgrimage festivals could be fulfilled in this way. What these postbiblical traditions do accomplish, however, is to show us the underlying theological significance of texts like Numbers 4:20 or the Ark Narrative in Samuel. We might think of these rabbinic traditions like artists who draw a caricature of a famous sports star, actor, or politician. The picture may present an unrealistic exaggeration of some facial feature, but it always builds on a peculiar aspect of the face itself. In fact, the caricature can be embarrassing because it highlights a characteristic that one would normally try to downplay or even cover up. In this sense, caricatures can be truer to life than some studio photographs that take great efforts to underplay said features. In my view, this is exactly how we should read the postbiblical traditions about the furniture of the tabernacle. They help draw our attention to a somewhat shocking theological position: something of God's very being is made manifest in the furniture adorning his home.

127–128) reads: "The tabernacle was covered with curtains woven of fine linen, in which the hues of purple and blue and crimson were blended. Of these the first [veil; i.e., the *parokhet*] measured ten cubits either way and was spread over the pillars which divided the temple and screened off the sanctuary; this it was which rendered the latter invisible to the eyes of any. . . . A second [veil; i.e., the *masakh*], corresponding to the first in dimensions, texture and hue, enveloped the five pillars that stood at the entrance, supported by rings at the corner of each pillar, it hung from the top to the middle of the pillar; the rest of the space was left as a passage for the priests entering beneath it. Above this was another covering of linen, of the same dimensions, which was drawn by cords to either side, the rings serving alike for curtain and cord, so that it could either be outspread or rolled together and stowed into a corner, in order that it should not intercept the view above all on the great days." The translation is from the Loeb edition, vol. 1 (Cambridge: Harvard University Press, 1930), 375–77.

28. Jon Levenson, *Sinai and Zion* (San Francisco: HarperSanFrancisco, 1985), 134.

Tabernacle Narrative as *Ekphrasis*?

The quasi-"divinization" of the furniture may afford the reader a new way to approach one of the most puzzling features of the Tabernacle Narrative: its length. Two things should be observed. First is the striking fact that the commands given to Moses regarding the structure of the tabernacle (Exod. 25–31) are repeated verbatim in the execution section (chs. 35–40). Second would be the numerous times that our author enumerates all the pieces of the tabernacle. Let us begin with the former.

Verbatim Repetition

In order to appreciate the extraordinary nature of the duplication, we will begin with the command to build the table of presence and its execution:

Exodus 25:23–30	Exodus 37:10–16
[23] You shall make a table of acacia wood, two cubits long, one cubit wide, and a cubit and a half high.	[10] He also made the table of acacia wood, two cubits long, one cubit wide, and a cubit and a half high.
[24] You shall overlay it with pure gold, and make a molding of gold around it.	[11] He overlaid it with pure gold, and made a molding of gold around it.
[25] You shall make around it a rim a handbreadth wide, and a molding of gold around the rim.	[12] He made around it a rim a handbreadth wide, and made a molding of gold around the rim.
[26] You shall make for it four rings of gold, and fasten the rings to the four corners at its four legs.	[13] He cast for it four rings of gold, and fastened the rings to the four corners at its four legs.
[27] The rings that hold the poles used for carrying the table shall be close to the rim.	[14] The rings that held the poles used for carrying the table were close to the rim.
[28] You shall make the poles of acacia wood, and overlay them with gold, and the table shall be carried with these.	[15] He made the poles of acacia wood to carry the table, and overlaid them with gold.
[29] You shall make its plates and dishes for incense, and its flagons and bowls with which to pour drink offerings; you shall make them of pure gold.	[16] And he made the vessels of pure gold that were to be on the table, its plates and dishes for incense, and its bowls and flagons with which to pour drink offerings.
[30] And you shall set the bread of the Presence on the table before me always.	

As is the rule across the Tabernacle Narrative, everything pertaining to the physical structure of the item in question is described twice, once as a command and then as an accomplished fact. The only details that are left out in the execution section are those that pertain to the usage of the item in question (see 25:30, the only sentence with no counterpart in the execution section).

Modern readers have found this literary feature of the Tabernacle Narrative to be very tedious. Goethe is certainly representative when he writes that these texts appear "completely unbearable due to a very sad and incomprehensible job of editing."[29] The contemporary Finnish scholar, Anneli Aejmelaeus, describes these chapters as a "tiresome account."[30] Some ascribe this verbosity to the overly scholastic character of the Priestly writer. But such a judgment would be wide of the mark. Indeed, just the opposite is more often the case; the Priestly writer abbreviates whenever the opportunity presents itself. Consider, for example, the command God gives to Noah to build an ark:

> [14] Make yourself an ark of cypress wood; make rooms in the ark, and cover it inside and out with pitch. [15] This is how you are to make it: the length of the ark three hundred cubits, its width fifty cubits, and its height thirty cubits. [16] Make a roof for the ark, and finish it to a cubit above; and put the door of the ark in its side; make it with lower, second, and third decks. (Gen. 6:14–16)

If our Priestly author held fast to the pattern established in the Tabernacle Narrative, we would have expected each of the items listed in vv. 14–16 to be repeated in the following execution section. Instead, the story concludes with great brevity: "Noah did this, he did all that the LORD commanded him" (v. 22). A similar pattern can be found in Numbers 1–4. Each chapter consists of a long set of commands extending over dozens of verses that conclude with a single verse informing the reader that Moses or Israel had executed every demand in a faithful manner (see Num. 1:54; 2:34; 3:51; and 4:49).

Clearly, the Priestly writer does not endlessly repeat himself as a general rule. Exodus 35–40 constitutes an enormous exception to his normal compo-

---

29. As cited in Dominik Markl, "Zur literarischen und theologischen: Funktion der Heiligtumstexte im Buch Exodus," in *Heiliger Raum: Exegese und Rezeption der Heiligtumtexte in Ex 24–40*, ed. M. Hopf, W. Oswald, and S. Seiler (Stuttgart: Kohlhammer, 2016), 79.

30. Anneli Aejmelaeus, "Septuagintal Translation Techniques: A Solution to the Problem of the Tabernacle Account," in *Septuagint, Scrolls, and Cognate Writings*, ed. George Brooke and Barnabas Linders (Atlanta: Scholars Press, 1992), 382.

sitional style. For this reason, a number of modern scholars have hypothesized that the earliest form of the Tabernacle Narrative would have conformed to this pattern. In such a reconstruction, all of the repetition found in 35:1–39:31 would disappear. What would have stood in its place is the simple concluding formula of Exodus 39:32: "In this way, all the work of the tabernacle of the tent of meeting was finished; the Israelites had done everything just as the Lord had commanded." Such a conclusion would be far more appealing to modern readers. And given the precedent for such a reconstruction in the story of Noah's ark, why did our writer not finish his story in this way?

Repeated Itemization

The second puzzling characteristic of this narrative is the striking tendency to repeat the list of materials found within the tabernacle whenever there is the occasion to do so. In chapter 31, when Moses appoints Bezalel as chief artisan, he does not simply inform the reader that he is to "make all that I have commanded you." Rather, he takes this opportunity to enumerate, once again, each and every item mentioned in the previous chapters.

> [7] [T]he tent of meeting, and the ark of the covenant, and the mercy seat that is on it, and all the furnishings of the tent, [8] the table and its utensils, and the pure lampstand with all its utensils, and the altar of incense, [9] and the altar of burnt offering with all its utensils, and the basin with its stand, [10] and the finely worked vestments, the holy vestments for the priest Aaron and the vestments of his sons, for their service as priests, [11] and the anointing oil and the fragrant incense for the holy place. They shall do just as I have commanded you. (Exod. 31:7–11)

And in chapter 35, when Moses fulfills the command to appoint the artisans, he lists all the items yet another time:

> [10] All who are skillful among you shall come and make all that the LORD has commanded: the tabernacle, [11] its tent and its covering, its clasps and its frames, its bars, its pillars, and its bases; [12] the ark with its poles, the mercy seat, and the curtain for the screen; [13] the table with its poles and all its utensils, and the bread of the Presence; [14] the lampstand also for the light, with its utensils and its lamps, and the oil for the light; [15] and the altar of incense, with its poles, and the anointing oil and the fragrant

incense, and the screen for the entrance, the entrance of the tabernacle; ¹⁶ the altar of burnt offering, with its grating of bronze, its poles, and all its utensils, the basin with its stand; ¹⁷ the hangings of the court, its pillars and its bases, and the screen for the gate of the court; ¹⁸ the pegs of the tabernacle and the pegs of the court, and their cords. (Exod. 35:10–18)

Perhaps the most surprising list is to be found at the very end of the construction process. After all the pieces of the tabernacle have been built, the narrator concludes by asserting that all has been executed according to the divine commandment:

> ³² In this way all the work of the tabernacle of the tent of meeting was finished; the Israelites had done everything just as the LORD had commanded Moses.

But then the story begins again with a description of the Israelites bringing the completed pieces to Moses:

> ³³ Then they brought the tabernacle to Moses, the tent and all its utensils, its hooks, its frames, its bars, its pillars, and its bases; ³⁴ the covering of tanned rams' skins and the covering of fine leather, and the curtain for the screen; ³⁵ the ark of the covenant with its poles and the mercy seat; ³⁶ the table with all its utensils, and the bread of the Presence; ³⁷ the pure lampstand with its lamps set on it and all its utensils, and the oil for the light; ³⁸ the golden altar, the anointing oil and the fragrant incense, and the screen for the entrance of the tent; ³⁹ the bronze altar, and its grating of bronze, its poles, and all its utensils; the basin with its stand; ⁴⁰ the hangings of the court, its pillars, and its bases, and the screen for the gate of the court, its cords, and its pegs; and all the utensils for the service of the tabernacle, for the tent of meeting; ⁴¹ the finely worked vestments for ministering in the holy place, the sacred vestments for the priest Aaron, and the vestments of his sons to serve as priests.

The unit then closes in chapter 39 with a repetition of what was said earlier in v. 32 and a concluding blessing on the part of Moses:

> ⁴² The Israelites had done all of the work just as the LORD had commanded Moses. ⁴³ When Moses saw that they had done all the work just as the LORD had commanded, he blessed them. (Exod. 39:32–42)

Abarbanel, a Jewish Bible scholar who lived in the fifteenth century, asks, "Why does scripture repeat every vessel and article which it already mentioned several times in the earlier chapters? This seems excessive. Would it have not been sufficient to have said more simply: 'Then they brought the [work of] the tabernacle to Moses (v. 33a) . . . [and when] Moses saw that they had done all the work just as the Lord had commanded, he blessed them (v. 43)?'"[31]

What Abarbanel playfully suggests is precisely what many modern commentators (far more earnestly) reconstruct. The original text would have consisted of just vv. 33a and 43—everything else was a pedantic secondary addition. Such a reconstruction would certainly eliminate a good bit of the tedium these texts create for their readers. But it would not answer the question as to why the author chose such a style in the first place.[32] The best explanation for its length, I would argue, would be its linkage to the God who resided within it. If the God who created heaven and earth has condescended to dwell among the people he so dearly loves, then those who love him in return will take delight in every detail pertaining to that dwelling. Though ordinary Israelites were forbidden from beholding their God, they could direct their spiritual attention to these sancta through a form of attentive reading or listening. If we are not sensitive to the awe-producing fact that God really inhabits the building, the attention that is showered upon it will feel excessive and downright tedious.

Dominik Markl has compared the Tabernacle Narrative to the classical genre of *ekphrasis* which has been defined as "descriptive speech which brings

31. This text can be found in many *Miqraot Gedolot* (rabbinic Bibles). I consulted the version at Alhatorah Library (library.alhatorah.org). As is the custom with his commentaries, he poses questions about the verses in question at the beginning of the weekly Torah portion. In this case, the question is located in relation to Exodus 38:21 (*Pekudei*).

32. When I read these lists, I am reminded of the assembly instruction booklets that furniture manufacturers ship. The first page lists all the items found in the box before taking the customer through a step-by-step procedure of assembling the whole. What would the reader of those instructions think if after every other stage in the process, he found all the items listed again (and again)? Certainly one would think that the manufacturer must have some special affection for the items contained in the box that went beyond their mere utility. This is the effect such lists have on the reader of the Tabernacle Narrative. Menahem Haran is certainly correct when he writes, "The priestly writers find [this] subject so fascinating that . . . [they are] prompted to recapitulate the list of its appurtenances time and again." See Menahem Haran, *Temples and Temple Service in Ancient Israel: An Inquiry into Biblical Cult Phenomena and the Historical Setting of the Priestly School*, 2nd ed. (Winona Lake, IN: Eisenbrauns, 1985), 149. The question that I am asking is just what made this subject so fascinating?

the thing shown vividly before the eyes."[33] The most famous example is the lengthy description of Achilles's shield in the *Iliad*. Closer, for our purposes, would be the description of the temple of Apollo at Delphi in Euripides's *Ion*.[34] As Markl notes, these visual descriptions do not provide enough information to allow one to reconstruct the appearance of the structure in question. Their intent is rather to shower praise on the building or its builder. Irene Winter has found this genre especially useful for articulating the importance of architectural descriptions in classical Mesopotamia. Gudea of Lagash (2127–2110 BCE), for example, when describing the Eninnu temple writes: "The temple, its awesome radiance was cast over the land; its praise-song reaching the mountains . . . [the temple], bearing allure, is established to be admired."[35] The term "admired," she argues, is aptly chosen as it literally means "enhanced (ad-) viewing (mirare)." This corresponds to the underlying Sumerian term which means "to look at something in wonder or astonishment."[36] "I find myself tending to think," Winter concludes,

> of the ad+miration/awe response in terms of a sort of WOW! effect on the people, parallel to, but different from the joy response of the gods. It is as if the impact of the work when viewed by the people is perceived as impressive, if not overwhelming, whereas when viewed by the gods, their own inherent power matches that of the work, and so their response is seen not in terms of being overwhelmed but rather well met. What to the gods produces delight, to those on a lower level evokes admiration and awe.[37]

In the Bible, the delight or, perhaps better, satisfaction of God is marked by his repeated approval of what Israel or Moses have done (". . . he did [action X] just as the LORD had commanded Moses"). The awe of Israel, on the

33. Markl, "Zur literarischen und theologischen Funktion," 56–87. The definition of *ekphrasis* is taken from an ancient Greek handbook on rhetoric, see Jaś Elsner, "The Genres of Ekphrasis," *Ramus* 31 (2002): 1–18.

34. For a discussion of this text see Irene Winter, "The Eyes Have It: Votive Statuary, Gilgamesh's Axe, and Cathected Viewing in the Ancient Near East," in *Visuality before and beyond the Renaissance: Seeing as Others Saw*, ed. Robert Nelson (Cambridge: Cambridge University Press, 2000), 22–23, and Froma Zeitlin, "The Artful Eye: Vision, Ecphrasis and Spectacle in Euripidean Theatre," in *Art and Text in Ancient Greek Culture*, ed. Simon Goldhill and Robin Osborne (Cambridge: Cambridge University Press, 1994), 138–96.

35. Winter, "Eyes Have It," 32.

36. Winter, "Eyes Have It," 30–31.

37. Winter, "Eyes Have It," 35.

other hand, is marked by the pilgrim gazing upon the temple or city in which it is located. As we have noted, the power of a god's presence in the temple is such that the divine aura radiates over the whole building and extends even to the surrounding city. The Epic of Gilgamesh opens with the hero exhorting his listeners to make a pilgrimage to the sacred Eanna Temple in Uruk:

> Behold its outer wall, whose cornice is like copper,
> Peer at the inner wall, which none can equal!
> Seize upon the threshold, which is from of old!
> Draw near to Eanna, the dwelling of Ishtar,
> Which no future king, no man, can equal.
> Go up and walk on the walls of Uruk,
> Inspect the base terrace, examine the brickwork.[38]

Though the focus of the speech is on Gilgamesh's accomplishment as a builder, the grounds for his pride rest on the fact of Ishtar's presence in the building. Accordingly, his praise for her dwelling is tantamount to praise for the goddess herself.

If we return to the Bible, we can find a close parallel to the speech of Gilgamesh in Psalm 48, where the pilgrims to Jerusalem are exhorted to "Walk about Zion, go all around about it . . . that you may tell the next generation that this is God." The attachment of some aspect of God's holiness to the city is evident in that gazing upon its buildings is equated with glimpsing something of the grandeur of God himself. Admiration of the holy city does have a "wow effect" on the pilgrims who come to visit. Israelite culture, however, has no immediate parallel to the votive statues we encounter in Mesopotamia. This is because Israelite religion was aniconic; there was no statue in the temple toward which a votive could direct its gaze. But as we have argued, the Bible retains a strong sense that the deity truly inhabits the building and as a result the most sacred pieces of the furniture absorb something of the divine presence such that it is potentially lethal for nonpriests to look upon them. This deeply Israelite and eventually Jewish sensibility came to inform Christian liturgical practices as well in that the vessels used to serve the Eucharist were also thought to bear a similar level of sanctity and should not be gazed upon unadvisedly.[39]

38. The translation is that of E. A. Speiser found in *Ancient Near Eastern Texts Relating to the Old Testament*, ed. J. Pritchard (Princeton: Princeton University Press, 1955), 2:72–99.
39. So Bovon, "Fragment," and, more recently and in greater detail, Harald Buchinger

Before closing we should perhaps note one way in which the "ekphrastic" presentation of the materials of the tabernacle differ from Psalm 48 (or Euripides's *Ion*). In the latter, our poet describes what any pilgrim who comes to Jerusalem would have actually seen. But there is a different strategy at play in the Tabernacle Narrative. Our author devotes more energy to those parts of the tabernacle that the pilgrim could *not* see. Consider what was said in our introduction about the courtyard (27:9–19) and the tabernacle proper (26:1–37). The outer perimeter, which was visible to all Israel, is described in the briefest form possible. It is the inner curtains of the tent itself—visible to no one save the attending high priest—that is subject to the most detailed account. Scholars have long noted that the holiness of the sancta is graded according to the value of the materials used (bronze, silver, and gold). But a gradient that is often ignored is that of literary detail. On the one hand, this befits the holiness of these items. That which is closest to God shares more deeply in his presence and merits a more detailed description. On the other hand, the detailed textual presentation has the advantage of allowing lay persons to feast their "literary" eyes on what they could not see in actual fact. Perhaps our author has accomplished, according to his own fashion, something similar to the talmudic tradition of displaying the furniture to pilgrims at the festivals: a means of beholding the grandeur of their God.[40]

---

and Elizabeth Hernitscheck, "P. Oxy. 840 and the Rites of Christian Initiation: Dating a Piece of Alleged Anti-sacramentalistic Polemics," *Early Christianity* 5 (2014): 117–24, especially 122–23.

40. See fig. 3.1 on p. 52 above.

CHAPTER 4

Serving God

The altar, and the priestly service in general, are not for sin offerings—better that a man should never sin and not have to bring one!—but for the Tamid offering, [a sacrifice given] in thanksgiving to God for what he has done for his people.

Abarbanel, *Commentary on Exodus* 29:38–42[1]

"But who am I, and what is my people, that we should be able to make this freewill offering? For all things come from you, and of your own have we given you. . . . [I]n the uprightness of my heart I have freely offered all these things, and now I have seen your people, who are present here, offering freely and joyously to you."

David's prayer over the first offerings at the temple
1 Chronicles 29:14, 17

Since the law has only a shadow of the good things to come and not the true form of these realities, it can never, by the same sacrifices which are continually offered year after year, make perfect those who approach. . . . For it is impossible for the blood of bulls and goats to take away sins.

Hebrews 10:1, 4

In our first chapter we pointed out that the Tabernacle Narrative had two major focal points, each marked by their own respective theophany. These two focal points, we explained, represent two distinctive ways of depicting

---

1. Michael Carasik, *The Commentator's Bible: The JPS Miqra'ot Gedolot* (Philadelphia: Jewish Publication Society, 2005), 262; translation has been slightly adjusted.

the agency of God in the liturgical life of ancient Israel. One way is nicely captured in Psalm 48:8–14, a poem describing the experience of a pilgrim who has traveled to Jerusalem. The religious disposition on display is that of vision. The act of contemplating the architecture of this holy city ("consider well its ramparts") is tantamount to seeing God Almighty ("this is God, our God forever"). In Psalm 96, on the other hand, a different dimension of Jerusalem is represented. On this viewpoint, the temple is the site where God is *served*:

> [7] Ascribe to the LORD, O families of the peoples,
>   ascribe to the LORD glory and strength.
> [8] Ascribe to the LORD the glory due his name;
>   bring an offering, and come into his courts.
> [9] Worship the LORD in holy splendor;
>   tremble before him, all the earth.

These two foci, obviously, cannot be fully disengaged. God is served in the location where he dwells. But the two psalms demonstrate that these focal points represent distinct dimensions of spiritual practice that can be developed independently.

Mosaic at Sepphoris

Let us begin our consideration of altar service with the fifth century carpet mosaic from a synagogue in the city of Sepphoris (see fig. 4.1). As scholars have argued, one way to understand the imagery on the floor is the hope it reflects concerning Israel's future redemption.[2] The panel in question depicts the origins of sacrifice as depicted in Exodus 29. But given the fact that the temple was destroyed several centuries earlier, this panel also looks forward to its restoration, a time at which the sons of Aaron can offer these sacrifices anew.

In the fourth century, the infamous Roman Emperor Julian (also known as "the Apostate" since he renounced the Christian faith in which he had been raised) set in motion an initiative to rebuild the temple in Jerusalem.[3] A prin-

---

2. Zeev Weiss, *The Sepphoris Synagogue: Deciphering an Ancient Message through Its Archaeological and Socio-Historical Contexts* (Jerusalem: Israel Exploration Society, 2005), 235–38.

3. For a discussion of Julian and his attempt to rebuild the temple, see Robert Wilken, *The First Thousand Years: A Global History of Christianity* (New Haven: Yale University Press, 2012), 118–26.

cipal motivating factor for Julian was the Christian claim that the temple had been destroyed by the Romans in 70 CE as a punishment for Jewish complicity in the death of Jesus and, as a result, would never be rebuilt. If the temple was rebuilt, this would have been a major setback for the church. As a result, Julian reasoned, the Christian claim to have superseded Judaism would be decisively disproven. Obviously, this would have been a major source of embarrassment for the church. No doubt the Jews themselves had strongly resisted this Christian claim about the temple's demise and continued to hope and pray for its restoration as well as the sacrificial service that took place there.[4] One way to read the top registers of the Sepphoris mosaic is as a visual expression of these fervent hopes. In this sense, the mosaic is of a piece with the coins we discussed that were issued during the Bar Kokhba revolt. The difference would be that the coins depicted the rebuilding of the temple in terms of the return of the furniture, a sign that Israel's God dwells there again.

Let us consider more carefully the character of the third panel of the mosaic. There are four elements to consider: the laver on the far right, the four-horned altar occupying the central axis of the panel, the high priest Aaron who stands to the immediate left of the altar, and a bull and a sheep on the far left. Immediately above the sheep we find a citation of Exodus 29:39, "one sheep [you shall offer in the morning]." The importance of the laver is described in Exodus 30:20–21 (cf. 40:30–32). Every time Aaron or his sons go into the tent of meeting or approach the altar "they shall wash with water, so that they may not die." But the central image within this panel is the altar itself. It is larger than Aaron and located dead center within the panel. The distinction is as subtle as it is important: the altar is the spot where Aaron serves rather than Aaron being the one who serves at the altar. As we have noted, the scene depicted in the panel is drawn from Exodus 29. The bulk of this chapter provides the commands for ordaining Aaron and his sons to the priesthood. But it concludes with the rite that will prove definitive for the priesthood—the offering of the morning and evening sacrifice or, as it is known in Hebrew, the tamid.

The Tamid Sacrifice in Exodus 29

The importance of the tamid rite (Exod. 29:38–46) is already anticipated in the last element of the ordination service (vv. 31–37).[5] This becomes clear by com-

4. Weiss, *Sepphoris*, 249–53.
5. Christophe Nihan, *From Priestly Torah to Pentateuch*, FAT 25 (Tübingen: Mohr

paring the text of Exodus 29 with Leviticus 8. In our first chapter we noted that the service could be divided into seven discrete units, each concluding with an approbatory formula. The first six commands found in Exodus 29 are repeated nearly verbatim in Leviticus 8 when they are executed. The seventh and final command, however, varies from this pattern. Both the command and execution demonstrate distinctive features that anticipate the narratives that will follow.

Exodus 29	Leviticus 8
[31] You shall take the ram of ordination, and boil its flesh in a holy place; [32] and Aaron and his sons shall eat the flesh of the ram and the bread that is in the basket, at the entrance of the tent of meeting. [33] They themselves shall eat the food by which atonement is made, to ordain and consecrate them, but no one else shall eat of them, because they are holy.	[31] And Moses said to Aaron and his sons, "Boil the flesh at the entrance of the tent of meeting, and eat it there with the bread that is in the basket of ordination offerings, as I was commanded, 'Aaron and his sons shall eat it';
[34] If any of the flesh for the ordination, or of the bread, remains until the morning, then you shall burn the remainder with fire; it shall not be eaten, because it is holy.	[32] and what remains of the flesh and the bread you shall burn with fire.
[35] Thus you shall do to Aaron and to his sons, just as I have commanded you; through seven days you shall ordain them.	[33] You shall not go outside the entrance of the tent of meeting for seven days, until the day when your period of ordination is completed. For it will take seven days to ordain you."

Siebeck, 2007), 34, observes that "almost all scholars agree that the conclusion to P[g] (the original form of the Priestly Narrative) in Exod 25–29 should be found in YHWH's final statement in 29:43–46 which takes up and continues YHWH's initial promise in Exod. 25:8 that he will 'dwell' (*shakan*) among the Israelites." A number of scholars make a further specification that connects 29:45–46 with the completion of the tabernacle in 26:30. On this view, the material regarding the altar (27:1–8) and the tamid sacrifice that takes place there (29:43–44) are secondary additions. The most extreme suggestion is that of Thomas Pola, *Die ursprüngliche Priesterschrift: Beobachtungen zur Literarkritik und Traditionsgeschichte von P[g]* (Neukirchen-Vluyn: Neukirchener, 1995), 224–97, who excises not only the references to sacrifice but all of the lengthy descriptions of the tabernacle structure as well. On this view, the original story is reduced to three elements: (1) the model which was shown to Moses (25:8a, 9), (2) the promise that God would indwell it (29:45–46), and (3) the erection of the tabernacle which Moses had seen (40:16, 33b).

³⁶ Also every day you shall offer a bull as a sin offering for atonement. Also you shall offer a sin offering for the altar, when you make atonement for it, and shall anoint it, to consecrate it.

³⁷ Seven days you shall make atonement for the altar, and consecrate it, and the altar shall be most holy; whatever touches the altar shall become holy.

³⁶ Aaron and his sons did all the things that the LORD commanded through Moses.

....

....

29:38–42a describes how to perform the tamid sacrifice

Leviticus 9 gives instructions for the rites of the eighth day

Let us begin with Leviticus 8. The key literary feature to bear in mind is that Aaron's ordination is preparing him to take over responsibilities at the sacrificial altar. Up to now, Moses has done all this, but in Leviticus 9, he will relinquish this role. In Exodus 29:1–37, God commands Moses to execute all seven actions of the ordination rite. The first six of those actions are carried out by Moses exactly as God had commanded him (Exod. 29:1–30 = Lev. 8:1–30). This point is given special emphasis with the repetition of the formula, "(Moses did) just as the Lord had commanded him" (vv. 5, 9, 13, 17, 21, 29). But in the seventh and final sequence of actions (see the text cited above), Moses diverges from the directions God has given (29:31) and issues a command to Aaron ("Moses said to Aaron and his sons, 'Boil the flesh at the entrance of the tent of meeting, and eat it there' [8:31]), who subsequently fulfills it. This transference of authority is reflected in the approbatory formula that closes the chapter. It is no longer Moses who has acted "just as God had commanded," but Aaron ("Aaron and his sons did all the things that the LORD commanded through Moses"). What is important to note is that this shift in agency away from Moses and toward Aaron is completely unexpected. The commands for this seventh ritual action (29:31–37) are addressed to Moses alone, exactly as all the others earlier in the chapter. Leviticus 8 exercises this sort of freedom in this last ritual action because it is highlighting the fact that Aaron is about to assume the reins of the cult. What will formally take place in chapter 9 is already underway at the end of chapter 8.

Exodus 29, as our presentation above reveals, includes some material that is absent from Leviticus 8. The command to offer a sin offering during each day of the ordination service in order to purge the altar of any impurities (see 29:36–37 in the table above), for example, has no parallel in Leviticus 8.[6] The command for a sin offering was first made in 29:10–14 and its execution is recounted in Leviticus 8:14–17. Why is this command repeated at the end of Exodus 29? Up to this point, one has the impression that the ordination rites will take place on a single day. But in v. 35 we learn that the ritual will continue over seven days. A logical question would be: will all the sacrificial rites be repeated or only some of them? One purpose of vv. 36–37 is to indicate that the sin offering must be offered on each of the seven days. But this logistical clarification is not the sole purpose of this verse. By repeating this command, the reader's attention is shifted from the figure of Aaron, who has been the center of attention for most of the chapter, to the altar at which he will serve. The significance of the altar as an actor in this portion of the chapter is made clear by repeating the word four times across these two verses. Like the other sacred pieces of furniture within the tabernacle, the altar will become most holy (*qodesh qadashim*) once it is consecrated. Extreme caution must be taken in its vicinity for anything that touches the altar will become holy (v. 37).[7]

This emphasis on the altar at the close of the ordination rite provides an excellent transition to the next narrative unit, the tamid offering. Here, the focal point is no longer Aaron but rather the altar and the sacrifices:

> [38] Now this is what you shall offer on the altar: two lambs a year old regularly each day. [39] One lamb you shall offer in the morning, and the other lamb you shall offer in the evening; [40] and with the first lamb one-tenth of a measure of choice flour mixed with one-fourth of a hin of beaten oil, and one-fourth of a hin of wine for a drink offering. [41] And the other lamb

6. William Propp, *Exodus 19–40: A New Translation with Introduction and Commentary*, AB 2A (New York: Doubleday, 2006), 469, asks whether this bull is the same as mandated in 29:10–14 or an additional animal as S. R. Driver, *The Book of Exodus* (Cambridge: Cambridge University Press, 1911), 324, had claimed. He assumes it is the same. Cornelius Houtman, *Historical Commentary on the Old Testament: Exodus*, trans. J. Rebel and S. Woudstra (Kampen: Kok, 1993–2000), 3:547, also explains its placement here to emphasize the need to cleanse and consecrate the altar.

7. The clause can be understood two ways. Jacob Milgrom, *Leviticus 1–16*, AB 3 (New York: Doubleday, 1991), 446–56, believes that the verse only refers to physical objects that might touch the altar. Cornelius Houtman, *Exodus*, 3:549, argues that the verse pertains to Aaron and his sons and "should be understood as a warning to them not to approach the altar unless they are in a state of holiness."

you shall offer in the evening, and shall offer with it a grain offering and its drink offering, as in the morning, for a pleasing odor, an offering by fire to the LORD. [42a] It shall be a regular burnt offering throughout your generations at the entrance of the tent of meeting before the LORD.

After describing the tamid, the author comes to the denouement of the entire chapter (if not the whole Tabernacle Narrative): God's decision to dwell among his people.

[42b] There I will meet with you, to speak to you there. [43] I will meet with the Israelites there, and it shall be sanctified by my glory; [44] I will consecrate the tent of meeting and the altar; Aaron also and his sons I will consecrate, to serve me as priests. [45] I will *dwell* [*shakhan*] among the Israelites, and I will be their God. [46] And they shall know that I am the LORD their God, who brought them out of the land of Egypt that I might *dwell* among them; I am the LORD their God.

This description of the indwelling in vv. 42b–46 recalls the promise God made to Moses at the start of the Tabernacle Narrative: "Let them make a sanctuary so that I may dwell [*shakhan*] among them" (25:8).[8] The fact that the statement of this goal (29:42b) follows directly from the laws for the tamid sacrifice (vv. 38–42a) shows that sacrificial worship is the means by which God is to be encountered at the sanctuary. The altar becomes the privileged spot for such an encounter. Amos Hacham observes that when God says "I will meet with the Israelites there" (v. 43a), he is referring to the altar which stands "at the entrance of the tent of meeting, before the Lord" (v. 42a).[9] "From the vantage

---

8. The observation of Jeffrey Tigay in *The Jewish Study Bible*, ed. Adele Berlin and Marc Zvi Brettler (Oxford: Oxford University Press, 2004), 178, bears mentioning: "The sanctuary will be ready to serve its various functions as the site of divine human communication, as a sanctuary, and as the focus of God's Presence among the Israelites. In this climatic passage, all these functions are alluded to by the verbs (each occurring at least twice) from which the three main terms for the sanctuary (25:8) are derived—thereby explaining these terms. God will *meet* (*'iva'ed, no'ad*) there with Moses and Israel, echoing 'Tent of Meeting' (*'ohel mo'ed*), it will be *sanctified* (*nikdash, kadesh*) echoing 'sanctuary' (*mikdash*), and God will *abide* (*shakhan*) there echoing 'abode' (*mishkan*). That these goals are mentioned after the regular daily sacrifice may reflect the idea that sacrificial worship is the means by which God is drawn to the sanctuary (20:21). Notably, however, sacrifice is presented as a means not as a goal in itself. The sanctuary is for the benefit of Israel, not God."
9. Amos Hacham, *Shemot*, Da'at Miqra (Jerusalem: Mossad Harav Kook, 1991),

Figure 4.1 Two panels of a mosaic floor from a synagogue in Sepphoris from the fifth century CE; drawing by Pnina Arad, courtesy of Zeev Weiss, the Sepphoris Excavations, the Hebrew University of Jerusalem

2:24ı. Note the transition between v. 42a and b. The JPS translation divides this verse into two independent sentences and makes the second sentence introduce a new paragraph. But the original Hebrew has linked the two clauses by means of the relative particle, *asher*. If we render this word in a locative sense as "where," then the antecedent is obviously a place that will in turn inform how we are to understand the reference to a "there" in v. 43. So Propp, *Exodus 19–40*, 473: "Vv. 38–42a are a digression; 42b–43 returns us to the altar, whose holiness is the subject of v. 37."

point of that altar," Hacham continues, "one can see the opening to the Tent and, along that same line of sight, the inner veil (*parokhet*) within which the Divine Presence dwells."

If we turn our attention back to the carpet mosaic from Sepphoris (fig. 4.1) we will notice the very same sight line is depicted across the second and third panels. The altar stands directly below the doors that guard the ark, which represents the dwelling of God within the holy of holies. In fact, the presence of the incense shovel at the base of those doors puts the incense altar (part of the larger tamid rite, see Exod. 30:1–10) directly above the altar. A similar alignment of the altar to the inner sanctum of the temple is depicted in a mosaic from the Christian church at Mount Nebo (fig. 4.2).[10] In this image, the doors found within the temple have been thrown open so that the line of vision from the altar fire to the holy of holies is unimpeded. It is worth noting that according to the Mishnah, the doors of the temple were opened every morning just prior to the offering of the tamid so that the sight line from the altar to the holy of holies was unimpeded (*Tamid* 3:7).

The Importance of the Tamid

It would be difficult to gather the full significance of the tamid rite from its brief description in vv. 38–42a. It is just a terse recipe for making the sacrifice. One way to gauge its importance is to consider the role it plays in the book of Daniel. This book was written in response to the crisis wrought by the Seleucid (Syrian) monarch Antiochus Epiphanes IV. In the mid-second century BCE, his armies invaded Judea, captured the city of Jerusalem, and profaned the temple and its altar. The loss of this central liturgical site was devastating for the Jews. On three separate occasions, Daniel summarizes the devastation wrought by Antiochus by focusing on the cessation of the tamid offering. In the excerpt that follows the "prince of the host" is the God of Israel while "it" refers to the horn of a goat, a symbol for Antiochus:

> [11] Even against the prince of the host it [= Antiochus] acted arrogantly; it took the regular burnt offering away from him and overthrew the place of his sanctuary. [12] Because of wickedness, the host was given over to it together with the regular burnt offering [tamid]; it cast truth to the ground,

---

10. See the discussion of Steven Fraade, "Facing the Holy Ark, in Words and in Images," *NEA* 82 (2019): 158–59.

Figure 4.2 A mosaic of the Jerusalem temple found in front of the apse and altar area of the Theotokos Chapel, Mount Nebo, Jordan (sixth century); photo © Photographic Archive of the Studium Biblicum Franciscanum, Jerusalem, courtesy of S. J. Saller, Head of the Archaeological Mission of the Studium Biblicum Franciscanum; published in S. J. Saller, *The Memorial of Moses on Mount Nebo*. Part I: The Text (Publications of the Studium Biblicum Franciscanum [Collectio Maior] 1), Jerusalem 1941, frontispiece

and kept prospering in what it did. [13] Then I heard a holy one speaking, and another holy one said to the one that spoke, "For how long is this vision concerning the regular burnt offering, the transgression that makes desolate, and the giving over of the sanctuary and host to be trampled?" (Dan. 8:11–13; cf. 11:31 and 12:11)

Carol Newsom aptly captures the significance of the loss of the tamid sacrifice: "Even though Antiochus's edict outlawed all traditional burnt offerings, sacrifices, and drink offerings (1 Macc 1:45), substituting instead offerings considered to be unfit abominations (1 Macc 1:59, 2 Macc 6:5), the author of Daniel focuses on the *tāmîd*, or daily whole offering, because it was the most frequent and the most important of the required sacrifices at the temple."[11] Her insights are seconded by Joseph Blenkinsopp, who writes that the tamid offering "signified by metonymy the sacrificial system as a whole."[12]

The importance of the tamid is also reflected in the sacrificial calendar of Numbers 28–29. It begins with a recitation of the laws for the tamid (28:3–8) that is clearly drawn from Exodus 29:38–42.[13] It then documents all of the sacrifices that will be required for the various sacred times of the year including the sabbath, new moon, and the three pilgrimage festivals. Besides documenting the sacrificial requirements for each and every sacred festival, it repeatedly observes that these additional rites do not displace the daily tamid (28:3, 6, 10, 15, 23, 31; 29:6, 11, 16, 19, 22, 25, 28, 31, 34, 38) but are in addition to it. Let us consider just one example.

[9] On the sabbath day: two male lambs a year old without blemish, and two-tenths of an ephah of choice flour for a grain offering, mixed with oil, and its drink offering— [10] this is the burnt offering for every sabbath, *in addition to the regular burnt offering and its drink offering.* (Num. 28:9–10)

In this lengthy roster of Israel's festival offerings, the tamid functions like a stabilizing "base line" to which the other sacrificial "voices" are added. Mishnah *Tamid* clarifies this important structural role by making clear that, as the first offering of the day, all subsequent sacrifices are additions to it. And, as the last

11. Carol Newsom, *Daniel* (Louisville: Westminster John Knox, 2014), 265.
12. Joseph Blenkinsopp, *Ezra–Nehemiah* (Louisville: Westminster John Knox, 1988), 98.
13. Shimon Bar-On, "The Development of the Tamid Offering and Its Place in the Priestly Calendar of Sacrifices" (Hebrew), in *Proceedings of the Twelfth World Congress of Jewish Studies, Jerusalem, July 29–August 5, 1997, Division A: The Bible and Its World* (Jerusalem: World Union of Jewish Studies, 1997), 143–53.

offering of the day, it guarantees that the sacred fire will remain lit until the following morning when the cycle is repeated.

Perhaps the best index of its importance can be found in a lengthy description of the ritual that comes near the end of the book of Ben Sira. Comparing Exodus 29 to Ben Sira is like reading the grocery list for a holiday dinner and sitting down to enjoy the meal itself.[14] Though the Priestly writers have put a premium on how a sacrifice is to be performed, the significance of the sacrificial experience cannot be limited to the ingredients required. For this reason, texts like Ben Sira and Mishnah *Tamid* are crucial supplements to what the Priestly writer has so tersely described.

As scholars have noted, the order of events in Ben Sira closely parallels the description of the ritual found in the Mishnah.[15] In order to draw attention to the respective parts of the ritual, I have added headings to the sections to the text of Ben Sira 50.

High Priest offers the sheep
¹² When he received the portions from the hands of the priests,
    as he stood by the hearth of the altar
  with a garland of brothers around him,
    he was like a young cedar on Lebanon
    surrounded by the trunks of palm trees.
¹³ All the sons of Aaron in their splendor
    held the Lord's offering in their hands
    before the whole congregation of Israel.

Drink offering
¹⁴ Finishing the service at the altars,
    and arranging the offering to the Most High, the Almighty,
¹⁵ he held out his hand for the cup

---

14. Also see Sirach 45:14, which singles out the role of the tamid just after addressing the vesting of Aaron.

15. Though some have argued that this chapter reflects the ritual of Yom Kippur, a consensus has emerged that the tamid offering is the better candidate. Most refer to the article of Fearghas O. Fearghail, "Sir 50,5–21: Yom Kippur or the Daily Whole-Offering?," *Biblica* 59 (1978): 301–16, to establish the case. See, for example, Benjamin G. Wright, *No Small Difference: Sirach's Relationship to Its Hebrew Parent Text* (Atlanta: Scholars Press, 1989), 177; Patrick Skehan and Alexander di Lella, *The Wisdom of Ben Sira*, AB 39 (New York: Doubleday, 1987), 550–52; and C. T. R. Hayward, *The Jewish Temple: A Non-Biblical Sourcebook* (New York: Routledge, 1996), 50.

and poured a drink offering of the blood of the grape;
he poured it out at the foot of the altar,
a pleasing odor to the Most High, the king of all.

Sounding the trumpets
[16] Then the sons of Aaron shouted;
they blew their trumpets of hammered metal;
they sounded a mighty fanfare
as a reminder before the Most High.

Public adoration
[17] Then all the people together quickly
fell to the ground on their faces
to worship their Lord,
the Almighty, God Most High.

Singing of psalms
[18] Then the singers praised him with their voices
in sweet and full-toned melody.
[19] And the people of the Lord Most High offered
their prayers before the Merciful One,
until the order of worship of the Lord was ended,
and they completed his ritual.

Blessing of the congregation, pronouncement of the Holy Name
[20] Then Simon came down and raised his hands
over the whole congregation of Israelites,
to pronounce the blessing of the Lord with his lips,
and to glory in his name;
[21] and they bowed down in worship a second time,
to receive the blessing from the Most High. (Sir. 50:12–21)

A number of the rubrics that we see in this liturgical celebration find parallels in the rites of the eighth day in Leviticus 9. These would include (1) the gathering of the congregation of Israel, (2) the public adoration at the offering of the sacrifices, and (3) the pronouncement of a blessing on the congregation. This is hardly surprising because the eighth day marks the onset of the tamid rite. In fact, there is a loose parallelism between Exodus 29 and Leviticus 8–9. Exodus 29 begins with the command to ordain Aaron and his sons (vv. 1–37), which is immediately followed by the command to offer the tamid and the promise that God will dwell among his people (vv. 38–46). Leviticus 8 is the fulfillment of the ordination commands in Exodus 29, and Leviticus 9 is an account of the rites of the eighth day, which includes the offering of the tamid (v. 17). Leviticus 9, then, corresponds to the close of Exodus 29 even as it adds additional sacrificial procedures to the onset of the daily tamid.

This similarity is often ignored by scholars because the tamid sacrifice is mentioned as something of an afterthought in Leviticus 9:17b (and for that reason many excise it as a secondary addition).[16] But it is worth recalling that the addition is described in terms very similar to Numbers 28–29, and in that calendar it was never an extraneous detail but an expression of the ritual that grounded all the others. I would suggest that the joyous celebration that marked the onset of the altar service in Leviticus 9 also conveyed something of the atmosphere that attended the daily tamid rite. Readers of this narrative should be sensitive to its singular character as a foundation narrative for the cult but at the same time be careful not to ignore its durative dimension.

The Meaning of Sacrifice

All of which brings us to the subject of the meaning of the tamid rite. This is a considerable challenge for though the text of Exodus 29:38–42a tells us *how* to prepare the tamid it tells us nothing about *why* such a sacrifice should be offered in the first place. Christian readers have the tendency to think of the sacrificial cult purely in terms of atonement. No doubt this is due to allowing texts such as Hebrews 10 (see the epigram to this chapter) to have a controlling voice over the entirety of the sacrificial system. Read this way, Christ's atoning sacrifice replaces the rhythm of the sacrificial cult "for it is impossible that the blood of bulls and goats should take away sins." But this text from Hebrews need not be read as a judgment on the entire cult of ancient Israel. If we review the legislation for sacrifice found in Leviticus 1–7, we will discover that atonement plays a surprisingly minor role in the priestly cult. Only two of these seven chapters address the concept directly. And even when this happens, the discussion centers on inadvertent sins, a small subset

16. See August Dillmann, *Die Bücher Exodus und Leviticus* (Leipzig: Hirzel, 1880), 469–70; Karl Elliger, *Leviticus*, HAT (Tübingen: Mohr Siebeck, 1966), 126; Milgrom, *Leviticus 1–16*, 584; and Nihan, *Priestly Torah*, 121.

of a much larger category.[17] Nor does atonement do justice to the description of the tamid in Ben Sira 50. There is no sorrow expressed for human sin in this chapter. We see, rather, just the opposite: a celebration of the gracious condescension of God to dwell among his people, as noted by Abarbanel in the epigraph to this chapter.

Jonathan Klawans has captured the problem of elevating atonement to center stage:

> The idea that sacrifice and sin are related in some way has long been recognized and emphasized. Indeed, many discussions of sacrifice are dominated by concerns with guilt, scapegoating, and expiation. It certainly cannot be denied that a number of sacrificial rituals described in Leviticus in particular serve an expiatory role on some level (Lev 1:4, Lev 4; Lev 16). But the typical understanding of the way daily sacrifice and grave sin are related is, I believe, backward. It is not that the daily sacrifice undoes the damage done by grave transgression. Quite the contrary: grave transgression undoes what the daily sacrifice produces. And the difference between the two formulations is important. What it boils down to is whether a sacrifice is considered, in and of itself, a productive act. Those who argue that expiation is at the core of all or most sacrificial rituals ultimately view sacrifice not as something productive in its own right but as a correction or a reversal of something else what was wrong. One well-known and useful commentary uses the following sequence of verbs in discussing sacrifice: "restore," "correct," "undo," "reverse," and "cleanse." That is typical of a host of scholars in biblical studies who view sacrifice as primarily a response to transgression.[18]

Two elements are worth special attention. First is the relationship of sacrifice to sin. The purpose of the daily sacrifice is not to eliminate human sin; nothing in the description of the tamid in Ben Sira would suggest such. Sin, rather, "undoes what the daily sacrifice produces." This concept is nicely illustrated in Psalm 51, the classic penitential prayer of ancient Israel. Having confessed his grave wrongdoings, the psalmist concludes his prayer with these words:

17. I should add that the "graded purification offering" (see Milgrom, *Leviticus 1–16*, 307–18) does deal with a small subset of intentional sins (see Lev. 5:1–4) but it should be noted that this is a subset. Intentional sins as a broader category are not dealt with in these chapters.

18. Jonathan Klawans, *Purity, Sacrifice and the Temple: Symbolism and Supersessionism in the Study of Ancient Judaism* (Oxford: Oxford University Press, 2006), 71.

¹⁶ For you have no delight in sacrifice;
>   if I were to give a burnt offering, you would not be pleased.
¹⁷ The sacrifice acceptable to God is a broken spirit;
>   a broken and contrite heart, O God, you will not despise.

Offerings are not understood to ameliorate sin, as that is the job of "a broken and contrite heart." But the last two lines of Psalm 51 (perhaps a later addition) abruptly return to the subject of the importance of sacrifices.

¹⁸ Do good to Zion in your good pleasure;
>   rebuild the walls of Jerusalem,
¹⁹ then you will delight in right sacrifices,
>   in burnt offerings and whole burnt offerings;
>   then bulls will be offered on your altar.

It is important to note that these verses do not reverse the words of judgment found earlier in vv. 16–17 but give them the theological context they require. In a time of sin and penitential reflection, a contrite heart is more important than any cultic act. But when that day has passed and God has accepted the proffered contrition, then the restoration of sacrificial service is not only licit but a supreme good. As a token of the harmony between creator and creature, God will again delight in burnt offerings. Grave sins, according to this psalm, undo the good wrought by sacrifice. But when those sins are dealt with, sacrificial practice regains its position of high esteem in God's eyes.

This leads us to Klawans's second point. If the tamid sacrifices are about removing sin, there would be no internal good to the sacrificial action itself. Its only function is to repair something. Perhaps an analogy will clarify this point. Consider the importance of bleach in the laundry room. It is without parallel for removing certain types of stains. No home can do without it. But absent the need to remove stains or disinfect surfaces, there would be no reason to keep bleach on hand. It has no good internal to itself.

Klawans puts the focus where it belongs—on the internal, "productive" good of the action. But if the act is productive, what does it produce? Or, to frame the question a bit differently, absent the need to atone for sin, why offer a sacrifice? To answer this question, let us recall what Menahem Haran has written about the ritual actions that take place within the tabernacle:

> The symbolical significance underlying this complex of inner ritual acts
> is simple and clear: the daily satisfaction of the "needs" of the deity. It is

these rites, performed regularly and continually, that give the tabernacle-temple its character of a dwelling-place of the deity. The ritual vessels that stand inside the temple—the table, lampstand, and incense-burner—are the furnishings of this "residence." With the aid of these furnishings the special priest, who, as already mentioned, is denominated "the Lord's servant," *mesharet YHWH*, ministers to all the requirements of the master of the residence.[19]

If we added the tamid sacrifices to Haran's list, it would be clear that it also serves the "needs" of the deity who resides there. Other idioms in the Hebrew Bible (e.g., "the food for my offerings . . . my pleasing aroma" [Num. 28:2]) suggest that God was "fed" at his sacrificial hearth. Jacob Milgrom builds on Haran's observations by comparing the tamid to the daily sacrifices in Egypt and Mesopotamia:

In outer form, the *Tāmîd* resembles the daily offering of Israel's neighbors, where—at least symbolically—it formed the daily diet of the gods. Thus in Egyptian temples there were three daily services, but only during the morning and evening were the gods served their meals (Sauneron 1960). In Mesopotamia the parallel is even more striking: "According to an explicit and detailed text of the Seleucid period, the images in the temple of Uruk were served two meals per day. The first and principal meal was brought in the morning when the temple opened, and the other was served at night, apparently immediately before the closing of the doors of the sanctuary" (Oppenheim 1964). Israel's *Tāmîd* also prescribed two offerings daily, a "main course" of a lamb with a meal offering and a libation as "side dishes" . . . Indeed, as (Medieval Jewish commentator) Abravanel has already observed, the *Tāmîd* was restricted to the essential staples of the Israelite diet: the flesh of lambs (the most inexpensive meat) and a portion of the three most abundant crops—from which firstfruits were prescribed (Num 18:12)—wheat, wine, and (olive) oil.[20]

19. Menahem Haran, *Temples and Temple Service in Ancient Israel: An Inquiry into Biblical Cult Phenomena and the Historical Setting of the Priestly School*, 2nd ed. (Winona Lake, IN: Eisenbrauns, 1985), 218–19.

20. Milgrom, *Leviticus 1–16*, 456. The citations within this quotation are from Serge Sauneron, *The Priests of Ancient Egypt* (New York: Grove, 1960), and A. Leo Oppenheim, *Ancient Mesopotamia: Portrait of a Dead Civilization* (Chicago: University of Chicago Press, 1964). He does not provide a citation for the medieval Jewish commentator Abarbanel, but it is presumably from his commentary to Exodus 29:38.

One might counter that this anthropomorphic language is just a vestigial reminder of an ancient conception of sacrifice that no longer had any real purchase on Israelite thinking. Consider, for example, the oft-cited words of the psalmist:

> [7] Hear, O my people, and I will speak,
>   O Israel, I will testify against you.
>   I am God, your God.
> [8] Not for your sacrifices do I rebuke you;
>   your burnt offerings are continually before me.
> [9] I will not accept a bull from your house,
>   or goats from your folds.
> [10] For every wild animal of the forest is mine,
>   the cattle on a thousand hills.
> [11] I know all the birds of the air,
>   and all that moves in the field is mine.
> [12] "If I were hungry, I would not tell you,
>   for the world and all that is in it is mine.
> [13] Do I eat the flesh of bulls,
>   or drink the blood of goats?" (Ps. 50:7–13)

The most common interpretation of this psalm is that it represents a more evolved view of sacrifice than the more literal description found in the Priestly writings. If God has no need for the "flesh of bulls" or the "blood of goats" then references to his "pleasure" in the aroma of their sacrificial flesh must be an archaic holdover from a distant, pagan past. Perhaps this sort of language could be compared to modern persons who continue to use the expression "sunrise" in spite of the knowledge that the sun does not really revolve around the earth.

As appealing as that perspective might be, we should exercise caution before completely dismissing the colorful language of the cult. Perhaps consideration of another dimension of the spiritual life will help put this anthropomorphic language in proper perspective. Consider the example of intercessory prayer. How does one explain the practice of soliciting individuals to pray for those undergoing some sort of trial? The motivating rhetoric is the need to implore God to act. But does God require such prompting? Does he forget or become indifferent to our plight? In short, why pray for others if God is all-knowing and all-powerful? The worries we have about a deity enjoying roasted flesh can be extended to other parts of Israel's spiritual life.

The importance of intercession is brought out well in Moses's prayer on behalf of Israel after the sin of the golden calf (Exod. 32:7–14). God is justly outraged by this high-handed act of disobedience and threatens to destroy the nation he has just liberated from Egypt. Yet at the same time, God subtly instructs Moses to step into the breach and make an impassioned appeal for the deliverance of Israel. Moses complies with this desire and persuades God to forsake his punitive intentions. God relents and Israel is saved.

How are we to understand this remarkable episode? The first step is to recognize that the strategy employed by Moses is not unique to him but underlies the rhetoric found in many intercessory psalms. It seems that God has ordered the life of prayer in such a way that it truly makes a difference in the world. Patrick Miller senses this dimension of biblical piety when he writes:

> God's purpose and action are involved with and affected by the purposes and actions of those whom God has created. God is independent of human control but has chosen to be responsive to the human situation. There is a kind of openness, a room for maneuvering, not just a willingness but an intention on God's part to be accessible to and responsive to the creation without being dependent upon it and controlled by it.[21]

The key insight is God's desire to be accessible and responsive to the human person. Or, to put it a different way, to stand in an *engaged* relationship with the human race, a relationship that has a dramatic character.[22]

The British novelist Evelyn Waugh knew the importance of this anthropomorphic dimension of God's identity and wove it into his *Sword of Honour* trilogy. The protagonist, Guy Crouchback, suffers from a form of spiritual sloth known as *acedia*. Though he still believes in God, he takes little account of the role God wishes to play in his everyday life. Waugh writes,

> For many years now the direction in the *Garden of the Soul*, "put yourself in the presence of God," had for Guy come to mean a mere act of respect, like the signing of the Visitors' Book at an Embassy or Government House. He reported for duty saying to God:

---

21. Patrick Miller, *Interpreting the Psalms* (Philadelphia: Fortress, 1986), 183.

22. I have addressed the "engaged" nature of the life of prayer in far more detail in *Christian Doctrine and the Old Testament: Theology in the Service of Biblical Exegesis* (Grand Rapids: Baker Academic, 2017), 23–38.

"I don't ask anything from you. I am here if you want me. I don't suppose I can be of any use, but if there is anything I can do, let me know," and left it at that.

"I don't ask anything from you": that was the deadly core of his apathy. . . . That emptiness had been with him for years now even in his days of enthusiasm and activity for the Halberdiers. Enthusiasm and activity were not enough. God required more than that. He had commanded all men to ask.[23]

Here we see the reason why the Bible makes Moses a nonnegotiable element in the drama of divine forgiveness. The religious life is not defined by simply signing a "Visitors' Book." As Miller puts it, God "has chosen to be responsive to the human condition." God commands us to ask, and in the context of intercessions such as that of Moses we see the results of this "engaged" relationship.

James Kugel reflects this engaged dimension of the religious life when he describes the act of offering a sacrifice as a "*prise de position*, a formal setting up of the worshiper as subject to God (one might almost say, in the royal sense, a subject of God, dependent, indebted), in every sense a devotee." "The point," Kugel continues, "is a subtle one, but worth insisting on: the deity is not . . . simply storing up oxidized calves and sheep in the supernal realm; but by acting the part of the domestic servant or humble courtier, the worshipper is, as it were, paying with himself, setting himself in a subservient relationship to the god."[24] What I like about this description is that it takes the liturgical action seriously without reducing the deity to the literal sense of the anthropomorphic image.

Ancient interpreters were sensitive to what we might call the "dramatic" dimension of religious life. Though all of these interpreters were well acquainted with the position articulated in Psalm 50 ("do I eat the flesh of bulls?"), they did not let it erase the engaged character of ritual life. Consider these lines from the fourth-century Christian interpreter, Ephrem the Syrian.

He Who is Lord of all, gives us all,
And He Who is the Enricher of all, borrows from all.
He is Giver of all as one without needs.

---

23. As cited in George Weigel, *The Truth of Catholicism* (San Francisco: Harper, 2001), 70.

24. James Kugel, "Topics in the History of the Spirituality of the Psalms," in *Jewish Spirituality from the Bible through the Middle Ages*, ed. Arthur Green (New York: Crossroad, 1988), 127–29.

> Yet He borrows back again as one deprived.
> Though He provided cattle and sheep as Creator,
> Yet He sought sacrifices as one deprived.
> (*Hymns on the Nativity* 4.203–205)[25]

Ephrem observes that God administers the providential order in such a way that he can be "responsive to creation." In the New Testament, God identifies with the pauper in need of material assistance. When one assists such a person, one is making a loan to him who is "without needs." Charity, on this view, is not simply an act of kindness but a way of "assisting" God (cf. Prov. 19:17: "Whoever is kind to the poor lends to the LORD and will be repaid in full"). In the Old Testament, on the other hand, God sought animal flesh as though he was "deprived" of food. Ephrem does not follow the modern evolutionary trajectory in which a God "without need" abandons "primitive" rituals. Rather, God presents himself to the human race as one in need so that a space is created for a living relationship with the deity. He knows all, but demands our prayers; he is beyond physical need, but takes pleasure in sacrificial flesh.

The rabbis make a similar move. In the Mekhilta de Rabbi Ishamel, an early commentary on the book of Exodus, they ponder how to fulfill the command not to appear before God "empty-handed" (Exod. 23:15). The text clearly demands that the worshipper bring a sacrifice, but which one? Perhaps the well-being offering (*shelamim*), a sacrifice in which most of the animal is consumed by the worshippers themselves? Or maybe the burnt offering (*olah*), an animal completely burned on the altar, its aroma rising (so the meaning of *olah*, "rising up") to the heavens? The rabbis conclude that both types must be offered.

> Behold, you must reason thus: "Rejoicing" is mentioned with reference to man and "rejoicing" is also implied with reference to God. Just as the rejoicing mentioned with reference to man means with something fit to be brought into the hands of man (well-being sacrifice), so also the rejoicing implied with reference to God must mean with something fit to be brought to God (burnt offering). It is not right that your own table be full while your Master's table be empty.[26]

25. The translation is taken from Kathleen McVey, *Ephrem the Syrian: Hymns*, Classics of Western Spirituality (Mahwah, NJ: Paulist, 1989), 103.

26. The translation comes from the edition of Jacob Lauterbach, *Mekhilta De-Rabbi*

The logic of this rabbinic text is worth pausing over. I think it is fair to say that the rabbis would share the viewpoint of Psalm 50 that God does not "eat the flesh of bulls or drink the blood of goats." But like St. Ephrem, they would also know that God accommodates himself to become accessible to the human race. If a central feature of the pilgrimage festivals was a large banquet in which food was broadly distributed ("Rejoice during your festival, you and your sons and your daughters, your male and female slaves, as well as the Levites, the strangers, the orphans, and the widows residing in your towns" [Deut. 16:14]), it would be altogether fitting to make God a partner to this celebration. Because the tabernacle was the house of God and the altar was his table, it was logical that God be served at his table as well.

We might want to compare this to what literary critics refer to as the tenor and vehicle of a metaphor. Everyone is familiar with Shakespeare's comparison of human life to a stage:

> All the world's a stage,
> And all the men and women merely players;
> They have their exits and their entrances;
> And one man in his time plays many parts,
> His acts being seven ages.
> (*As You Like it*, Act 2, scene 7)

In these lines, the concept ("tenor") being addressed is the nature of a human life. The mystery of that life is explored through the image ("vehicle") of the stage. This speech is so compelling not because human life is completely reducible to a theatrical performance. The stage, to be more accurate, provides a profound access point for contemplating human life. But the point I wish to make is this: as rational animals, we require metaphors like this to grapple with abstract concepts such as the nature of human life. If not the stage, then another image would be required, *mutatis mutandis*, for enacting one's relationship to God. We require a liturgical metaphor (vehicle) to provide an access point that will allow us to relate to God (tenor). The altar, as the spot where God is served, provides exactly that. In bringing an animal to the altar, the worshipper is pulled into a circle of giving that God, in his immeasurable grace, has initiated.

For the anthropologist Marcel Mauss (1872–1950), sacrificial ritual is grounded in the notion of an exchange, a process he tersely summarized by

---

Ishmael (Philadelphia: Jewish Publication Society, 2004), 2:483. The text is commenting on Exodus 23:17.

the formula *do ut des*, "I give [to you] so that you will give [to me]."[27] Taken too literally, this expression reduces the act of worship to the naked pursuit of one's self-advantage. Bernd Janowski has suggested that we modify the formula to read *do quia dedisti*, "I give because you have first given."[28] King David reflects this principle when he initiates the process of building the temple. He begins by extolling the grandeur of God.

> [11] Yours, O LORD, are the greatness, the power, the glory, the victory, and the majesty; for all that is in the heavens and on the earth is yours; yours is the kingdom, O LORD, and you are exalted as head above all. [12] Riches and honor come from you, and you rule over all. In your hand are power and might; and it is in your hand to make great and to give strength to all. [13] And now, our God, we give thanks to you and praise your glorious name. (1 Chron. 29:11–13)

But then he turns to the theme Janowski addressed: "But who am I, and what is my people, that we should be able to make this freewill offering? For all things come from you, and of your own have we given you" (v. 14). Sacrifice, in this prayer, is a public demonstration of thanksgiving for the gifts one has received. It is true that all things belong to God; he is in need of nothing. But in his grace he condescends to our level so that we may offer him something in gratitude for all that he has given.

I think that the idea of thanksgiving is a crucial piece of the equation; it softens the overly mercantile and self-interested dimension of the Maussian formula. Yet it is striking that the Bible takes great care to describe the tabernacle as the place where God dwells. As Haran notes, this would include provisioning his table. Language, in this context, fails us for this particular cultic act—like the notion of intercessory prayer that we discussed earlier—is only intelligible if the deity is truly affected. To return to Ephrem, God plays the role of the hungry person to open up a space for a form of religious service that constitutes more than simply "signing the Visitors' book."

I am personally drawn to the work of the anthropologist Valerio Valeri who writes, "as a gift, sacrifice is effective because it is a token of the relationship between god and man—*because it creates that relationship by instantiating it*. In other words, by being presented as a token, the sacrificial gift evokes the presence of

27. Henri Hubert and Marcel Mauss, *Sacrifice: Its Nature and Function* (Chicago: University of Chicago Press, 1964).

28. B. Janowski, *Sühne als Heilsgeschehen* (Neukirchen-Vluyn: Neukirchener, 1982), vii.

the type (the relation) that it presupposes."[29] At the sacrificial hearth, God condescends to the human community in such a way that their ritual actions make a material difference in the relationship that the deity wishes to establish with his people. It is not the case that somehow the offerer has some type of control over the deity. The relationship that is "instantiated" in the cult, Valeri concludes, underscores the dramatic dependence of humankind on the God they serve:

> The value of the thing given is inversely proportional to that of the giver. In other words, for a god, giving much is giving little; for man, giving little is giving much. Hence man's small gift to the god is as valuable as god's big gift to man, but at the same time this equivalence of the gifts signifies and establishes the nonequivalence of the givers, of god and man. It is in this way that reciprocity can coexist with hierarchy and that the sacrificial exchange can represent the gods' superiority over men."[30]

According to Valeri, the Latin phrase *do ut des* could be paraphrased, "I give you so little yet you give me so much."

Conclusion

We began this chapter with the depiction of Aaron's first sacrifice in the carpet mosaic from Sepphoris. One of the reasons for doing this was to provide a vivid visual contrast to the theme of divine indwelling that we encountered in our previous chapter. But even more important was the emphasis this picture put on the tamid sacrifice, a rite that is often overlooked in standard handbooks of Israelite religion. This is due to the disparity between Exodus 29 and Leviticus 8–10. The former provides the prescriptions for ordaining the priests and the onset of the tamid. The latter, however, does not follow this script in every detail. The tamid, a central feature of Exodus 29, is reduced to just a half-verse—almost an afterthought—in Leviticus 9:17b. In its place stands the lengthy rite of the eighth day, something that is not even hinted at in Exodus 29. It is the first unscripted story in the Tabernacle Narrative.

Because of the centrality of the eighth day rite and the negligible contribution of Leviticus 9:17b, many scholars have eliminated this half-verse as a secondary addition. Others go a step further and delete the tamid rite in

---

29. Valerio Valeri, *Kingship and Sacrifice* (Chicago: University of Chicago Press, 1985), 63.
30. Valeri, *Kingship*, 65.

Exodus 29 as well. (In part because it seems ill-suited to the conclusion of that chapter, which focuses on the notion of indwelling rather than sacrifice.) The task of this book is not to produce yet another hypothesis about the diachronic development of these chapters (though I would not deny such), but rather to deal with the text in its final canonical form. I suggested two reasons why Leviticus 9:17b is not as odd as one might think. First, its appearance as something of an "afterthought" conforms to the way it appears in Numbers 28–29. Second, the celebratory character of the eighth day rite has some structural similarities to the festivities of the tamid rite, at least as it is described in Ben Sira 50 and Mishnah *Tamid*. I could add a third as well. One of the purposes of the eighth day rite is to provide the occasion on which the divine fire can emerge and consume the first sacrifices. Because of its divine origin, the priests were obligated to make sure it never went out (Lev. 6:8–13). This meant refreshing that fire in the early morning in conjunction with the tamid and making sure sufficient wood was in place during the evening tamid to last throughout the night. The fire was imbued with such sacramental importance that the author of 2 Maccabees records that some of it was taken into exile and subsequently reused to light the altar upon their return (2 Macc. 1:19–23).

Having disposed with the literary structure of Exodus 29, we turned to a second issue, the meaning of the sacrificial rite itself. This is a challenge because the Tabernacle Narrative in general, and the laws for the tamid in particular, only reveal how to prepare the sacrifice; they say nothing about what the rite means. Two things, however, are clear. First, as Klawans rightly emphasizes, this sacrifice has nothing to do with atoning for sins. Second, the sacrifice should be understood as part of the "care and feeding" of the deity who resides in the tabernacle. Nevertheless, it remains an open question as to how literally ancient Israelites understood this idiom. Though it is impossible to enter the head of an ancient Israelite, I suggested reasons why the realistic, anthropomorphic tenor should not be dismissed out of hand. The metaphor of "feeding the gods" allows a place for Israelites to "position themselves" (a *prise de position* as Kugel expressed it) in a subordinate, reverential posture toward the deity. In a word, it provided a framework for offering a gift to God in return for the many blessings he had bestowed. "Sacrifice is effective," Valeri argued, "because it creates [a] relationship by instantiating it."

CHAPTER 5

Liturgical Beginnings and Immediate Sin

After two chapters of repeating "as the Lord commanded," Lev 10:1 announces that Nadab and Abihu did "what had *not* been commanded." The intrusion of the negative [particle] "not," in the familiar refrain comes like a thunderclap, an aural shock to a listening audience just as Yhwh's consuming fire presented a visual shock to the watching Israelites in the story.

James Watts[1]

[In regard to] the Tabernacle, any sin, in so far as it is a sin is serious. If one must distinguish between grave and light sins, grave sins concern the area closest to the Holy and not in a more distant arena such as idolatry.

Aryeh Toeg[2]

In the next two chapters I would like to return to the story of the theophany that concludes Leviticus 9, but this time I will consider an important detail that we have not yet addressed. One of the striking features of the Tabernacle Narrative is that it does not conclude with a moment of beatitude after the divine fire has consumed the sacrifices that Israel has offered. This literary unit ends on a much more discordant note. All four of Aaron's sons commit errors of one kind or another; the two oldest sons die as a result and the two others are subject to a sharp reprimand by Moses. In other words, no sooner is God's domicile inaugurated than it is in need of repair. Most readers of the Bible presume that the laws governing the Day of Atonement address a ritual created to deal with the sins of

---

1. James Watts, *Ritual and Rhetoric in Leviticus: From Sacrifice to Scripture* (Cambridge: Cambridge University Press, 2007), 106–7.
2. Aryeh Toeg, *The Giving of the Torah at Sinai* (Jerusalem: Magnes, 1977), 150 (Hebrew).

Israel on an annual basis. After all, that is what the rite becomes in the postbiblical era. But surprisingly that is not the story that the Bible tells. According to the opening verses of Leviticus 16 the purpose of this atonement rite is far more specific: to deal with the aftereffects of what Aaron's sons have done wrong.

Because the sins of the four sons are not identical and reveal different theological facets of the tabernacle, we will dedicate a chapter to each of the two offending actions. The present chapter will have two foci. On the one hand, we will be interested in the larger structural problem of a foundation narrative (Lev. 8–9) that is abruptly interrupted by cultic error (Lev. 10), a pattern that I will identify as the doctrine of "immediate sin." In this larger frame, distinguishing between the sins of the four sons is not crucial; the point to be made is that *all* of Aaron's sons fail as soon as the daily liturgy commences. On the other hand, we shall examine the specific sins of the two younger sons and the peculiar way in which their wrongdoing is narrated. I should warn my readers in advance that the narrative logic of this portion of Leviticus is a challenge to follow, not because of my prose (I hope!) but because the biblical authors themselves did not intend to clarify the specific character of the sins. Part of the burden of this chapter and the next will be to explain why these narratives are intentionally opaque and have perplexed readers for two millennia.

The Tabernacle as the Goal of Creation

As we pointed out in our first chapter, the account of the erection of the tabernacle follows the structure of the creation narrative in Genesis 1. But there is a significant advance in this Sinaitic moment. Whereas in creation God's sacralizing of the sabbath takes place apart from human knowledge and participation, *at Sinai God involves humanity in bringing creation to its goal.* It is striking that whereas God finishes the creation of the world in seven days, it is Moses who constructs the tabernacle through seven deeds. At Sinai, unlike creation, God approaches Israel and draws her near to himself. The rabbis caught the high valuation of this human act of world-building when they described the purpose of Moses's action as causing the divine presence (*Shekinah*) to dwell within *a work of human hands.* As Peter Schäfer summarizes the rabbinic position: "The creation of the world is not, if one accepts this view, solely the work of God but also the work of man: only when the man Moses erects the tabernacle is God's created order brought to completion."[3] Subsequently, when explaining

3. Peter Schäfer, "Tempel und Schöpfung," *Kairos* 16 (1974): 132–33.

why the completion of the tabernacle was necessary to complete creation itself, Schäfer concludes: "The world, from its beginning onward, requires that God be in relationship with mankind; without such a relationship between God and man, the creation of the world would be senseless and superfluous."

According to the theology of the Priestly school, once the tabernacle and its altar had been consecrated by Moses, the preparatory work of the liturgy was finished. When the daily sacrifices began (Exod. 29:38–42 = Lev. 9:17), the goal of all creation was consummated. The promise of God had been realized: "I will dwell among the Israelites, and I will be their God" (Exod. 29:45). The people responded in kind, falling on their knees in praise and trembling at his awesome appearance:

> [23] As [Moses and Aaron] came out from the tent of meeting, they blessed the people and the glory of the LORD appeared to all the people. [24] Fire came out from the LORD and consumed the burnt offerings and the fat on the altar. When all the people saw it, they gave a loud shout and fell on their faces. (Lev. 9:23–24)

The erection of the tabernacle and the lighting of the sacrificial pyre constitute the apogee of the Torah. And, as Avigdor Hurowitz has so carefully shown, this moment of wonder and glory has ample parallels in the ancient Near East.[4] Because the temple was the world in microcosm, ancient Near Eastern texts are quite happy to compare the erection of a temple to the act of creating the world. The moment of temple building *always* ushers in an age of peace and tranquility.

This is nicely reflected in the stories about Solomon's erection of the temple in the books of Kings and Chronicles. Let us consider the version found in 2 Chronicles 7, which, as we have seen,[5] relies on Exodus 40:34–35 and Leviticus 9:23–24 to describe the event:

> [1] When Solomon had ended his prayer, fire came down from heaven and consumed the burnt offering and the sacrifices; and the glory of the LORD filled the temple. [2] The priests could not enter the house of the LORD,

---

4. Avigdor Hurowitz, "The Priestly Account of Building the Tabernacle," *JAOS* 105 (1985): 21–30, and Hurowitz, *I Have Built You an Exalted House: Temple Building in the Bible in the Light of Mesopotamian and North-West Semitic Writings*, JSOTSup 115 (Sheffield: JSOT, 1992).

5. See chapter 2, p. 43 n. 25.

because the glory of the LORD filled the LORD's house. ³ When all the people of Israel saw the fire come down and the glory of the LORD on the temple, they bowed down on the pavement with their faces to the ground, and worshiped and gave thanks to the LORD, saying, "For he is good, for his steadfast love endures forever."

⁴ Then the king and all the people offered sacrifice before the LORD. ⁵ King Solomon offered as a sacrifice twenty-two thousand oxen and one hundred twenty thousand sheep. So the king and all the people dedicated the house of God. ⁶ The priests stood at their posts; the Levites also, with the instruments for music to the LORD that King David had made for giving thanks to the LORD—for his steadfast love endures forever—whenever David offered praises by their ministry. Opposite them the priests sounded trumpets; and all Israel stood.

⁷ Solomon consecrated the middle of the court that was in front of the house of the LORD; for there he offered the burnt offerings and the fat of the offerings of well-being because the bronze altar Solomon had made could not hold the burnt offering and the grain offering and the fat parts.

⁸ At that time Solomon held the festival for seven days, and all Israel with him, a very great congregation, from Lebo-hamath to the Wadi of Egypt. ⁹ On the eighth day they held a solemn assembly; for they had observed the dedication of the altar seven days and the festival seven days. ¹⁰ On the twenty-third day of the seventh month he sent the people away to their homes, joyful and in good spirits because of the goodness that the LORD had shown to David and to Solomon and to his people Israel.

¹¹ Thus Solomon finished the house of the LORD and the king's house; all that Solomon had planned to do in the house of the LORD and in his own house he successfully accomplished. (2 Chron. 7:1–11)

What should be noted here is the celebratory atmosphere that follows from the dedication of the temple. Sacrifices were offered (vv. 4–5), songs were sung, and Israel stood in rapt attention (v. 6). Afterward there were eight days of festivities (vv. 8–9) and everyone then departed for their homes "joyful and in good spirits" (v. 10). Solomon had carried out his responsibilities impeccably (v. 11).

Many scholars have suggested, on the basis of this ancient Near Eastern pattern, that the Priestly narrative at one time also ended with the lighting of the sacrificial pyre before the assembled crowd (Lev. 9:23–24).⁶ On this view,

6. For a good survey of where various scholars have situtated the original conclusion

the story of the founding of the tabernacle has much in common with similar tales about the temple in Jerusalem or elsewhere in Mesopotamia. Although this hypothetical reconstruction has a lot to commend it, the final form of the story does not respect it. One of the most striking features of the Tabernacle Narrative is that *immediately* after the sacrificial pyre was sanctified by fire, it was profaned. Or, to put it in a slightly different way: this foundational moment did not culminate in beatitude but priestly error. Unlike the story of Solomon's temple, the foundational moment did not give way to festal celebrations but a reckoning with grave cultic error.

The way the story unfolds emphasizes a single point: cultic error is immediate. Just as fire issued from the temple to consume the first sacrifices, so fire miraculously and immediately issues forth and devours the first offenders of the liturgy.

Fire came out from before the LORD and consumed the burnt offering . . . (Lev. 9:24)

Fire came out from before the LORD and consumed them . . . (Lev. 10:2)

It is easy to see from the parallelism of these two verses why the Jewish medieval commentator, Rashbam argued that it was one and the same fire that consumed both the sacrifices and Nadab and Abihu.[7] On this reading, there was hardly a millisecond of joy; as soon as God draws near, human sin threatens to drive him away.

The Error of Eleazar and Ithamar

So far we have documented the striking way in which the Bible presents the origins of the cult—and cultic error—in the wilderness of Sinai. When viewed against comparable material elsewhere in the Bible and the ancient

---

of the Priestly narrative, see Christophe Nihan, *From Priestly Torah to Pentateuch*, FAT 25 (Tübingen: Mohr Siebeck, 2007), 31. German scholarship, in particular, has been characterized by a high degree of confidence in being able to discern what the primitive form ("Grundschrift" or P^g for short) of the Priestly narrative would have looked like. Though I do not deny that the narrative went through a number of redactional stages, I have much less confidence in being able to lay them out in any detail. In the end, I have chosen to interpret the final canonical form of the text.

7. Rashbam, *Commentary on Leviticus*, ad 10:1.

Near East, it is somewhat shocking to see this foundational moment besmirched in this way. In the remainder of the chapter we will bore down a bit deeper and explore the character of the sin of Eleazar and Ithamar. This will require careful attention to detail because almost no reader would ever guess that something has gone wrong. The sacrificial ritual requires two sin offerings, one for the priests and another for the people. After a detailed description of the procedure used for the priestly sacrifice, our story ends with the expected formula of approval: "[Aaron had acted] as the LORD commanded Moses" (8:10). When the text turns to the people's offering, our author abbreviates. Rather than repeating all the ritual actions, he writes: "He took the goat of the sin offering that was for the people, and slaughtered it, and presented it as a sin offering, like the first one" (Lev. 9:15). There is no hint in this verse that anything has gone wrong. Yet in the subsequent chapter, Moses issues a sharp reprimand to Eleazar and Ithamar regarding the way they handled that very offering:

> [16] Then Moses made inquiry about the goat of the sin offering [i.e., the people's offering], and—it had already been burned! He was angry with Eleazar and Ithamar, Aaron's remaining sons, and said, [17] "Why did you not eat the sin offering in the sacred area? For it is most holy, and God has given it to you that you may remove the guilt of the congregation, to make atonement on their behalf before the LORD. [18] Its blood was not brought into the inner part of the sanctuary. You should certainly have eaten it in the sanctuary, as I commanded." (Lev. 10:16–18)

What is peculiar here is that the reader would never have guessed that anything had gone wrong in Leviticus 9. The procedures followed there parallel almost exactly what happened in Leviticus 8. Yet clearly a mistake has been made, as Moses explains. An animal that was supposed to be eaten by those who offered it was burned outside the camp (10:16–18). Embedded in this reprimand is a loose citation of a law found in Leviticus 6:30. The only way to understand the actions of the priests and the subsequent ire of Moses is to attend carefully to the role played by the sacrificial laws found in Leviticus 1–7, a portion of the Tabernacle Narrative that we have not yet examined.

The Challenge of Leviticus 1-7

Up to this point, we have examined the way the sacrificial actions described in Leviticus 8-10 are related to the laws found in Exodus 29 and 40. We have not attended to the role played by the sacrificial laws found in Leviticus 1-7. In doing so we have followed the lead of the overwhelming majority of modern scholars who have argued that these laws are the result of a late scribal insertion. Several reasons are given for this hypothesis. First of all, as we will see later in the chapter, the laws that govern the sin offering in Leviticus are not followed in the ordination rites of Leviticus 8 and are inconsistently applied in the eighth day rites in Leviticus 9. In the present form of the text, this inconsistency creates a challenge for the reader. What laws are Moses and Aaron to follow—the ones revealed in Exodus 29 or in Leviticus 4? If we posit an earlier form of the narrative without Leviticus 4, this difficulty will disappear. Milgrom suggested a second reason when he noted that the completion of the priestly vestments (Exod. 39), the assemblage of the tabernacle (Exod. 40), and the ordination of the priesthood (Lev. 8) are all marked by a sevenfold approbatory formula: "Moses did [said action] as the Lord commanded him." If the laws of sacrifice (Lev. 1-7) were dropped, these approbatory sequences would follow in a strict sequential fashion.[8] Finally, we should note that the summoning of Moses in Leviticus 1:1 initiates the rubric of *general* law-giving. Because the laws that Moses will receive include the commandments in Leviticus 11-27, it would make sense that they would be grouped together and not interrupted by extraneous narrative material. This is actually the solution adopted by a number of ancient readers, who retold the narrative in such a way that the laws of Leviticus 1-7 followed the narration of the eighth day rites.[9]

---

8. Jacob Milgrom, *Leviticus 1-16*, AB 3 (New York: Doubleday, 1991), 61 and 542-43.

9. Ancient readers were also sensitive to the difference between the narrated order in scripture and the way things actually unfolded in time and space. But rather than positing an earlier, more pristine version of the story, they felt free to move these sacrificial laws to a location that they imagined more fitting. Let us consider once more Pseudo-Philo's retelling of the biblical story in the Biblical Antiquities 13.1-14.1).

> [13.1a] And Moses hastened and did everything that God had commanded him. [1b] And he went down and made the tent of meeting and its vessels and the ark and the lamp and the table and the altar of holocausts and the altar of incense and the ephod and the breastplate and the precious stones and the laver and the basins and everything that was shown to him. [1c] And he arranged all the vestments of the priests, the belt and the robe and the headdress and the golden plate and the holy crown [= Exodus 35-39]. [1d]

Whatever the value might be of such efforts to reconstruct a putative original, it must be acknowledged that the final form of our text has not respected them. The most obvious explanation of the placement of Leviticus 1–7 is that these laws will govern the routine cultic regimen that will begin once the altar is dedicated.[10] Though, at the end of the day, I agree with this position, it is not without its challenges. And one of those challenges concerns the intelligibility of the rites found in Leviticus 9.

The Problem of the Sin Offering

The laws that govern the sin offering provide a great test case for the supposed intelligibility of the eighth day rites. The laws in Leviticus 4 and 6 make a distinction between the sin offering brought by the high priest and congregation on the one hand and those brought by the chieftains and ordinary individuals on the other. In the former, one must sprinkle the blood on the golden incense altar found inside the tabernacle (4:5–7) and burn the carcass outside the camp (4:11–12); in the latter, the blood is sprinkled on the outer bronze altar (4:25) and the flesh is consumed by the priests (6:30). One would expect these laws to govern the rituals that follow. But that is not the case.

The procedure commanded In Exodus 29 and executed in Leviticus 8 follows a different protocol. In this case, the blood is placed on the outer altar while the animal is burned outside the camp.

And the oil for anointing priests as well as the priests themselves he consecrated [= Leviticus 8]. [1e] And when all this was done, the cloud covered them all [= Exod. 40:34–35].

[14.1] Then Moses called to the LORD, and God spoke to him from the tent of meeting, saying, "This is the law of the altar . . ." [= Lev. 1:1].

Earlier we noted that Pseudo-Philo retells the story in a way that combines the theophanies of Exodus 40 and Leviticus 9. But in order to do that, he had to skip the sacrificial laws that intervene. He does this by moving them to the period after the theophany of Leviticus 9:23 (so 14:1 and following). In other words, after the tabernacle is assembled, the priests are ordained, and the first public sacrifices are consumed, God then calls Moses forward to reveal the rest of the laws. On this understanding, Leviticus 1–7 is grouped with 11–27 as a single, continuous episode of revelation that begins after the lighting of the sacrificial pyre. A similar understanding of the order of events can be found in Josephus, the rabbis, and some medieval Jewish commentators.

10. Thomas Hieke, *Levitikus 1–15*, HThKAT (Freiburg: Herder, 2014), 331.

Exodus 29:10–14	Leviticus 8:14–17
¹⁰ You shall bring the bull in front of the tent of meeting. Aaron and his sons shall lay their hands on the head of the bull, ¹¹ and you shall slaughter the bull before the LORD, at the entrance of the tent of meeting, ¹² and *shall take some of the blood of the bull and put it on the horns of the altar with your finger*, and all the rest of the blood you shall pour out at the base of the altar. ¹³ You shall take all the fat that covers the entrails, and the appendage of the liver, and the two kidneys with the fat that is on them, and turn them into smoke on the altar. ¹⁴ *But the flesh of the bull, and its skin, and its dung, you shall burn with fire outside the camp*; it is a sin offering.	¹⁴ He led forward the bull of sin offering; and Aaron and his sons laid their hands upon the head of the bull of sin offering, ¹⁵ and it was slaughtered. *Moses took the blood and with his finger put some on each of the horns of the [bronze] altar*, purifying the altar; then he poured out the blood at the base of the altar. Thus he consecrated it, to make atonement for it. ¹⁶ Moses took all the fat that was around the entrails, and the appendage of the liver, and the two kidneys with their fat, and turned them into smoke on the altar. ¹⁷ *But the bull itself, its skin and flesh and its dung, he burned with fire outside the camp*, as the LORD commanded Moses.

It is significant that our narrator remarks that Moses acted "as the LORD commanded [him]" (8:17). But the point to be emphasized is that the command in question is that of Exodus 29:10–14, not Leviticus 4. In this particular case, the inclusion of the sacrificial laws in chapters 1–7 creates a sense of dissonance for the reader. One can readily understand why scholars have suggested that Leviticus 1–7 is a late scribal insertion. The story reads much more smoothly if one skips from the end of Exodus 40 to the beginning of Leviticus 8.

The Chasm between Leviticus 8 and 9

If the laws found in Leviticus 1–7 have no function for the rites of ordination in chapter 8, the situation changes dramatically in chapter 9. Now that the ordination service has been completed and Aaron and his sons are acting as priests, they can begin to carry out their routine responsibilities at the altar. Their supreme responsibility will be to offer the tamid (Lev. 9:17), a sacrifice that constituted the denouement of the ordination rite in Exodus 29.

Most readers of Leviticus do not notice the major disjuncture that exists between Leviticus 8 and 9. In Leviticus 8 Aaron and his sons have been, more or less, passive participants in a seven-day rite of consecration. It is Moses who brings them forward to the altar, washes them, and clothes them, and it is Moses who supervises and performs nearly all the rites at the altar. We should also add that Moses performs these actions according to the rules given in Exodus 29:1–37. Seven times, the narrator underscores, each step of the ritual has been performed "just as the LORD had commanded."

Enter Leviticus 9 and the mold is broken. The foundation rites end as does the sequence of seven-fold cultic actions. Moreover, unlike Leviticus 8, the ritual narrated in Leviticus 9 has no corresponding command section and so *it is the first act in the priestly narrative that has not been carefully pre-scripted.* The period of careful design, oversight, and execution through the agency of Moses and the deity has drawn to a close. Aaron and his sons are poised to take the reins and inaugurate the routine functions of the daily cult.

My presentation of the text below distinguishes between the command and execution sections, the sacrifices that pertain to Aaron and his sons and those of Israel. I have also italicized the various approbatory formulae used in the execution section.

Commands for Sacrifices

(A) Aaron's Sacrifices
[1] On the eighth day Moses summoned Aaron and his sons, and the elders of Israel. [2] He said to Aaron, "Take a bull calf for a sin offering, and a ram for a burnt offering, without blemish, and offer them before the LORD.

(B) Israel's Sacrifices
[3] And say to the people of Israel: Take a male goat for a sin offering; a calf and a lamb, yearlings without blemish, for a burnt offering; [4] and an ox and a ram for an offering of well-being to sacrifice before the LORD; and a grain offering with oil mixed in. For today the LORD will appear to you."

(C) Drawing Near to the Altar
[5] They brought what Moses commanded to the front of the tent of meeting; and the whole congregation drew near and stood before the LORD. [6] And Moses said, "This is the thing which the LORD commanded you to do, so that the glory of the LORD may appear to you." [7] Then Moses said to Aaron, "Draw near to the altar, and sacrifice your sin offering and your burnt offering, and make atonement for yourself and for the people; and sacrifice the offering of the people, and make atonement for them; as the LORD has commanded."

Execution of Sacrifices:

(A) Aaron's Sacrifices

[8] Aaron drew near to the altar, and slaughtered the calf of the sin offering, which was for himself. [9] The sons of Aaron presented the blood to him, and he dipped his finger in the blood and put it on the horns of the altar, and the rest of the blood he poured out at the base of the altar. [10] But the fat and the kidneys and the appendage of the liver from the sin offering he turned into smoke on the altar, *as the LORD commanded Moses*; [11] and the flesh and the skin he burned with fire outside the camp.

[12] And he slaughtered the burnt offering. Aaron's sons brought him the blood, and he dashed it against all sides of the altar. [13] And they brought him the burnt offering piece by piece, and the head which he turned into smoke on the altar. [14] He washed the entrails and the legs and, with the burnt offering, turned them into smoke on the altar.

(B) Israel's Sacrifices

[15] Next he presented the people's offering. He took the goat of the sin offering that was for the people, and slaughtered it, and presented it as a sin offering, *like the first one.*

[16] He presented the burnt offering, and sacrificed it *according to the regulation.*

[17] He presented the grain offering and, taking a handful of it, he turned it into smoke on the altar, in addition to the burnt offering [= tamid] of the morning.

[18] He slaughtered the ox also and the ram as a sacrifice of well-being for the people. Aaron's sons brought him the blood, which he dashed against all sides of the altar, [19] and the fat of the ox and of the ram—the broad tail, the fat which covers the entrails, the two kidneys and the fat on them, and the appendage of the liver. [20] They first laid the fat on the breasts, and the fat was turned into smoke on the altar; [21] and the breasts and the right thigh Aaron raised as an elevation offering before the LORD; *as Moses commanded.* (Lev. 9:1–21)

There are a number of features that should be pointed out. First of all, Moses appears to summon Aaron and his sons to the altar and issue a set of commands on his own recognizance (v. 1). Unlike Leviticus 8, there is no command section in Exodus that points forward to these rituals. These ritual requirements emerge as a complete surprise to the reader. Yet just few verses into the chapter we learn that everything that Moses asks of Aaron and Israel is the result of a divine command he had heard previously: "This is the thing which the LORD commanded you to do, so that the glory of the LORD may appear to you" (v. 16). Evidently, God relayed these commands to Moses off the record. Unlike what we have seen elsewhere in Exodus 25–40, the reader is not privy to this information. Second, the approbatory statements in this chapter are quite different from those in the previous chapter. Whereas in chapter 8 each of the seven sacrificial actions was marked by the observation that it was carried out exactly as commanded, in this chapter only the first and the last sacrifices are so marked (vv. 10 and 21). A few of the sacrifices are described without any evaluation at all (vv. 12–14, 17). And two of the sacrifices—Israel's sin and burnt offerings (vv. 15–16)—are marked in novel ways.[11]

Priestly Shorthand

Let us look more closely at the sin and burnt offerings in Leviticus 9. The priests and the people share these two sacrifices but there are some significant differences in how they are presented. Those differences demand our careful attention.

Priest	People
[8] Aaron drew near to the altar, and slaughtered the calf of the sin offering, which was for himself. [9] The sons of Aaron presented the blood to him, and he dipped his finger in the blood and put it on the horns of the altar, and the rest of the blood he poured out at the base of the altar. [10] But the fat and the kidneys and the appendage of the liver from the sin offering he turned into smoke on the altar, *as the LORD commanded Moses*; [11] and the flesh and the skin he burned with fire outside the camp.	[15] Next he presented the people's offering. He took the goat of the sin offering that was for the people, and slaughtered it, and presented it as a sin offering, *like the first one.*

11. It is worth noting that those sacrifices that have no appended evaluation are wholly burnt on the altar; those that are evaluated include actions that extend beyond the theophany at the end of the chapter.

¹² And he slaughtered the burnt offering. Aaron's sons brought him the blood, and he dashed it against all sides of the altar. ¹³ And they brought him the burnt offering piece by piece, and the head which he turned into smoke on the altar. ¹⁴ He washed the entrails and the legs and, with the burnt offering, turned them into smoke on the altar.

¹⁶ He presented the burnt offering, and sacrificed it *according to the regulation.*

If we look first at the priestly sacrifices in the left column (vv. 8–11 and 12–14), we notice that each is described in the same detailed manner that we saw in Leviticus 8. The people's sacrifices in the right column have been drastically abbreviated, something that we have not seen in any of our narrative texts so far. Indeed quite the opposite: up to this point, whenever our author has the chance to repeat verbatim a command that he has received, he does so!

For the sin offering, our author abbreviates the rite by saying that it was carried out "like the first one." In other words, if you want to know more, go back and reread the procedure described in vv. 8–11. The second formula of evaluation, "[he did it] according to the regulation," refers us back to a law previously revealed in Leviticus 1. This sort of narrative "shorthand" is standard elsewhere in the Priestly writings.

A good example of this can be found in the instructions regarding birds for a sin offering (Lev. 5:7–10). The text begins by mentioning that the person who cannot afford a sheep (5:7) can substitute either two turtledoves or two pigeons, one for a sin offering, the other for a burnt offering. Because no regulations have been given for a sin offering involving a bird, the ritual must be described in full:

> ⁸ You shall bring them to the priest, who shall offer first the one for the sin offering, wringing its head at the nape without severing it. ⁹ He shall sprinkle some of the blood of the sin offering on the side of the altar, while the rest of the blood shall be drained out at the base of the altar; it is a sin offering. (Lev. 5:8–9)

But in the case of the bird offered as a burnt offering, the ritual is abbreviated: "And the second he shall offer for a burnt offering *according to the regulation*" (5:10). The abbreviation refers the reader back to the first chapter of Leviticus where the rite is described in full:

[14] If your offering to the LORD is a burnt offering of birds, you shall choose your offering from turtledoves or pigeons. [15] The priest shall bring it to the altar and wring off its head, and turn it into smoke on the altar; and its blood shall be drained out against the side of the altar. [16] He shall remove its crop with its contents and throw it at the east side of the altar, in the place for ashes. [17] He shall tear it open by its wings without severing it. Then the priest shall turn it into smoke on the altar, on the wood that is on the fire; it is a burnt offering, an offering by fire of pleasing odor to the LORD. (Lev. 1:14–17)

I have taken the time to lay out this common priestly practice of abbreviating a cultic regulation after it has been introduced in a fuller form in order to highlight the singular character of Leviticus 8 (and, by extension, all of the execution narratives in Exod. 25–40). For each sacrifice in this chapter, the author repeats nearly verbatim what had been prescribed in Exodus 29. There is no use of abbreviation. It is analogous to a building contractor who must check with the city inspectors at every major stage of the construction process to make sure that the building will be safe for habitation. Once the inspector has done his job, he fills out a form documenting that the work has been done according to specification. Leviticus 8, we might say, is a compilation of such inspections, documenting in detail that the work has been done according to spec. Because the cult mimes creation and directly involves the deity, its founding cannot be derailed by human error. Careful oversight is the order of the day.

When we get to Leviticus 9, all of this changes. The priests are beginning to take charge of the liturgical process.[12] They are no longer subject solely to a set of special laws that Moses has received; from now on they will need to consult the "manual" (= Lev. 1–7) that God has revealed through the mediation of Moses. Yet, as soon as the closely superintending hand of God is removed and a space is created for human autonomy, things begin to unravel. We have left the rigor and exactitude of those foundation rites where careful attention to detail is necessitated to assure that the cult not be established on shifting sands. In the more quotidian world of Leviticus 9, the priests begin to act on their own, practicing their craft according to what will become received legal custom. This, I would like to claim, is the significance of the abbreviations found in Le-

---

12. Though in Leviticus 9:8–14 things are a bit more complicated. Aaron offers the sacrifice, unlike Leviticus 8, but still in accordance with a divine commandment. But this time that command is not part of the public, written record. It has been vouchsafed to Moses alone.

viticus 9:15–16. They alert the reader that the time of explicit Mosaic oversight is over and the priests must turn to the "manual" for guidance (Lev. 1–7).

Immediate Sin

Yet strikingly, as soon as this element of human autonomy is introduced, so is human error. But the nature of this error is revealed in a mysterious fashion. As I indicated earlier, I do not think that even the most careful reader would have guessed that something was amiss when he or she read that the priests offered the sacrifice of the people "like the first one" (v. 15). Yet in Leviticus 10, when Moses is surveying the work of the priests to make sure that the animals in question have all been disposed of properly, we learn that a gross error had been made. Moses issues an angry indictment. Moses justifies his outrage by citing the rule found in the priestly manual. According to Leviticus 6:30 there are two types of sin offerings. In one case, when the blood is brought inside the tabernacle to be daubed on the golden incense altar, the flesh cannot be eaten but must be burned. In the other case, when the blood is daubed on the bronze outer altar, the animal must be eaten and should not be burned. The priests violated this norm by burning flesh that should have been eaten. With this piece of information in hand, we can now understand the distinction between the description of Israel's sin offering being offered "like the first" and Israel's burnt offering being done "according to the regulation." The latter marks obedience, the former violation.[13]

The picture drawn here is striking. Although creation began with an account of what took place during the first six days in Genesis 1, it did not reach

13. But full understanding of this passage still eludes us. If Israel's sacrifice was performed just like Aaron's, why was his not also in violation of the law? On this question there is no easy answer. But one should observe, however, that the approbatory formula (v. 10) precedes the act of burning the carcass (v. 11). Perhaps this is a hint as to its irregular nature. An irregularity, it turns out, that was licit for the priests but not for laypeople. Crucial to note here is that the rites of the eighth day were not scripted in Exodus 29. One would have guessed that once Aaron and his sons were ordained, the routine daily sacrifices would begin. The rites of the eighth day are unexpected for the reader but evidently not for Moses. As we learn from 9:6, these rites were revealed to the participants but not the reader. This is fitting in its own way because once the cult is set in motion, a curtain is drawn between the general public and the priesthood. Certain rites and procedures were publicly known, but not all. We must presume that on the eighth day special rules still applied to the priestly offerings whereas the general rubrics for the same offerings applied to the people. The priests erred, according to the reprimand of Moses, in applying the laws of the priesthood to the people at large.

its true climax until Moses and the Israelites had arrived at Mount Sinai. When the priesthood was consecrated and the altar lit, God's purpose for the world was completed. He had elected the nation Israel and commanded them to draw near to his presence and tend his daily needs. But no sooner has creation come to closure than its very centerpiece, the tabernacle, becomes violated. Eleazar and Ithamar failed to offer the sin offering for the people correctly and Nadab and Abihu offered incense in a way that violated the Lord's commands. In sum, by the time we reach the end of this inaugural celebration, we learn that all four of Aaron's sons are guilty of an infraction of cultic law.

But it is important to underscore what the text does not say as well. Although our writer will not allow the story of the founding of the cult to end in beatitude, he is also loath to assert in any dogmatic way that the errors of the sons of Aaron were acts of obstreperous rebellion against, or even wanton disregard for, the God of Israel.[14] But this ambiguity about the character of these errors should not blind us to their structural significance. From a priestly perspective, the prescriptions for behavior around sancta are not graded as to weight of sin or level of human intentionality. Aryeh Toeg catches this sensibility well when he writes: "in as much as a complex and detailed set of laws oversee the promise that God shall dwell within the tabernacle, any sin, in so far as it is a sin is serious. For all that, if there is room to distinguish between a grave and a light sin, the grave sins can be found precisely in the area closest to the focal point of holiness and not in a far distant arena such as that of idolatry."[15] In other words, all errors in close proximity to the holy are grave. The sons of Aaron have marred the otherworldly beatitude that should have attended the inauguration of the cult. As a consequence of this priestly sin, Leviticus 16 demands a set of atonement rites to set creation aright.[16]

Conclusion

When I introduced the problem of cultic error at the beginning of this chapter, I noted that the problem had a number of complexities that would make the presentation of all the data a challenge for the reader. Now that we have

14. We are left, as Edward Greenstein has shown so ably, completely in the dark about the motivation of these two wayward priests and the specific nature of their sin. See "Deconstruction and Biblical Narrative," *Prooftexts* 9 (1989): 43–71.

15. Toeg, *Giving of the Torah at Sinai*, 150.

16. Note how Israel's rite of atonement begins: "The Lord spoke to Moses *after the death of the two sons of Aaron* [= Lev. 10:1] when they drew near before the Lord and died."

run through all the relevant textual issues, let me summarize the findings in the hope that any nagging points of unclarity might be removed. Perhaps the most important point to master is what I have called the "textual chasm" that stands between Leviticus 8 and 9. For readers who do not have much affection for biblical law and ritual, this will be difficult to appreciate because they will not have the patience to attend carefully to the significant changes that occur across these two chapters. Perhaps I could bring out the importance of what is transpiring in these chapters by way of an illustration. Imagine that you have a teenage son or daughter who wants to learn to drive. Initially they will take driving lessons, which are carefully supervised by an instructor accompanying the student on each excursion. Everything the novice does will be subject to direct oversight. Yet eventually, the student must master the required rules of the road and skills in order to drive the car on their own. Just so for Leviticus 8 and 9. Initially, while the foundation of cultic life is being prepared, the priests will conduct their craft under the careful supervision of Moses. For seven days they will be subject to his strict guidance and only in the seventh action of each of those seven days do they become actors in their own right.[17] On the eighth day, they will begin to act on their own. From then on there will be no need to document the fulfillment of every cultic action. The image of the contractor is again fitting. During construction, the builder must seek approval from city officials at numerous stages (e.g., installation of the plumbing, electric). But once the home is built, one can use all of that infrastructure without recourse to any approval. Such is the case in our Priestly source: we move from detailed accounts of the execution of each comment to the employment of what I have called "Priestly shorthand." Tragically, as soon as Aaron and his sons have their "priestly licenses," they suffer their first "accident." There is no extended period in which they can enjoy the beatitude offered by their God. No sooner is the "vehicle" in motion than we are witness to its first "fender-bender." That this cultic "accident" takes place so quickly is a striking feature of the Bible's

---

17. It should be noted that over the first six actions of the ordination sequence (8:1–30), Moses executes the commands he received in Exodus 29. However, for the seventh action—the consumption of the sacrificial flesh (8:31–36)—Aaron and his sons take over. This is unexpected because Exodus 29 presumes that Moses will perform *all* the commands. How do we explain this anomaly? I would suggest that these last verses of Leviticus 8 transfer the focus of attention to Aaron as a way of anticipating the role he must assume in Leviticus 9 when responsibility for the cult will be fully his. For a fuller explanation of this surprising detail, see Anderson, "Inauguration of the Tabernacle Service at Sinai," in *The Temple of Jerusalem: From Moses to the Messiah*, ed. Steven Fine (Leiden: Brill, 2010), 2–6.

presentation of this formative event. Whereas the Christian tradition has used the term "original sin" to mark human frailty in the face of divine commands, the notion of "immediate sin" is perhaps a better phrase to describe what we find in the Priestly account.

So far the driver's training analogy is apt, but there are some problems. Unlike students in driver's training—who can imitate the rules they learned in driver's education courses when they hit the road—the priest must learn a set of protocols for making a sacrifice during his ordination period but then follow a different set once he has assumed full reins on the cult. In other words, the procedures laid down in the priestly manual of Leviticus 1–7 stand in tension with the actions that take place in Leviticus 8. Once the routine of the daily cult begins, the special practices of Leviticus 8 must be set aside and the rules laid down in chapters 1–7 must be followed.

But the problem is even more complicated. For Leviticus 9 represents something of a transition from complete Mosaic oversight to independent action on the part of the priests. We can see this in the way in which the sin offering is handled. When Aaron and his sons prepare their own animal, they must follow the protocol laid down in Leviticus 8. When they offer the people's animal they are obligated to the rules laid down in Leviticus 1–7. For the reader, this distinction comes as a complete surprise (which was probably the case for the sons of Aaron as well). Nothing in the description found in Leviticus 9:15 would prepare us for the reprimand that Moses delivers in 10:16–18.

So one last conundrum remains: Why has our narrator built this sort of opacity into the story? Why do we have no clue that something has gone wrong in Leviticus 9:15? One explanation has been offered by historical critics: originally the story of dedicating the altar ended with the theophany at the end of Leviticus 9. On this view, there was no error earlier in the chapter. Aaron and his sons offered the sin offering of the people exactly like their own sin offering and this was in accordance with biblical law in this early stage of the narrative. In favor of this view is the reuse of Leviticus 9 in the temple dedication story found in 2 Chronicles 7 that we examined in our first chapter. That dedication clearly draws on the vocabulary of the Tabernacle Narrative to create a story in which altar dedication occurs without any sort of priestly error. Beatitude abounds! On this view a later scribe added the material we find in Leviticus 10 (German scholars refer to this sort of thing as *Fortschreibung*, the ongoing writing and rewriting of biblical narrative that occurred over the centuries) and transformed a moment of beatitude into tragedy.[18]

18. See the discussion of Nihan, *From Priestly Torah to Pentateuch*, 598–607, for a

But why would a scribe introduce a priestly error that had no immediate explanation in the text? One possible explanation for this strategy is that it further develops the notion of a chasm between Leviticus 8 and 9. In the former chapter the lay reader is equipped to be able to follow almost every detail that transpires. In chapter 9, however, a veil is drawn between that reader and the sacerdotal experts who are now assuming the responsibilities proper to their vocation. On this view, the knowledge that is proper to the priesthood and which is not shared with laypersons is realized in the way in which the narrative itself unfolds.[19] Moses is privy to a revelation about which the reader knows nothing, and the priests are expected to know how to apply various protocols of which the reader also has no comparable knowledge. Though I cannot prove that this is the reason, it makes good sense of the chapters and fits nicely with what we know about the character of the priesthood and the role it plays in Israelite culture. It is a professional guild and possesses a knowledge proper to its profession.

---

learned argument that Leviticus 10 is an example of late "inner-biblical exegesis" on the part of the Priestly circle.

19. My suggestion is similar, in some ways, to that of James Watts (*Ritual and Rhetoric in Leviticus* [Cambridge: Cambridge University Press, 2007], 97–129, but esp. 127–29). He believes the notion of special knowledge is ordered to a claim on the priestly office ("We are professionals doing a necessary and dangerous job, and only we can do it right"). Although he is not altogether wrong, the emphasis, I believe, is misplaced. The interest of the author is to underscore the radical dangers that attend serving the living God. The chapter, in other words, is motivated by a profound theological sensitivity, not the self-serving interests of a parochial priestly group.

CHAPTER 6

Nadab and Abihu and Apophatic Theology

[The story of Nadab and Abihu] is a model of undecidability. . . . [It] looks to most readers like a punishment in search of a crime.

Edward Greenstein[1]

One of the strangest stories in the Bible is that of Nadab and Abihu in Leviticus 10. Immediately after the consecration of the priesthood (Lev. 8) and the miraculous consumption of the sacrifices on the eighth day (Lev. 9:24), these two priests offer *esh zarah*, "strange fire" and are incinerated on the spot (Lev. 10:1-2). In the Jewish tradition, this tale is paired with the death of Uzzah when he tries to steady the ark in 2 Samuel 6 in the postbiblical liturgical reading cycle of the synagogue.[2] But Edward Greenstein has argued that there are innerbiblical grounds for this association: "Uzzah was the son of Abinadab, and this name has been constructed from Abi[hu] and Nadab."[3] Though my emphasis will be on Nadab and Abihu, I would like to claim that both stories explore the theme of divine holiness within the framework of God's choice to dwell among the Israelites.

The Ark Narrative in the Book of Samuel

The first thing that the reader must bear in mind is the Bible's assumption that God has really taken up residence in the tabernacle. But this radical act

1. Edward Greenstein, "Deconstruction and Biblical Narrative," *Prooftexts* 9 (1989): 43-71, here 56.
2. See Michael Fishbane, *Haftarot: The Traditional Hebrew Text with the New JPS Translation* (Philadelphia: Jewish Publication Society, 2002), 120-21.
3. Edward Greenstein, "An Inner-Biblical Midrash of the Nadab and Abihu Episode" (Hebrew), in *Proceedings of the Eleventh World Congress of Jewish Studies, Jerusalem, June 22-29, 1993* (Jerusalem: World Union of Jewish Studies, 1994), 71-78, here 71.

of condescension on the part of God carries a particular danger along with it: individuals will be tempted to coopt either the building itself (cf. Jer. 7) or its most important artifact—the ark—to their own political or religious advantage and so compromise the freedom of God. We can see this danger enacted in the so-called Ark Narrative in the books of Samuel.[4] This narrative opens up with Israel suffering a terrible defeat at the hands of Philistines. The troops subsequently return to camp and the elders pose the obvious question: "Why has the LORD put us to rout today before the Philistines?" (1 Sam. 4:3a). The reader knows the answer: the sins of Hophni and Phineas, the sons of Eli. But the elders do not share this knowledge. Though they ask the proper question, they do not wait for an answer. Their inquiry turns out to be less a lament over Israel's sin than a (subtle) challenge that God take immediate action: "Let us bring the ark of the covenant of the LORD here from Shiloh, so that he may come among us and save us from the power of our enemies" (4:3b). As André Caquot and Philippe de Robert conclude: "All this seems to suggest a certain arrogance in the attitude of the elders of Israel."[5]

This stratagem appears promising at first, for when the Philistines learn of the arrival of the ark, they quake in fear: "Woe to us! Who can deliver us from the power of these mighty gods? These are the gods who struck the Egyptians with every sort of plague in the wilderness" (4:8). But calmer heads prevail, and they venture forth to battle. The results for the Israelites, however, are

4. The classic treatment is that of Leonhard Rost, *The Succession to the Throne of David*, trans. Michael D. Rutter and David M. Gunn (Sheffield: Almond, 1982). Still one of the best treatments would be that of Patrick D. Miller and J. J. M. Roberts, *The Hand of the Lord: A Reassessment of the "Ark Narrative" in 1 Samuel* (Baltimore: Johns Hopkins University Press, 1977). For a recent survey of the literature, see Keith Bodner, "Ark-Eology: Shifting Emphases in 'Ark Narrative' Scholarship," *CBR* 4 (2006): 169–97. The analysis found below was first expressed in Gary A. Anderson, "Towards a Theology of the Tabernacle and its Furniture," in *Text, Thought, and Practice in Qumran and Early Christianity*, ed. Ruth A. Clements and Daniel R. Schwartz, STDJ 84 (Leiden: Brill, 2009), 161–94, here 164–66. It has subsequently been expanded in the dissertation of Mark Enemali, "The Danger of Transgression against Divine Presence" (PhD diss., University of Notre Dame, 2014).

5. This quotation and the proposal that bringing the ark constitutes a challenge to the deity to act can be found in André Caquot and Philippe de Robert, *Les livres de Samuel*, CAT 6 (Geneva: Labor et Fides, 1994), 77. They also make the astute observation that the elders' proposal to bring the ark into battle constitutes a sin at least as, if not more, grave than that of Hophni and Phineas: "But the taking of the ark, which appears as an exceptional act, a sort of last resort before a failure, will cause a much more serious failure, and the author wants to accent the respective responsibilities" (78).

devastating: "So the Philistines fought; Israel was defeated, and they fled, everyone to his home. There was a very great slaughter, for there fell of Israel thirty thousand foot soldiers. The ark of God was captured; and the two sons of Eli, Hophni and Phinehas, died" (4:10–11).

The precise character and gravity of Israel's sin becomes clearer when we compare the Israelite reaction to their initial defeat at Ai (Josh. 7).[6] Just as in 1 Samuel 4, the Israelites suffer a terrible defeat due to an unknown sin: Achan, the narrator informs us, had taken booty for himself in violation of Mosaic law (7:1–5). After the return of the defeated soldiers, Joshua and the tribal elders tear their clothes, put ashes on their heads, and fall on their faces before the ark imploring God to explain the reason for the defeat:

> [6] Then Joshua tore his clothes, and fell to the ground on his face before the ark of the LORD until the evening, he and the elders of Israel; and they put dust on their heads. [7] Joshua said, "Ah, Lord GOD! Why have you brought this people across the Jordan at all, to hand us over to the Amorites so as to destroy us? Would that we had been content to settle beyond the Jordan! [8] O LORD, what can I say, now that Israel has turned their backs to their enemies! [9] The Canaanites and all the inhabitants of the land will hear of it, and surround us, and cut off our name from the earth. Then what will you do for your great name?" (Josh. 7:6–9)

God is quick to answer: it is the sin of Achan that has led to Israel's defeat. This misdeed must be attended to before any other military action can be attempted (7:12–26).

It is striking how differently the Israelites behave in 1 Samuel 4. Instead of taking the opportunity to appeal to God in the deliberate and solemn fashion we find in Joshua (i.e., tearing of clothes, placing ashes on their heads, and falling on their faces before the ark) they simply pose what appears to be a perfunctory question: "Why has the LORD put us to rout?" Eschewing a posture of penance and allowing God no time to respond, the elders concoct their own solution: they race to the shrine and remove the ark of the covenant, believing its sacramental agency can assure them a victory. By failing to address the sin that occasioned the terrible defeat, the elders have unwittingly turned the ark into something of a lucky charm.

---

6. The importance of this intertext has been neglected in much of the secondary literature. The only reference I could find was that of Robert Chisholm, *1 and 2 Samuel* (Grand Rapids: Baker, 2013), 27.

We can contrast this aberrant understanding of the power of the ark with that of David in 2 Samuel 15:23. David possesses a divine promise regarding the eternal character of his kingdom (2 Sam. 7). But even with this promissory note in hand, when his upstart son Absalom drives him from Jerusalem, David refuses to use the ark as a guarantee of his safe return:

> ²⁶ Abiathar came up, and Zadok also, with all the Levites, carrying the ark of the covenant of God. They set down the ark of God, until the people had all passed out of the city. ²⁵ Then the king said to Zadok, "*Carry the ark of God back into the city. If I find favor in the eyes of the* L ORD, *he will bring me back and let me see both it and the place where it stays.* ²⁶ But if he says, 'I take no pleasure in you,' here I am, let him do to me what seems good to him." . . . ²⁹ So Zadok and Abiathar carried the ark of God back to Jerusalem, and they remained there. (2 Sam. 15:24–26, 29)

David realizes that everything that is taking place is the result of his dalliance with Bathsheba, just as the prophet Nathan had predicted. Though David has no doubts about the power of the ark, he is spiritually mature enough to realize that it will provide no advantage in his penitential state.[7] The freedom of God is honored precisely in respect to the object to which God has tied God's being.

It is for this reason that the Ark Narrative comes to a preliminary conclusion in 1 Samuel 6 with the story of the ark's return to Israel and the slaying of those in Beth Shemesh who greeted its arrival improperly.[8] In response to their grave misdeed, the people cry out: "Who is able to stand before the LORD, this holy God?" (1 Sam. 6:20). The implied answer is obvious: no mortal should presume him- or herself safe when standing before the God of Isra-

---

7. This is not to say that David has altogether set aside any concern for his future. His advice that Hushai return to Jerusalem to counter the counsel of Ahitophel indicates that David knows that divine providence requires his own active agency. But this action only sets in broader relief David's refusal to use the ark as an aid in securing his restoration to the throne.

8. The text in question (1 Sam. 6:13) is quite difficult. See the commentaries for a discussion of the text-critical problems. In this instance, lower and higher criticism cannot be separated. The fact that I call this a preliminary conclusion is intentional. Miller and Roberts claim that the relocation of the ark to Kiriath-jearim brings the narrative to full closure; see *Hand of the Lord*, 35–36. To be sure, a lesson has been learned about the danger of using the ark as "lucky charm," but the Israelites remain uneasy as to the nature and character of the ark. The close of 1 Samuel 6 points logically toward 2 Samuel 6 when the ark will find its final resting spot in Jerusalem.

el.[9] This is the lesson to be learned from the improper treatment of the ark back at the beginning of the Ark Narrative. God's presence in the ark is not to be taken lightly. The ark is no lucky charm. The men of Beth Shemesh do the rational thing: they forward this dangerous cargo to the inhabitants of Kiriath-jearim.

The Literary Structure of Leviticus 10

This brings me to the subject of the present chapter: the incense offering of Nadab and Abihu. The story follows the theophanic climax of the eighth day: "Fire came out from the LORD and consumed the burnt offering and the fat on the altar; and when all the people saw it, they shouted and fell on their faces" (Lev. 9:24). Immediately thereafter we read:

> [1] Now Aaron's sons, Nadab and Abihu, each took his censer, put fire in it, and laid incense on it; and they offered strange fire (*esh zarah*) before the LORD, such as he had not commanded them. [2] And fire came out from the presence of the LORD and consumed them, and they died before the LORD. [3] Then Moses said to Aaron, "This is what the LORD meant when he said,
>
> 'Through those who are near me I will show myself holy,
> and before all the people I will be glorified.'"
> And Aaron was silent. (Lev. 10:1–3)

The story about Nadab and Abihu's cultic error has puzzled interpreters for centuries, going all the way back to Philo of Alexandria.[10] Christophe Frevel sums things up well when he writes: "This short episode provides more questions than answers."[11] Before entertaining some of the proposed solutions to

---

9. The connection of this question to that posed to pilgrims in Psalms 15:1 and 24:3 is obvious and important. All three of these texts inscribe within the reader the concern not to presume on the LORD's presence within the ark.

10. The literature on the reception history of this pericope is rather large. For a survey, see Robert Kirschner, "The Rabbinic and Philonic Exegeses of the Nadab and Abihu Incident (Lev 10:1–6)," *JQR* 73 (1983): 375–93; Avigdor Shinan, "The Sin of Nadab and Abihu in Rabbinic Literature" (Hebrew), *Tarbiz* 48 (1978–1979): 201–14; and Jacob Milgrom, *Leviticus 1–16*, AB 3 (New York: Doubleday, 1991), 633–35.

11. Christian Frevel, "Und Mose hörte (es), und es war gut in seinen Augen (Lev 10,20): Zum Verhältnis von Literargeschichte, Theologiegeschichte und innerbiblischer

the challenges posed by this text, let us place this story within its present canonical environment.

There are a few basic structural factors that must be borne in mind before we can address the question of what Nadab and Abihu have done wrong. First of all, it is important to note that chapters 8, 9 and 10 open with a reference to the "taking" of various materials that are necessary for the ritual in question:[12]

The LORD spoke to Moses saying: "*Take* Aaron and his sons with him, the vestments, the anointing oil, the bull of sin offering . . ." (Lev. 8:1–2)

On the eighth day . . . Moses said to Aaron: "*Take* a bull calf for a sin offering . . ." (Lev. 9:1–2)

Now Aaron's sons, Nadab and Abihu, each *took* his censer . . . (Lev. 10:1)

The first two narrative examples take special care to underscore that the "taking" in question was done according to a legitimate command:

And Moses did as the LORD commanded him. (Lev 8:4)

They brought what Moses commanded . . . (Lev 9:5)

But our third example, Leviticus 10, diverges abruptly from this pattern:

Nadab and Abihu each *took* his censer . . . such as [the LORD] had *not* commanded them. (Lev. 10:1)

James Watt has noted that the last clause of 10:1 ("as [the LORD] had not commanded them") is not simply at variance with what had been said in 8:4 and 9:5. Rather, it stands athwart seven citations of this compliance formula ("Moses/Aaron did as the LORD commanded him") in chapter 8 and three more in chapter 9. Watt captures the literary effect quite well: "the intrusion of the negative particle ["such as he had *not* commanded them"] comes like a

---

Auslegung am Beispiel von Lev 10," in *Gottes Name(n): Zum Gedenken an Erich Zenger*, ed. Ilse Müllner et al., HBS 71 (Freiburg: Herder, 2012), 104–36, here 114.

12. Thomas Hieke, *Levitikus 1–15*, HThKAT (Freiburg: Herder, 2014), 377–78; cf. Milgrom, *Leviticus 1–16*, 596.

thunderclap, an aural shock to a listening audience just as YHWH's consuming fire presented a visual shock to the watching Israelites in the story."[13] This raises an important question: Why did Nadab and Abihu bring incense in the first place?

For some interpreters the fact that Nadab and Abihu did something that was not commanded is all we need to know to explain the punishment. Because the cult stands squarely under the authority of the God, any freelancing is strictly forbidden. Nadab and Abihu are punished for going beyond what was prescribed. This sounds eminently reasonable, but the literary character of Leviticus 9 suggests another way of understanding the problem.

Ritually we must distinguish Leviticus 8 from chapters 9–10. Leviticus 8 describes the ordination of Aaron and his sons to the priesthood that takes place over seven days. Leviticus 9, on the other hand, describes the rituals of the eighth day that lead to the dramatic theophany that climaxes the entire Tabernacle Narrative. Leviticus 8 is distinctive in that every ritual action has been carefully scripted in Exodus 29:1–37.[14] In Leviticus 9, Aaron and his sons must consult the general rules for sacrifice that have been laid out in Leviticus 1–7 and discern which ones apply to the current circumstances.[15]

---

13. James Watts, *Leviticus 1–10*, HCOT (Leuven: Peeters, 2013), 512–13. Gordon Wenham, *The Book of Leviticus*, NICOT (Grand Rapids: Eerdmans, 1979), 134, says much the same thing: "Throughout chs. 8 and 9 the obedience of Moses and Aaron is constantly stressed (8:4, 9, 13, 17, 21, 29, 36; 9:5, 7, 10, 21). Every step they take is in obedience to a divine command directly given or mediated by Moses. Both chapters open with such a word (v. 2). But the action in ch. 10 commences without any divine directives. In language very reminiscent of ch. 8 we learn of Nadab and Abihu taking the initiative themselves. The alert listener or reader at once senses that there is something wrong. This scene does not begin like the previous two. It is structured differently. Almost immediately the narrative explains what is wrong: the fire they offered was 'not commanded.'"

14. On the enormous difference between these two chapters, see Andreas Ruwe "The Structure of the Book of Leviticus in the Narrative Outline of the Priestly Sinai Story (Exod 19:1–Num 10:10*)," in *The Book of Leviticus: Composition and Reception*, ed. Rolf Rendtorff and Robert A. Kugler, VTSup 93 (Leiden: Brill, 2002), 55–78, here 67. But it should be noted that I do not agree with Ruwe's claim that the book of Leviticus, as a whole, should be divided into two parts: chapters 1–8 and 9–26. Chapters 8–10 remain something of a unity in my mind notwithstanding the significant caesura between 8 and 9.

15. See Rolf Rendtorff, *Leviticus*, BKAT 3 (Neukirchen-Vluyn: Neukirchener, 1985), 298, and Andreas Ruwe, "Structure," 68: "The sacrificial regulations in 1:1–7:37, however, refer only to the first offering of Israel through Aaron and the Aaronites, celebrated *following the consecration*, and all further offerings of the people." Of course, we should not overstate the matter: the sin offering that the priests offer for themselves will vary from what was prescribed in Leviticus 4.

This is no small difference. In a word, the period of Mosaic supervision has drawn to a close and from now on the responsibility will rest on the priests to "check the manual," so to speak, as to what comes next. As we saw in our previous chapter, this was exemplified in the case of the people's burnt offering ("he presented the burnt offering, and sacrificed it *according to the* regulation" [Lev. 9:16]). But we could argue similarly with respect to the incense offering of Nadab and Abihu. As scholars have long noted, the telos of the Tabernacle Narrative is described in Exodus 29:42b–46, a text sandwiched between the laws for the daily animal and incense offerings (Exod. 29:38–42a and 30:1–10).[16] Indeed, the laws for the animal tamid blend almost imperceptibly into a description of God's indwelling the tabernacle complex—the presumption being that once the tabernacle has been constructed (Exod. 40) and the priests ordained (Lev. 8, fulfilling the commands of Exod. 29:1–37) the morning and evening tamid ("regular") offerings can begin. This would include the sheep offering that took place at the outer bronze altar (Exod. 29:38–41) and the incense at the inner golden altar (Exod. 30:7–10).[17] Given the structure of Exodus 29:1–30:10 (seven days of ordination followed immediately by the two tamid offerings), one might have expected that once the commands regarding priestly ordination had been completed in Leviticus 8 that Aaron and his sons would commence their regular daily routine with respect to the tamid offerings. The synagogue mosaic at Sepphoris depicts the rites of Leviticus 9 in just this fashion.[18] To our surprise, however, Leviticus 9 opens with a set of

16. Among others, see Erhard Blum, *Studien zur Komposition des Pentateuch*, BZAW 189 (Berlin: de Gruyter, 1990), 297; Christophe Nihan, *From Priestly Torah to Pentateuch*, FAT 25 (Tübingen: Mohr Siebeck, 2007), 34; and Benjamin Sommer, *The Bodies of God and the World of Ancient Israel* (Cambridge: Cambridge University Press, 2009), 100.

17. Many modern readers have been misled by the chapter divisions to think of Exodus 30:1–10 as a new literary unit. But the Masoretes were sensitive to the Priestly writer's own division when they identified 30:11 as the next literary unit. P divides the discourse of Exodus 25:1–31:18 into seven discrete units, the first of which is the longest and extends from 25:1 to 30:10. On this, see Peter Kearney, "Creation and Liturgy: The P Redaction of Ex 25–40," *ZAW* 89 (1977): 375–87. Critical scholarship has been so focused on the "misplacement" of the instructions to build the incense altar (30:1–6)—positing that they should have been found in Exodus 25—that it has overlooked the fittingness of the instructions to offer incense (30:7–10). Strikingly the Samaritan version, which does relocate the incense legislation, attaches it to 26:35 rather than chapter 25.

18. Zeev Weiss, *The Sepphoris Synagogue: Deciphering an Ancient Message through Its Archaeological and Socio-Historical Contexts* (Jerusalem: Israel Exploration Society, 2005), 77–94, especially 91–94.

unexpected commands regarding the eighth day rituals ordered to secure the public theophany at the close of the chapter (v. 24).

The animal tamid offerings, however, have not been forgotten, just displaced. In an offhand remark in the middle of the eighth day ceremony we learn that Aaron has attended to the requirements of the animal tamid:[19] "He presented the grain offering, and, taking a handful of it, he turned it into smoke on the altar, *in addition to the burnt offering of the morning.*" Since the animal tamid had already been offered (Lev. 9:17b), and clearly in accord with a divine command, one could infer that the incense tamid should follow. This position was suggested by Rashbam and followed by the late medieval Jewish interpreter Seforno (d. 1550).[20] Though I think this is the best explanation, it is by no means conclusive (as little is in the first few verses of Lev. 10!). David Hoffman rejects this view on the supposition that the daily incense offering was offered by one priest rather than two. He concludes that "it is more accurate to explain the offering along the lines found in the Rabbinic tractate Mekhilta de-Millu'im that the sons of Aaron wanted to bring a special freewill offering of incense in order to express their joy."[21] But whatever position one takes, it is clear that Nadab and Abihu did not intend to stray from divine teaching. In any event, the question becomes: What did they do wrong?

What Did Nadab and Abihu Do Wrong?

This is a challenging matter. After some two millennia of inquiry no consensus has emerged. One common solution locates the problem with the fire. Menahem Haran, for example, explains: "Nadab and Abihu intended to make an offering of incense in their censers (Lev. 10:1–3). They were punished because they offered it to Yahweh in 'strange fire,' that is, fire other than that which was kept burning on the altar for the daily sacrifice. Nadab and Abihu *apparently* [emphasis added] took their fire from somewhere outside the altar-area and

19. Milgrom notes that it is unusual that our text has mentioned the daily tamid in association with the grain offering (v. 17) rather than with the burnt offering in the previous verse (v. 16). But he offers the reasonable explanation that "the writer presumes that the burnt offering and cereal offering are an inseparable pair and are sacrificed together." See *Leviticus 1–16*, 584.

20. Rashbam can be found in *Miqra'ot Gedolot: Wayyiqra* (Ramat Gan: Bar-Ilan Press, 2013), *ad* Lev. 10:1, for Seforno see, *Bi'ur al Ha-Torah le-Rabbi Obadiah Seforno* (Jerusalem: Mossad Harav Kook, 1980), *ad* Lev. 10:1.

21. David Hoffman, *Das Buch Leviticus* (Berlin: Poppelauer, 1905–1906), 1:292.

placed it in their censers, as it is stated: 'each took his censer and put fire in it.'"[22] At first blush, this explanation seems obvious. But Edward Greenstein has called our attention to Haran's use of the word "apparently." Assumptions are being made here; a closer inspection reveals that the text says nothing about the *source* of the fire.

But the difficulty goes deeper. "Indeed, a persistent problem with this reading," Greenstein explains, "is the fact that the 'fire' is presented first as mere, unqualified 'fire' (so 10:1a: 'put fire in it'). It is modified as 'strange' only after it had been offered with incense before YHWH (10:1b)."[23] This suggests that the fire, in and of itself, was not the problem. Accordingly, the medieval Jewish commentary known as the Hizquni (thirteenth century) remarks: "All incense offerings involve fire; it was in fact the incense, not the fire, that was 'alien.'"[24] Baruch Levine echoes this sentiment when he writes: "Hebrew *'ēš zārāh* 'alien fire' refers to the incense itself. [This phrase] could be translated 'an alien [incense offering by] fire.'"[25] Additional, but certainly not conclusive, support for this explanation can be found in the law for the incense offering itself. In Exodus 30:9 Moses explicitly warns the priests not to offer "strange incense" (*qetoreth zarah*) at the altar. Some have suggested that the offering of Nadab and Abihu falls under the umbrella of this specific warning.[26]

22. Menaham Haran, *Temples and Temple Service in Ancient Israel: An Inquiry into Biblical Cult Phenomena and the Historical Setting of the Priestly School*, 2nd ed. (Winona Lake, IN: Eisenbrauns, 1985), 232. This interpretation is found already in Bruno Baentsch, *Exodus-Leviticus-Numeri* (Göttingen: Vandenhoeck & Ruprecht, 1903), 349, and in many others since: Roland Gradwohl, "Das 'fremde Feur' von Nadab und Abihu," *ZAW* 75 (1963): 288–96, here 290–91; John C. H. Laughlin, "The 'Strange Fire' of Nadab and Avihu," *JBL* 95 (1976): 559–65, here 560–61; and Milgrom, *Leviticus 1–16*, 598.

23. Greenstein, "Deconstruction," 58. Nihan, *Priestly Torah*, 581–82, has noted the same thing. He writes: "Yet as already observed by Dillmann, if the same notion was intended in Lev 10, the profane provenance of the fire used by Nadab and Abihu should have been specified at the *beginning*, not at the end of the description of the ritual act undertaken by Aaron's sons, when the fire they used was mentioned for the first time, exactly as is the case in the instructions of Lev 16:12–13 and Num 17:11. Instead, the formulation of 10:1 suggests that the 'profane fire' results from the addition of incense (*qatoret*) on the fire burning in Nadab's and Abihu's censers."

24. See *Hizquni: Perush al ha-Torah* (Jerusalem: Mossad Harav Kook, 1981) *ad* Lev. 10:1.

25. Baruch Levine, *The JPS Torah Commentary: Leviticus* (Philadelphia: Jewish Publication Society, 1989), 58.

26. So, Levine, *Leviticus*, 59.

Another reason for not adopting Haran's suggestion too quickly is found in Leviticus 16. Prior to laying out the rules for the rites of Yom Kippur, we read: "The LORD spoke to Moses after the death of the two sons of Aaron, when they *drew [too] near* before the LORD and died" (16:1).[27] This verse suggests that it was neither the incense nor the fire that were problematic but rather the decision by these two minor priests to encroach upon an area they did not have privilege to enter. In this respect, the sin of Nadab and Abihu looks a lot like that of Korah in Numbers 16–17, a favored point of comparison for many modern interpreters. Arie Noordtzij, for example, has argued: "*Apparently* they intended to offer daily incense that only the high priest was authorized to do."[28] But as Greenstein quickly adds: "The telltale 'apparently' admits to a high degree of doubt, leaving room for the contrary claim [of Gordon Wenham]: 'Along with Aaron and their brothers, Eleazar and Ithamar, [Nadab and Abihu] had just been ordained as priests. It *may be assumed*, therefore, that they had the right to offer incense.'" "The need to 'assume,'" Greenstein concludes, "bespeaks the undecidability of the sense."[29]

An Unanswerable Problem

So far we have examined several plausible explanations as to what Nadab and Abihu did wrong so as to merit the penalty they suffered. Other proposals have been made but I see no reason to provide a complete catalogue. But perhaps it is worth noting that several commentators have suggested that the real grounds for the incineration of Nadab and Abihu has to do with an inter-

27. I am following the lead of the Masoretic Text, the *lectio difficilior*. Numbers 3:4 and 26:61 offer a different understanding. The matter would be different if we followed the LXX or the Targums, which have adjusted the text of Leviticus 16:1 to harmonize it with Numbers 3:4 and 26:61. On this problem see Milgrom, *Leviticus 1–16*, 598, though Milgrom adopts the reading of the LXX.

28. Arie Noordtzij, *Leviticus* (Grand Rapids: Zondervan, 1982), 108 (emphasis added). The comparison of Leviticus 10:1–3 with the narrative of Numbers 16–17 is frequent. See most recently Benedikt Jürgens, *Heiligkeit und Versöhnung. Levitikus 16 in seinem literarischen Kontext* (Freiburg: Herder, 2001), 280–83; Reinhard Achenbach, *Die Vollendung der Torah: Studien zur Redaktiongeschichte des Numeribuches im Kontext von Hexateuch und Pentateuch* (Wiesbaden: Harrassowitz, 2003), 93–97; and Hieke, *Levitikus 1–15*, 385.

29. Greenstein, "Deconstruction," 58 (emphasis added), citing Wenham, *Book of Leviticus*, 154.

nal dispute between two rival priestly parties.[30] Such a view, ironically, often follows from the observation about how difficult it is to discern the nature of the sin.[31] Accordingly, Erhard Gerstenberger writes: "In the case of Nadab and Abihu, there was a divine death sentence involving death by fire for the guilty parties. Put plainly: A formerly influential, rival priestly group was eliminated. *The alleged occasion for their elimination is of no interest as such*. One need only allude to it, and not really designate it."[32]

The point I wish to make is that no single explanation has garnered a consensus, and it is highly unlikely that after centuries of reflection any of them will ever do so. That most modern commentators reflexively append words such as "apparently" or "it may be assumed" to their explanations says about all one needs to know about the nature of the problem. The claim that the text is really about tensions between different priestly parties is also a form of testimony to the difficulty of resolving the nature of the crime (so, Gerstenberger). A few recent commentators, however, have been more forthright about the intractable nature of the problem. Benjamin Sommer, for example, concludes that the various solutions are unpersuasive due to "the severely enigmatic nature of Leviticus 10."[33] James Watts is sharper still: "the endless attempt by interpreters to explain what

---

30. Frank Moore Cross, *Canaanite Myth and Hebrew Epic* (Cambridge: Harvard University Press, 1973), 204–5; Martin Noth, *Leviticus: A Commentary*, OTL (Philadelphia: Westminster, 1977), 84; and Erhard Gerstenberger, *Leviticus: A Commentary*, OTL (Philadelphia: Westminster John Knox, 1996), 117. I find this explanation hard to accept because the chapter, as a whole, finds fault with all four of Aaron's sons. Can we really imagine that the Priestly source polemicized against its entire line? But just such a case has been made recently by Reinhard Achenbach, "Das Versagen der Aaroniden. Erwägungen zum literarhistorischen Ort von Leviticus 10," in *"Basel und Bibel": Collected Communications to the XVIIth Congress of the International Organization for the Study of the Old Testament, Basel, 2001*, ed. M. Augustin and H. M. Niemann, BEATAJ 51 (Frankfurt am Main: Lang, 2004), 55–70. On this claim, see the weighty critique of Nihan, *From Priestly Torah to Pentateuch*, 606–7.

31. So Cross, *Canaanite Myth*, 204, writes: "Nadab and Abihu . . . offered 'strange fire,' whatever that may be, before Yahweh."

32. Gerstenberger, *Leviticus*, 117 (emphasis added). Finally, I might mention the attractive suggestion of David Damrosch, *The Narrative Covenant: Transformations of Genre in the Growth of Biblical Literature* (Ithaca, NY: Cornell University Press, 1991), 267–78, regarding various points of overlap between the account of Leviticus 10 and the sin of Jeroboam in 1 Kings 13–15. But as this approach is mainly interested in literary parallels and has little to nothing to say about the nature of the sin in Leviticus 10, I will not give it consideration.

33. Sommer, *Bodies of God*, 112. Note that he cites Greenstein's work with approval.

Nadab and Abihu did wrong is pointless."[34] Such comments remind me of what Robert Jenson once said about the doctrine of the atonement: "It is one of the most remarkable and remarked-upon aspects of theological history that no theory of atonement has ever been universally accepted. By now, this phenomenon is itself among the things that a proposed theory of atonement must explain."[35]

This is actually the approach Greenstein takes. He starts from the premise that the biblical text intentionally withholds the reason and then asks why this might be. It would be difficult to establish such a thesis solely on the grounds that scholars have not agreed. In this sense our text would be no different than hundreds of others in the Hebrew Bible. A lack of consensus is not a rare thing in biblical scholarship. To be persuasive, we must establish a good reason why the text would be silent about such an important question. We will turn to the matter of a material cause shortly. But let us look for a moment at some formal features of our text that may confirm Greenstein's thesis. Commentators often divide Leviticus 10 into two parts: the first half pertains to the sin of Nadab and Abihu and its aftermath (vv. 1–11) while the second deals with the consumption of the various sacrificial pieces and concludes with the apparent error of Eleazar and Ithamar (vv. 12–20).[36] What is most striking about the second half of the chapter is the way Moses inspects the activity of priesthood in regard to their sacrificial responsibilities. In each of the subunits (meal offering [vv. 12–13], offering of well-being [vv. 14–15], sin offering [vv. 16–20]) Moses documents how their actions tally with the laws given in Leviticus 1–7 (another reference back to "the manual") and explicitly notes whether the actions accord with the divine commandments or not.

This last point is worth bearing in mind as we consider another point of structural congruity. As has often been noted, the chapter provides two very different pictures of how Aaron reacts to the errors done by his children.[37] In the first he acquiesces to the divine punishment; in the second he argues strongly on behalf of his sons against the claims of Moses and his words carry the day.

34. Watts, *Leviticus 1–10*, 187.

35. Robert Jenson, *Systematic Theology*, vol. 1, *The Triune God* (Oxford: Oxford University Press, 1997), 186.

36. See Achenbach, "Das Versagen," 63.

37. On Aaron's response to Moses at the end of the chapter see the recent contribution of Frevel, "Und Mose hörte (es)," 104–35, and the literature cited therein.

Leviticus 10:3	Leviticus 10:16–20
[Error of Nadab and Abihu]	[Error of Eleazar and Ithamar]
³ Then Moses said to Aaron, "This is what the Lᴏʀᴅ meant when he said, 'Through those who are near me I will show myself holy, and before all the people I will be glorified.'"	¹⁷ "Why did you not eat the sin offering in the sacred area? For it is most holy, and God has given it to you that you may remove the guilt of the congregation, to make atonement on their behalf before the Lᴏʀᴅ. ¹⁸ Its blood was not brought into the inner part of the sanctuary. You should certainly have eaten it in the sanctuary, as I commanded."
And Aaron was silent.	¹⁹ And Aaron spoke to Moses, "See, today they offered their sin offering and their burnt offering before the Lᴏʀᴅ; and yet such things as these have befallen me! If I had eaten the sin offering today, would it have been agreeable to the Lᴏʀᴅ?" ²⁰ And when Moses heard that, he agreed.

What is striking is that in the case of Eleazar and Ithamar, Moses spells out very specifically what law has been violated ("Its blood was not brought into the inner part of the sanctuary," cf. Lev. 6:23). But this careful correlation of sacrificial law with its subsequent execution is precisely what is missing in the first few verses of the chapter. Moses's explanation of the affair is just as mysterious as the sin itself: "This is what the Lᴏʀᴅ meant when he said, 'Through those who are near me I will show myself holy, and before all the people I will be glorified.'"³⁸ When did God say this and how does it clarify the character of Nadab and Abihu's sin? These questions cannot be answered.

One should also observe that the author had antecedent material before him that could have explained the error. Exodus 30:7–10 documents how the incense offering is to be made and explicitly warns against desecration

---

38. Milgrom poses the obvious question in *Leviticus 1–16*, 600: "But where did he say [this]?" Recognizing that there is no clear antecedent, Milgrom interprets the clause prospectively: "This is what the Lord has decreed, saying: 'through those near to me.'" Yet this interpretation—which says nothing about the nature of deed but only something of what it reflects about the deity—only further underscores the fact that our narrator is withholding from the reader the cause of the punishment.

(v. 9). It is striking and hardly accidental that our author makes no reference to this text. The contrast between the errors committed by these two sets of sons is vividly drawn. The literary structure of Leviticus 10 confirms Greenstein's contention that Nadab and Abihu's error is cloaked in mystery.[39]

Deconstruction or Apophatic Theology?

Let us return to the question as to why this should be the case. Greenstein has suggested that a deconstructive reading strategy may be of assistance. Deconstruction is a valuable tool for a text like this because it openly acknowledges structural limitations of all human knowing. No single reading, no matter how well conceived philologically or trenchantly argued historically, can provide a "stable or impregnable meaning."[40] The integrity of the story will always thwart any attempt to domesticate it. Hebrew narrative "is as stubborn as Job in the face of his friends' contentions," Greenstein writes. "In the end God supported Job. Interpretation runs into difficulty—Derrida's *aporia*—at precisely those points at which it seeks to impose order."[41]

But Greenstein does not follow Derrida to the letter (nor will I).[42] For Derrida believes that *every* text we encounter—no matter what the author may intend—resists domestication because *all* meaning is subject to endless deferment. Greenstein, however, contends that there is a particular reason (or "logos") that conditions the difficulty of discerning the nature of Nadab and Abihu's cultic error. In order to appreciate this nondeconstructive detail we

39. It is worth noting that the end of the chapter has its own enigma. It is by no means clear what the force of Aaron's explanation is that eventually assuages the anger of Moses. Commentators have, for the most part, thrown up their hands. It would appear that the narrator has drawn a curtain between the (implied) lay-reader and the sacerdotal office. I agree with Watts when he writes in Leviticus *1–10*, 515: "[T]he text's ambiguity indicates that the authors' interests lie elsewhere. The writers of Leviticus 10 did not intend to decide a particular issue of ritual practice by telling this story, but instead wanted to demonstrate Aaron's newly granted authority in action."

40. Greenstein, "Deconstruction," 62.

41. Greenstein, "Deconstruction," 60.

42. Watts, *Leviticus 1–10*, 513, makes a similar criticism. But he then proceeds to dismiss the rest of Greenstein's arguments. The text's purpose is not to make a claim about the character of God, Watts argues, but to buttress priestly claims to power. As I will claim below, almost all of what Greenstein has argued can be retained if we just recast his Derridean terminology into its Dionysian counterpart.

need to step back for a moment and look at Leviticus 10 in light of the lengthy tabernacle account that precedes it.

The first thing to be observed is the parallelism between the creation of the world in Genesis 1 and the building of the tabernacle in Exodus 25–Leviticus 9. As Peter Schäfer has put the matter: "The creation of the world is not, if one accepts this view, solely the work of God but also the work of man: only when Moses erects the tabernacle is God's created order brought to completion."[43] The role ascribed to human agency in this narrative is not to be overlooked. Human actions have become a nonnegotiable part of the way God has chosen to direct human history. A second, and closely related point, is the manner in which this building project succeeds in capturing the presence of God. Moses opens the eighth day rites with the warning to do exactly as God has commanded (Lev. 9:6–7). Aaron complies with complete obedience and succeeds in attracting the divine presence to the sacrificial altar ("Fire came out from the presence of the LORD and consumed the burnt offering and the fat on the altar" [9:24]). In allowing the tabernacle to be built and the cult to begin, God has invited Israel to participate in the divine life. But along with this gracious condescension comes a considerable risk. By allowing Israel's liturgical actions to attain such theurgic capabilities, God's freedom is put at risk. Has the priesthood gained the upper hand over the being of God? Can the mastery of cultic law allow the priesthood to conjure the divine presence at will? *Mē genoito*! As Thomas Hieke puts the matter: "This dramatic narrative dispels the misunderstanding that one can compel God to behave in a certain way through human—or more exactly—ritual action."[44]

Greenstein would certainly agree with this sentiment, but he would want to say more. Because of the limitations inherent to human knowing, every approach toward God will be dangerous. (One thinks of the conclusion reached at the close of the Korah episode in Numbers 16–17. The Israelites cry out in fear: "Anyone who approaches the tabernacle of the LORD will die. Are we all to perish?" [17:13].) God lessens this danger by revealing a protocol for draw-

---

43. Peter Schäfer, "Tempel und Schöpfung," *Kairos* 16 (1974): 132.

44. Hieke, *Levitikus 1–15*, 379. Also see his remarks on 332: "The narrative of the dramatic death of Nadab and Abihu in Leviticus 10 form a contrast to the ideal-cult and serve as an example of warning that the careful observance of liturgical rites should not lead the priest to think he can manipulate God through ritual actions." Sommer, *Bodies of God*, 120–21, registers similar concerns about the theurgic dimensions of Priestly theology. In his opinion the non-Priestly sources have better resources for dealing with this challenge; but if my argument about Leviticus 10 holds, the Priestly source holds its own on this matter.

ing near to his presence (Lev. 1–7). But the danger involved in approaching God will always exceed any finite list of precautionary measures. *However much law a priest may master, every approach to the altar constitutes a potential danger.* The spirituality of Psalm 24 and the Ark Narrative return with a vengeance: "Who can ascend the mountain of the LORD, who may stand in his holy place?" Hieke captures this well when he writes: "[Leviticus 1–9] gives the impression that the priests have a marvelous world at their disposal with their own office at the center in which they can flourish. Leviticus 10, however, makes it clear that the priests have been given the dangerous task of drawing near to God again and again as the representatives of the people."[45]

Though Greenstein has chosen to express these theological ideas in Derridean vocabulary, I think that his approach finds a better vehicle in the realm of negative or apophatic theology. According to Jaroslav Pelikan, apophatic theology was designed to safeguard the mystery of the divine being. "By its clarity," Pelikan explains, "cataphatic language gave the illusion of saying something affirmative concerning transcendent reality, but that was always unfitting to the hiddenness of the inexpressible. Therefore the apophatic way of speaking appears to be more suitable to the realm of the divine."[46] Following this view we could interpret the numerous commands that God has given Moses about the foundation and operation of the cult as a witness to the *cataphatic* side of revelation. That is, God has provided enough information about himself and the world he has created so that the priesthood can attract his physical presence to a structure built by human hands and tend to his daily needs. But *cataphasis* always requires an *apophatic* corrective.[47] There remains an infinite gap between creature and Creator and no matter how much cultic law one might master, God will not be reduced to an object subject to human control. Lest the priesthood become inebriated by the power God has conferred upon it, the radical otherness of God's majestic glory breaks out and reestablishes God's utter transcendence.

Let us look at how Greenstein concludes his argument but allow me to gloss his Derridean vocabulary with words that could have been drawn from

---

45. Hieke, *Levitikus 1–15*, 379. Also, see Watts, *Leviticus 1–10*, 513–17.

46. Jaroslav Pelikan, *The Melody of Theology: A Philosophical Dictionary* (Cambridge: Harvard University Press, 1988), 7.

47. For a gentle introduction to the themes of apophatic theology see Bernard McGinn, *The Foundations of Mysticism: Origins to the Fifth Century* (New York: Crossroads, 1994), 157–82; Denys Turner, *The Darkness of God: Negativity in Christian Mysticism* (Cambridge: Cambridge University Press, 1995), 19–49. For the briefest primer possible, see Pelikan, *Melody of Theology*, s.v. "apophatic."

the father of apophatic theology: St. Denys (or, as he is more commonly referred to, Pseudo-Dionysius). Derrida's thoughts are "under erasure" while
the words of St. Denys are in italics:

> The story of Nadab and Abihu, as narrative, intrudes into the exposi-
> tion of cultic law that precedes and follows it. It may strike the reader as
> disrupting the text as violently as the flash of fire annihilated the young
> priests. As the narrative genre of the episode disturbs the legal land-
> scape by its otherness, so does its representation of a possibly opaque
> and nonverbal—*suprarational* ~~irrational~~—God upset the orderliness of
> the cultic system. Notwithstanding the cultic regulations . . . God has not
> in fact explained everything. The system contains terrible dark secrets;
> YHWH may strike without warning. . . In our reading [the disruption on
> the eighth day shows us that] God is *greater than* ~~above/beyond~~ the cul-
> tic order. A God worthy of name cannot be *wholly contained* ~~trammeled~~
> by rules any more than an infinite God can be contained by names, by
> language. . . . The priest can only control what the priest does; he can-
> not control God. Behind the orderly veneer of priestly ritual, behind the
> *parokhet* that screens off YHWH's quasi-condensed presence from the
> human observer, is the unscrutable Other. YHWH can hardly be better
> comprehended than the motives of Nadab and Abihu and the question of
> whether they had done anything amiss.[48]

It is striking how minor these corrections are. We get nearly the same results
with Pseudo-Dionysius but avoid the theological (and literary!) errors that
accompany Derrida.[49]

I would like to emphasize, before concluding, that on this view we will
never know what Nadab and Abihu did wrong. Because if we could, our propensity to theurgic hubris would not be lessened (which is the intention of
our text), but rather abetted. The biblical author does not want us so much to
"learn" from their example (that is, they did X wrong and I will never do that

---

48. Greenstein, "Deconstruction," 63–64.

49. For a similar point, see Bryan Bibb, "Nadab and Abihu Attempt to Fill a Gap: Law
and Narrative in Leviticus 10:1–7," *JSOT* 96 (2001): 83–99. He says that God "reminds the
people that the problem is not that there is no order in his divinity. The problem is that
the limited understanding and ability of humans can only take a few steps toward com-
prehending the true reality, with its blessings and dangers. The narrative not only exposes
the depth of the problem, it also motivates them to think more about the limitations of
their cultic system" (95–96).

again) as to develop a sense of wariness about the altar of God (I will never master all that is required for this job).[50] The lesson learned at the close of the Ark Narrative in Samuel applies here as well: "Who is able to stand before the LORD, this holy God?" The implied answer: no one.

In a certain sense, the story of Nadab and Abihu is similar to that of Cain and Abel. For God's acceptance of Abel's sacrifice and the rejection of Cain's raises problems very comparable to those of Nadab and Abihu. The text provides no clear explanation as to the character of Cain's error. Not surprisingly, commentators have provided a variety of competing explanations, none of them satisfactory. The text itself, some have concluded, does not wish to disclose the motive. The preference for Abel over Cain, like that of Jacob over Esau, is grounded in the mystery of election, a domain of divine activity closed off to full human comprehension.[51]

There is good reason, then, why interpreters have found it difficult to locate the precise character of the error of Nadab and Abihu. Our text, which hitherto has been so deeply invested in the *cataphatic* process of revelation, recoils in worry that the reader who has mastered the many details of Levitical law may believe that he or she has acquired the formula for conjuring the divine presence. In some senses, the story of Nadab and Abihu and that of the ark in the books of Samuel are of a piece as the lectionary cycle of the synagogue

---

50. Which is not to say that there is no lesson to be learned here. Obviously Nadab and Abihu did violate some law—God does not act irrationally when taking their lives. But for reasons that I have spelled out, the text is not interested in providing the reader with an explanation. The point of the author is to instill within the reader the sense of danger that should attend every approach to the altar. As Milgrom notes, the *Sifra* had a feeling for the wariness that overtook Aaron as he prepared to assume his priestly office; see *Leviticus 1–16*, 577. One could also compare Aaron's worries to the young Martin Luther, who confessed that he shook in fear the first time he approached the altar to offer the eucharistic sacrifice. He said that had he not been restrained he would have fled and never raised the host. See Martin Brecht, *Martin Luther: His Road to the Reformation, 1483–1521* (Philadelphia: Fortress, 1985), 70–76. My suspicion is that many modern commentators lack the necessary theological imagination that attends the real presence of the deity to appreciate the religious world of the Bible. On precisely this point see the perceptive comments of Mary Douglas in her essay "The Bog Irish," in *Natural Symbols. Explorations in Cosmology* (New York: Pantheon, 1970), 37–53. Her comparison of Pope Paul's comments on the Eucharist in *Mysterium Fidei* to West African practices on pp. 47–48 is right to the point.

51. On the impossibility of determining Cain's error and its significance for the book of Genesis see Jon D. Levenson, *Death and Resurrection of the Beloved Son* (New Haven: Yale University Press, 1993), 71–75.

has long suggested.[52] Both narratives address the question of divine freedom from a context in which God has apparently given human beings considerable control over his person. In Samuel the issue is: What is the role of God's saving presence in the ark? Scripture is clear about God's condescension to dwell on the ark and his intention to venture forth with Israel's armies to victory in battle. This raises the obvious question. Will the ark "work its magic" regardless of the moral status of those who attend it? The Ark Narrative answers that question with a resounding "No."

In Leviticus 10 the theological challenge is slightly different. Here God's condescension through ritual law has granted the priesthood the power to conjure God's presence. Rashi captures this aptly when he comments on the promise Moses makes at Leviticus 9:6: "Through the works of [Aaron's] hands, God will make his presence manifest." This grants a considerable degree of power to the cultic procedures that Moses is about to hand over to Aaron and his sons. But Leviticus 10 shows us that the power granted to the priesthood is far more complex than it may have appeared at first. Not only do the commands require human discernment in order to be obeyed, but the cost of even the slightest error is frightfully high. No wonder the Israelites in a subsequent narrative will recoil in fear at the prospect of attending the altar: "anyone who approaches the tabernacle of the LORD will die" (Num. 17:13).

Let me conclude by saying that my thesis can be articulated in both a softer and stronger sense. At the softer end, I hope I have cogently argued that the final canonical form of our text is patient of this apophatic reading. If Rashi is to be trusted, one of the prominent issues at stake in Leviticus 8–10 is the liturgical power placed in the hands of the clergy. The reader who is sensitive to these theurgic possibilities cannot help but wonder what checks are in place to remind the priest of his status as a vulnerable and radically dependent creature. "Who would ascend the mountain of the Lord?" is a question for not only the lay-pilgrim but the servant of the altar as well. As Greenstein argues, "[A] God worthy of the name cannot be *wholly contained* ~~trammeled~~ by rules any more than an infinite God can be contained by names, by language. . . . The priest can only control what the priest does; he cannot control God."[53]

But my claim, truth be told, has been slightly stronger than this. I have suggested that the text is not only patient of such a reading but invites or even solicits it (but note, that I do not claim that the text demands it). To that end I suggested that the irresolvability of the episode is reflected in the literary

52. Fishbane, *Haftarot*, 120–21.
53. Greenstein, "Deconstruction and Biblical Narrative," 64.

character of the chapter as a whole. It is important to note how the author *underscores* obedience or disobedience to very specific sacrificial requirements: incense, meal, well-being, and sin offerings (vv. 1, 13, 15, 18). In each of the final three instances—the meal, well-being, and sin offerings—the requirements in question are easily traceable to laws found in the priestly manual of Leviticus 1–7. Only the incense offering departs from this pattern. In this instance alone we do not learn about the specifics but are simply told that the violation is testimony to the holiness of God: "This is what the LORD meant," Moses explains, "when he said, 'Through those who are near me I will show myself holy, and before all the people I will be glorified.'" This is, of course, an answer that explains nothing (check the commentaries!). And that is precisely my point. Recourse to apophatic theology, I have suggested, provides a way to make sense of the striking literary character of this story.

PART TWO

The Priestly Narrative in Its Larger Canonical Setting

CHAPTER 7

The Sin of the Golden Calf

[On the sin of the golden calf:] At the very moment that God was giving Moses the Tablets of the Pact, which forbids idolatry (Exod 20:4–5), the people were demanding just that. In modern terms, "the ink was not yet dry" on the covenant when the people violated it.

Jeffrey Tigay[1]

Over the course of chapters 2–6 we have examined a portion of the Bible that scholars have attributed to the Priestly source. Although this document shows signs of different hands at work in its composition, there is widespread agreement that the final product is sufficiently uniform and can be attributed to a single school known as the "P" source. Great interpretive progress has been made over the past century and a half in isolating the portions of Exodus and Leviticus that can be labeled "Priestly" and attempting to understand the specific theological program that this circle of authors favored. But as productive as this strategy has been, some considerable losses accrue if we limit our interpretive responsibilities to the isolation and description of individual sources. Whoever assembled the Bible into the final canonical form that we possess did not respect such divisions and took care to integrate a variety of materials into the story. For roughly a hundred years or so, the guild of biblical scholars ignored the final form in order to devote itself wholeheartedly to the isolation of individual sources. But beginning in the 1970s an interest in turning to the final form of the Bible began to emerge. Brevard Childs in North America and Rolf Rendtorff in Europe were the pioneers in this push to return to the form of the Bible read in the synagogue and the church. Some refer to this proposal of Childs as "canonical criticism," and thereby set it be-

---

1. *The Jewish Study Bible*, ed. Adele Berlin and Marc Zvi Brettler (Oxford: Oxford University Press, 2004), 183, includes Tigay's comment on 31:18.

side other forms of higher criticism such as literary, form, and redaction criticism. In other words, another one of the many tools contained in the scholar's toolbox. Childs, however, was not happy with this sort of nomenclature. For Childs, reading canonically was not just one method cast among many others; rather it constituted a stance toward the Bible that took cognizance of its divine inspiration.

In Childs's mind the canonical approach did not ignore the results of historical criticism with its diachronic interest—that is, tracking the contingencies of the historical process in order to delineate the human factors that contributed to the writing of the biblical books. Some have labeled his approach "synchronic," that is, viewing the final form as the *sole* variable to consider in determining the text's meaning. But nothing could be farther from the truth. The solid results of historical analysis were extremely important for Childs and marked the path he would follow in tracing the shape and character of the text's final form.

In the present chapter we will examine the way in which the story of the golden calf (Exod. 32–34) fits within the confines of the Tabernacle Narrative (Exod. 25–31 and 35–40). Canonical readers are in complete agreement that these two accounts derive from authors who composed their tales independently from one another. Though that independence must be respected, one's task as a reader is not finished until a way is found to appreciate how the two stories work together. And to the task of that sort of reading we shall now turn.

The Priestly and Non-Priestly Narratives

If one surveys the vast literature that has been produced on the literary sources of the Pentateuch, one would find conflicting proposals on almost every problem. A recent international conference in Jerusalem devoted itself to these questions and produced a thousand-page volume.[2] It is a good place to start if one wishes to survey the various proposals competing for attention. But it should be noted that the volume does not arrive at anything approaching a consensus; its purpose is rather to illustrate the vast methodological differences. Yet for all this variety, there is one area of near unanimous agreement: the distinction between the Priestly and non-Priestly writings. I think it is fair to say that if we took a random sampling of the leading scholars in the Americas, Europe, and Israel,

2. Jan C. Gertz, Bernard M. Levinson, Dalit Rom-Shiloni, and Konrad Schmid, eds., *The Formation of the Pentateuch: Bridging the Academic Cultures of Europe, Israel, and North America*, FAT 111 (Tübingen: Mohr Siebeck, 2016).

we would find broad agreement regarding those texts assigned to the Priestly (P) source. This would be especially true regarding the distinction between the story of the golden calf and the Tabernacle Narrative that surrounds it. Outside of biblical literalists, everyone agrees that different authors created these separate accounts and could identify what belongs to P and what does not.

One of the reasons for this unanimous judgment is that these stories have virtually no explicit verbal points of contact between them, even though they share a number of thematic concerns. If we wished to hold firm to the traditional view that Moses wrote the entire narrative sequence, we would have to grant that he altered his vocabulary when he left the account of command to build the tabernacle (Exod. 25–31) to narrate the apostasy of the calf (chs. 32–34), and returned to that same vocabulary when he described the construction of the tabernacle (chs. 35–40).

But for all the truth of this source-critical distinction, there are a few qualifications to be made. First, we should note that the story of the golden calf does not begin at 32:1 as most translations of the Bible would suggest, but with the last verse of chapter 31. The Hebrew text places a caesura between 31:17 and 18 and that division has been followed by many modern scholars.

What is significant about 31:18 is that it serves as a bridge between the Tabernacle Narrative (P) and the story of the golden calf (non-P). This can be demonstrated by taking a closer look at the diction of 31:18 and comparing it to its Priestly and non-Priestly antecedents.

Priestly Narrative: Law Regarding the Sabbath
31:12 The LORD said to Moses: 13 You yourself are to speak to the Israelites: "You shall keep my sabbaths, for this is a sign between me and you throughout your generations, given in order that you may know that I, the LORD, sanctify you. . . . 17 It is a sign forever between me and the people of Israel that in six days the LORD made heaven and earth, and on the seventh day he rested, and was refreshed."

Redactional Transition
31:18 When God finished speaking with Moses on Mount Sinai, he gave him the two tablets of the covenant, tablets of stone, written with the finger of God.

Non-Priestly Narrative: Golden Calf
32:1 When the people saw that Moses delayed to come down from the mountain, the people gathered around Aaron, and said to him, "Come,

make gods for us, who shall go before us; as for this Moses, the man who brought us up out of the land of Egypt, we do not know what has become of him." (Exod. 31:12–32:1)

The Priestly story, as we saw in chapter 2, has Moses ascend Mount Sinai, where he hears God address him seven times. The first six deal with the tabernacle, the seventh, which we cited above, with the sabbath (31:12–17). Not by accident, the description of the sabbath overlaps considerably with the account in Genesis 2:1–3, demonstrating that these two stories come from the same hand.

The non-Priestly story of the calf begins in 31:18 with an account of Moses's receipt of the tablets of the law. This is a flash back to Exodus 24 when those tablets were first given to Moses:

> [12] The LORD said to Moses, "Come up to me on the mountain, and wait there; and I will give you the *tablets of stone*, with the law and the commandment, which I have written for their instruction." [13] So Moses set out with his assistant Joshua, and Moses went up into the mountain of God. [14] To the elders he had said, "Wait here for us, until we come to you again; for Aaron and Hur are with you; whoever has a dispute may go to them." (Exod. 24:12–14)

The important detail to observe is that the tablets of stone which Moses receives in 24:12 are not spoken of again until we reach 31:18.

But if we look more closely at the diction of that verse, we will notice an awkward repetition. The tablets are described in two different ways, first as "the two tablets of the covenant [*edut*]" and second as "tablets of stone." The first description is a clear reference back to the Priestly account ("You shall put the mercy seat on the top of the ark; and in the ark you shall put the *covenant* [*edut*] that I shall give you" [25:21]). The second is taken from the non-Priestly narrative ("tablets of stone" [24:12]), but now functions as a gloss on the Priestly term. The awkward expression is a telltale sign of the hand of a later redactor. The scribe who assembled the final form of the Bible had two different stories in front of him, and in order to weld them together he added this linking verse. The result was a transition that allowed one to read these two stories as a single narrative. As an aside, it is worth pointing out that this is very similar to what happens in the redactional join between the two creation stories in Genesis 1–3. Genesis 2:4a is an editorial addition that links the Priestly creation story (Gen. 1:1–2:3) to the non-Priestly garden of Eden story

(2:4b–3:24). By inserting this transitional verse (2:4a), our scribe intended his readers to see the second story of creation as a logical extension of the first.[3]

The important lesson to be learned from the compositional history of these stories is that the editors who brought the Bible into its final canonical form recognized the independent character of these episodes but created a meaningful transition between them. The shapers of the Bible's final form wanted their readers to discern a deeper unity. Yet it should also be noted that they did not emend the internal content of the stories themselves to achieve that goal. The discordant features that emerged from juxtaposing these very different literary sources were allowed to stand. The key to a modern reading of these chapters is to respect their distinct and independent points of origin while at the same time recognizing the larger thematic or theological unity that the final editors intended. Reading the stories in complete isolation from one another is just as big a mistake as mindlessly harmonizing the competing details.[4]

The Original Literary Context of the Golden Calf

Before considering how the two stories can be read together, let us consider the stories on their own. We will begin by looking at the way the story of the golden calf is linked to the non-Priestly account of covenant making in Exodus 24.

Ratifying the Covenant

[24:3] Moses came and told the people all the words of the LORD and all the ordinances; and all the people answered with one voice, and said, "All the words that the LORD has spoken we will do." [4] And Moses wrote down all the words of the LORD. (1) *He rose early in the morning*, and built an altar (3) *at the foot of the mountain*, and set up twelve pillars, corresponding

---

3. Brevard Childs, *Introduction to the Old Testament as Scripture* (Philadelphia: Fortress, 1979), 148–50, and Jan Gertz, "The Formation of the Primeval History," in *The Book of Genesis: Composition, Reception, and Interpretation*, ed. Craig A. Evans, Joel N. Lohr, and David L. Petersen, VTSup 152 (Leiden: Brill, 2012), 107–35, esp. 114–18.

4. An outstanding example of how to treat this problem can be found in the way Brevard Childs understands the placement of Exodus 33:7–11 within its current literary setting. He acknowledges that this pericope had an independent origin but shows how it was reread when placed in its current location. See his *The Book of Exodus: A Commentary*, OTL (Philadelphia: Westminster, 1974), 589–93.

to the twelve tribes of Israel. ⁵ He sent young men of the people of Israel, who offered (2) *burnt offerings and sacrificed oxen as offerings of well-being* to the LORD. ⁶ Moses took half of the blood and put it in basins, and half of the blood he dashed against the altar. ⁷ Then he took the book of the covenant, and read it in the hearing of the people; and they said, "All that the LORD has spoken we will do, and we will be obedient." ⁸ Moses took the blood and dashed it on the people, and said, "See the blood of the covenant that the LORD has made with you in accordance with all these words." (Exod. 24:3–8)

Golden Calf
³²:² Aaron said to them, "Take off the gold rings that are on the ears of your wives, your sons, and your daughters, and bring them to me." ³ So all the people took off the gold rings from their ears, and brought them to Aaron. ⁴ He took the gold from them, formed it in a mold, and cast an image of a calf; and they said, "These are your gods, O Israel, who brought you up out of the land of Egypt!" ⁵ When Aaron saw this, he built an altar before it; and Aaron made proclamation and said, "Tomorrow shall be a festival to the LORD." ⁶ (1) *They rose early the next day*, and offered (2) *burnt offerings and brought sacrifices of well-being*; and the people sat down to eat and drink, and rose up to revel.
    ¹⁵ Then Moses turned and went down from the mountain . . .¹⁹ [and] as soon as he came near the camp . . . he threw the tablets from his hands and broke them (3) *at the foot of the mountain*. (Exod. 32:2–6, 15, 19)

There are several points of contact between the initial celebration that attended the making of the covenant and the feasting that accompanied the erection of the golden calf. First, just as Moses rose "early in the morning and built an altar" (24:4), so Aaron builds an altar in order that Israel might "rise early" to offer her sacrifices (32:5). Second, to solemnize the covenant, Moses calls for a public celebration that included burnt and well-being offerings, the latter providing the meat that Israel would feast on (24:5). This matches the festival announced by Aaron to honor the creation of the calf (32:5–6). Third, when Moses hears of Israel's disobedience, "he threw down the tablets from his hands and broke them *at the foot of the mountain*" (32:19). This is the precise location where Moses had built the altar to confirm the covenant he had revealed to Israel ("and built an altar *at the foot of the mountain*" [24:4]). E. Aurelius aptly summarizes the logical force of these parallels, "the worship before the image of the bull (chapter 32) counteracts the first true worship (chapter

24) of Israel's God."[5] What is crucial to note is that these correspondences relate to *specific details* in the two stories and often employ *identical vocabulary*. This is strong evidence that they come from the pen of a single author.

Canonical Context

If we accept the hypothesis that the story of the golden calf in chapter 32 originally followed the making of the covenant in chapter 24, then we can appreciate the change that occurs once a portion of the Tabernacle Narrative is dropped in between. The close correspondences between chapters 24 and 32 recede into the background as the readers' attention is drawn to the more immediate transition from the tabernacle (chs. 25–31) to the calf (chs. 32–34). The veneration of the calf is not simply the violation of the covenant made in Exodus 24 but the spurning of the type of sanctuary (and the adoration it requires) that God desires for Israel. This also transforms how we read the conclusion of the story of the calf. Within the context of Exodus 32–34, forgiveness for that sin is marked by the remaking of the covenant in Exodus 34, a story that has many linkages back to Exodus 19–24. But within the larger canonical frame of the book of Exodus, the story of the building of the tabernacle (Exod. 35–40) marks the ultimate termination point for a long process of penitence.

Jeffrey Tigay has highlighted five points of contact that are created once the building of the tabernacle (35–40) follows the sin of the golden calf.[6]

> 1. The people command Aaron to make a god (32:1)
>   1'. God commands Moses to make the tabernacle (Exod 25–31)
> 2. Aaron responds with an appeal for gold (32:2)
>   2'. Moses appeals for gold among other materials (35:4–9)
> 3. People bring gold (32:3)
>   3'. People bring requested materials (35:20–29)
> 4. Aaron makes the calf (32:4)
>   4'. Moses builds the shrine (36:8–38)
> 5. Altar is built, sacrifices are offered, celebration ensues (32:5–6)
>   5'. Altar inaugurated, public celebration (Exod. 40/Lev. 9)

5. As cited by Jan Gertz, "Beobachtungen zu Komposition und Redaktion in Exod 32–34," in *Gottes Volk am Sinai: Untersuchungen zu Ex 32–34 und Dtn 9–10*, ed. M. Köckert and E. Blum (Gütersloh: Gütersloher Verlagshaus, 2001), 88–106, esp. 89.

6. See Berlin and Brettler, *Jewish Study Bible*, 183.

It is important to observe that these correspondences are broadly thematic. Unlike the linkages between Exodus 24 and 32, which came from a single author, these redactional correspondences do not share a common vocabulary. Yet the narrative fit is surprisingly close; surely the redactor wanted the reader to pay attention to them.

The Penalty Imposed

An additional irony is worth noting. After the golden calf has been fashioned, Israel says: "These are your gods, O Israel, *who brought you up out of the land of Egypt!*" (32:4). This contrasts with the role of the true shrine that houses the ark of the covenant and the other pieces of sacred furniture: "And they shall know that I am the LORD their God, *who brought them out of the land of Egypt* that I might dwell among them; I am the LORD their God" (29:46). By erecting the calf, Israel threatens to undo the salvific work God had wrought in Egypt and puts in danger the very existence of the promised nation. This is precisely what God threatens to do when he says to Moses: "I have seen this people, how stiff-necked they are. Now let me alone, so that my wrath may burn hot against them and I may consume them" (32:9–10).

As the story unfolds, Moses steps into the breach between God and his people and tries to negotiate a reduced sentence. He succeeds initially; God rescinds his threat to destroy the nation (32:14). But the forgiveness is not complete. In his pique over the rebellion, God decides to send an angel before the people instead of accompanying them personally. "Go up to a land flowing with milk and honey," God declares, "but I will not go up among you, or I would consume you on the way, for you are a stiff-necked people" (33:3). Moses, however, boldly refuses to accept this decision. He tries (and eventually succeeds) to persuade God to restore the intimate relationship he had once enjoyed with his favored nation. It is against the background of this dispute that we are to read the second half of the Tabernacle Narrative (Exod. 35–40). Jeffrey Tigay represents a widely held view when he writes:

> The people's change of heart following their rebellion is shown by their punctilious obedience to God's commands, highlighted by near verbatim correspondences between the instructions in chs 25–31 and their execution in 35–40, and by the recurring phrase "as the Lord had commanded Moses" in 38:32, 42, 43, and ch 39, and by their enthusiasm, indicated by the recurrent references in ch 35 to their hearts and spirits moving them to

give, to their freewill offerings (35:29; 36:3), and by their giving so much that they had to be stopped (36:3–7).[7]

To these points, the observation is often made that the entrance of God into the tabernacle at the close of chapter 40 marks the successful conclusion to the repair of this grievous sin. God had threatened to remove himself from the people as a result of this tragic infidelity, but now, as a sign of reconciliation, he condescends to dwell in their midst.

Indwelling or Guidance?

There is a good deal of truth to this observation about the significance of the moment of indwelling (40:34–35), but it does not quite capture everything. It is important to realize that the forgiveness described in Exodus 32–34 is multistaged. It begins with the famous confrontation between God and Moses. God opens with the case he wishes to prosecute against Israel.

> [7] The LORD said to Moses, "Go down at once! Your people, whom you brought up out of the land of Egypt, have acted perversely; [8] they have been quick to turn aside from the way that I commanded them; they have cast for themselves an image of a calf, and have worshiped it and sacrificed to it, and said, 'These are your gods, O Israel, who brought you up out of the land of Egypt!'" [9] The LORD said to Moses, "I have seen this people, how stiff-necked they are. [10] Now let me alone, so that my wrath may burn hot against them and I may consume them; and of you I will make a great nation." (Exod. 32:7–10)

God's anger appears to be unquenchable. His threat to destroy the entire nation and build a new one from the loins of Moses looks like the tale of the flood in which God destroyed the whole world and started over with Noah. Yet God's decision is not as final as it seems. As commentators, both traditional and modern, have noted, God's request of Moses—"now let me alone"—is actually a subtle hint that Moses must step up and argue against the verdict.[8] Moreover, when God promises Moses that he will "make a great

---

7. Berlin and Brettler, *Jewish Study Bible*, 191.

8. The best discussion of this point is to be found in Yohanan Muffs's classic article, "Who Will Stand in the Breach? A Study of Prophetic Intercession," in *Love and Joy:*

nation of him," he is alluding to the promise made to Abraham back in Genesis 12:1–3. Moses picks up on this hint in the closing words of his response (v. 13).

> [11] But Moses implored the LORD his God, and said, "O LORD, why does your wrath burn hot against your people, whom you brought out of the land of Egypt with great power and with a mighty hand? . . . [13] Remember Abraham, Isaac, and Israel, your servants, how you swore to them by your own self, saying to them, 'I will multiply your descendants like the stars of heaven, and all this land that I have promised I will give to your descendants, and they shall inherit it forever.'" (Exod. 32:11, 13)

Having been reminded of the oath he swore, God acquiesces and withdraws the threat to eradicate the people: "And the LORD changed his mind about the disaster that he planned to bring on his people" (Exod. 32:14).

But Moses's work is not yet over. Another hurdle must be overcome. Although the lives of the Israelites have been spared, not all the effects of Israel's sin have been erased. In anger over the gravity of their actions, God withdraws his pledge to accompany Israel to the promised land:

> [1] The LORD said to Moses, "Go, leave this place, you and the people whom you have brought up out of the land of Egypt, and go to the land of which I swore to Abraham, Isaac, and Jacob, saying, 'To your descendants I will give it.' [2] I will send an angel before you, and I will drive out the Canaanites, the Amorites, the Hittites, the Perizzites, the Hivites, and the Jebusites. [3] Go up to a land flowing with milk and honey; but I will not go up among you, or I would consume you on the way, for you are a stiff-necked people." (Exod. 33:1–3)

Moses, however, cannot abide by this divine decision. A tug of war between God and his prophet ensues over the remainder of the chapter. Moses proves quite stubborn in his defense of Israel. As to God's decision to send a surrogate instead of himself, Moses pushes back bravely and intensely: "how shall it be known that I have found favor in your sight . . . unless you go with us?" (v. 16). In the end, God relents, and the restoration of the covenant is

---

Law, Language, and Religion in Ancient Israel (New York: Jewish Theological Seminary, 1992), 9–48.

marked by the fashioning of two new stone tablets to replace the ones that had been shattered:

> [1] The LORD said to Moses, "Cut two tablets of stone like the former ones, and I will write on the tablets the words that were on the former tablets, which you broke. [2] Be ready in the morning, and come up in the morning to Mount Sinai and present yourself there to me, on the top of the mountain. [3] No one shall come up with you, and do not let anyone be seen throughout all the mountain; and do not let flocks or herds graze in front of that mountain." [4] So Moses cut two tablets of stone like the former ones; and he rose early in the morning and went up on Mount Sinai, as the LORD had commanded him, and took in his hand the two tablets of stone. (Exod. 34:1–4)

At one level, the narrative comes to a proper conclusion with the remaking of the covenant that had been broken by Israel's flagrant idolatry. Yet, another issue remains unresolved: the refusal of God to accompany Israel to the promised land. It is commonplace among scholars to point to the entrance of God into the tabernacle in Exodus 40:34 as the fitting conclusion to the penance for the golden calf. But this is only a partial truth. The issue on the table is not simply the restoration of God's presence among the people. Moses's concern is much more specific, namely, whether God will *guide* Israel to the promised land (33:16). This particular question is answered at the close of Exodus 40. But in order to appreciate this, we will need to pay close attention to the complex literary structure of the text:

> [34] Then the cloud covered the tent of meeting, and the glory of the LORD filled the tabernacle. [35] Moses was not able to enter the tent of meeting because the cloud settled upon it, and the glory of the LORD filled the tabernacle.
> ([36] Whenever the cloud was taken up from the tabernacle, the Israelites would set out on each stage of their journey; [37] but if the cloud was not taken up, then they did not set out until the day that it was taken up. [38] For the cloud of the LORD was on the tabernacle by day, and fire was in the cloud by night, before the eyes of all the house of Israel at each stage of their journey.) (Exod. 40:34–38)

> [1] The LORD summoned Moses and spoke to him from the tent of meeting, saying: [2] Speak to the people of Israel and say to them: When any of you

bring an offering of livestock to the LORD, you shall bring your offering from the herd or from the flock. (Lev. 1:1–2)

Two things should be noticed about this text: its external frame (Exod. 40:34–35 and Lev. 1:1–2) and the description of the tabernacle's role in guiding Israel to the promised land embedded in the middle (40:36–38). Let me begin with the outer frame. The depiction of Moses being summoned to hear the revelation of the law is patterned on the prior revelation that took place at Mount Sinai, as the following chart makes clear.[9]

Exodus 24:15–25:1	Exodus 40:34–Leviticus 1:1
[15b] The cloud covered the mountain	[34a] Then the cloud covered the tent of meeting
[16a] The glory of the LORD settled on Mount Sinai	[34b] and the glory of the LORD filled the tabernacle
[16b] on the seventh day he summoned Moses out of the cloud.	[Lev. 1:1] The LORD summoned Moses . . . from the tent of meeting.
[17] Now the appearance of the glory of the LORD was like a devouring fire on the top of the mountain in the sight of the people of Israel.	[Exod. 40:38] For the cloud of the LORD was on the tabernacle by day, and fire was in the cloud by night, before the eyes of all the house of Israel.
[18] Moses entered the cloud	[35] Moses was not able to enter the tent of meeting.
[25:1] The LORD said to Moses saying . . .	[Lev. 1:1] The LORD . . . spoke to him saying . . .

This chart reveals that the tabernacle functions as a moveable Mount Sinai. Though the foundational, one-time appearance of God took place at that mountain, God will continue to reveal himself through the mediation of the tabernacle. The tabernacle, one could say, becomes a traveling Mount Sinai.

This leads us to our second point: the description of the portable nature of this shrine. If we cast a glance back to the text itself, we will notice that vv. 36–38 have been put in parentheses. Hebrew, of course, has no graphic convention for this. But this interpretive decision can be justified. A close look at the grammar of Leviticus 1:1 reveals a problem. The verse literally reads: "He summoned Moses and the LORD spoke to him." In Hebrew, as in English, one

---

9. Translation modified slightly from NRSV.

would have expected, "The LORD summoned Moses and *he* spoke to him," with the personal pronoun following the citation of the proper name. In the Hebrew original, however, that convention is reversed. All modern translations smooth over this difficulty by moving the proper name to the beginning of the sentence ("The LORD summoned Moses and (he) spoke to him"). Why this curious word order? The most common and convincing explanation is that Lev. 1:1 was originally meant to follow Exodus 40:35 ("the glory of the LORD filled the tabernacle and summoned Moses whereupon the LORD spoke to him"). Because that sentence closes with the divine name ("the glory of the LORD"), it would be understandable, and perhaps even expected, that the next clause would use the pronoun. The problem emerges when the story of the tabernacle's journey (vv. 36–38) is inserted. This creates a considerable textual distance between the mention of the "glory of the LORD" in Exodus 40:35b and the use of the pronoun in Leviticus 1:1. For this reason scholars believe that vv. 36–38 are a late addition to the story, perhaps being added just before the Torah emerged in its final published form.[10]

But establishing the secondary character of these verses should not be confused with explaining their literary function. As Jacob Milgrom has noted, this unit "is crucial to an understanding of the redaction of Leviticus and its place within the Hexateuch."[11] Exodus 40:36–38 serves as a literary anticipation of the tabernacle's role in guiding Israel to the promised land. The specific text that these verses are anticipating is found in the book of Numbers:

[15] On the day the TABERNACLE was set up, the cloud covered the TABERNACLE, the tent of the covenant; and from evening until morning it was over the TABERNACLE, having the appearance of fire. [16] It was always so: the cloud covered it by day and the appearance of fire by night. [17] Whenever the cloud lifted from over the tent, then the Israelites would set out; and in the place where the cloud settled down, there the Israelites would camp. [18] (1) *At the command of the LORD* the Israelites would set out, and (2) *at the command of the LORD* they would camp. As long as the cloud rested over the TABERNACLE, they would remain in camp. [19] Even when the cloud continued over the TABERNACLE many days, the Israelites would keep the charge of the LORD, and would not set out. [20]

10. But it is also possible that a single author marked these verses as parenthetical so that the reader would realize that Leviticus 1:1 connects back to v. 35. Solving this puzzle need not detain us. What is important is that they do not quite fit in their present context.

11. Jacob Milgrom, *Leviticus 1–16*, AB 3 (New York: Doubleday, 1991), 139.

Sometimes the cloud would remain a few days over the TABERNACLE, and (3) *at the command of the LORD* they would remain in camp; then (4) *at the command of the LORD* they would set out. [21] Sometimes the cloud would remain from evening until morning; and when the cloud lifted in the morning, they would set out, or if it continued for a day and a night, when the cloud lifted they would set out. [22] Whether it was two days, or a month, or a longer time, that the cloud continued over the TABERNA- CLE, resting upon it, the Israelites would remain in camp and would not set out; but when it lifted they would set out. [23] (5) *At the command of the LORD* they would camp, and (6) *at the command of the LORD* they would set out. They kept the charge of the LORD, (7) *at the command of the LORD* by Moses. (Num. 9:15–23)[12]

Several features of this text should be noted. First, the close similarity of Numbers 9:15–23 to Exodus 40:36–38 demonstrates that the author of the latter knows the former and is consciously using its vocabulary to create his text. Second, the *Leitwort* "tabernacle," as well as the approbatory formula "at the command of the LORD," occur seven times. This also appears to be intentional given the fact that the repetitions are not necessary. For example, the clause, "On the day the tabernacle was set up, the cloud covered the taber- nacle" could easily be reduced to, "On the day the tabernacle was set up, the cloud covered it." And similarly the phrase, "At the command of the LORD they would camp, and at the command of the LORD they would set out," could be reduced to: "At the command of the LORD they would camp, and set out." The repetition of the word "tabernacle" reflects the sevenfold usage of key terms in both Genesis 1 and Exodus 40, while the repetition of the phrase "at the command of the Lord" recalls the sevenfold approbatory scheme of Genesis 1, Exodus 40, and Leviticus 8. If the purpose of the sevenfold scheme is to show divine supervision and approval, then we can say that the theme of guidance to the promised land has the same theological importance and value as indwelling and sacrificial service. God was not going to leave Israel's guidance to the promised land to chance; as in the creation of the world, he would be directly involved.

Everything we have said to this point about Exodus 40 and Numbers 9 has to do with the Priestly composition considered as an isolated literary work. But if we step back and look at these texts in their present canonical location, another meaning emerges. After Israel venerated the golden calf,

12. NRSV translation slightly altered.

God threatened to abandon Israel and appoint a surrogate to lead his people to the promised land. Moses, however, opposed this decision. He insisted that God accompany the Israelites himself. Eventually God capitulated to his persistent pleas. If we focus our attention on Exodus 32–34 alone, the only sign of forgiveness is the remaking of the covenant at 34:10–27. When scholars cast their glance a bit further and consider the story of the tabernacle's construction, they often suggest that God's decision to indwell the tabernacle at 40:34 marks a better conclusion of the penitential sequence. Moses has secured the intimacy of the divine presence that appeared to have been lost. I would contend, however, that the clearest indicator of God's forgiveness is the description of the tabernacle's role in guiding the Israelites to the promised land (40:36–38). After all, Moses's own formulation of the problem in Exodus 33 focused on the act of divine *accompaniment* to the promised land. Only in Numbers 9 do we get testimony to the success of Moses's petitionary efforts. And just as important, the repetition of Israel acting in obedience to the divine directives seven times indicates both the transformation of Israel's character and God's honoring of that change. The role of these verses, which dramatically interrupt the transition from indwelling (Exod. 40:34–35) to the revelation of the laws for sacrifice (Lev. 1:1 and following) is more than just a formalistic, literary anticipation of the journey that will begin in Numbers 9. Milgrom's assertion that these verses are "a pivot in [the] palistrophic structure" of the Pentateuch says too little. The introduction of the theme of guidance through the wilderness at this point in the story brings the penitential sequence over the sin of the golden calf to its appropriate termination. A tragic moment has a comedic end.

The Golden Calf and Original Sin

The placement of the story of the golden calf in the middle of the Tabernacle Narrative is a striking editorial and theological decision. If we were to consider the character of this Priestly story alone (Exod. 25–31 and 35–40) we would be impressed by the strict obedience of Israel to all of the commands they receive from God. But once the story of the golden calf is placed in the middle of this account, its beatific character is turned upside down. The obedience of Israel is abruptly preceded by a penitential sequence. Our attention is no longer drawn to the virtue of this people but the startling act of disobedience inscribed into the story of her very founding. The German theological Karl Barth is quite sensitive to the effect the final form of the story has on the reader:

In the preceding narrative [Exod. 25–31] there is nothing to prepare us for what is recorded in these verses. In the light of it, it is simply a senseless and causeless act of apostasy. And if the act is presupposed in all its seriousness in the texts which follow, when we have regard to their culmination in the revelation of the name of God, it seems if anything all the more inconceivable—a refusal in face of these pre-conditions, an unfaithfulness in face of this faithfulness of Yahweh, a withdrawal of Israel from the covenant which He has so securely grounded. The contrast is, if anything, *even more clamant than that of the story of the fall.* It is quite understandable that the tradition which viewed the beginning of the history of Israel in this way—as indelibly blotted in this way—should only be able to view the beginning of the whole race, of history, as it is, in fact viewed in Genesis 3. Here in Exodus 32 the tradition of Israel speaks from direct knowledge. *Here is the setting of the view of man in relation to God which is attested in Gen 3, being there projected backwards and referred to the beginnings of all peoples.* Here we have a typical picture—a kind of cross-section—for it is against Ex 32 that we obviously have to see texts like I Kings 12:28ff [the sin of Jeroboam] and the corresponding passages in the prophets—of what always takes place in the history of Israel as the counterpart to the faithfulness and grace and mercy of God, the painful contradiction of its whole existence. No wonder that the contours and colours of Gen 3 seem to be mild compared with what we find here. Here it comes home with a vengeance.[13]

In the patristic period there was a lamentable tendency to view the story of the calf as a revelation of the unparalleled sinfulness of the people of Israel. But Barth captures the message of the Bible more accurately when he compares the story to the fall of humanity in Genesis 3. Through the vehicle of Israel's apostasy, the Bible is saying something about the character of the human person in general. Brevard Childs concurs that this text diagnoses a propensity of sin larger than just the Jewish people when he writes: "Israel *and the church* have their existence because God picked up the pieces. There was no golden period of unblemished saintliness."[14]

13. See Karl Barth, *Church Dogmatics*, IV/1, trans. G. W. Bromiley (Edinburgh: T&T Clark, 1956), 423–32, quotation 427 (emphasis added).

14. Childs, *Exodus*, 580 (emphasis added). Also, see Joel Kaminsky, "Paradise Regained: Rabbinic Reflections on Israel at Sinai," in *Jews, Christians, and the Theology of the Hebrew Scriptures*, ed. A. Bellis and J. Kaminsky (Atlanta: Scholars Press, 2000), 15–43. Kaminsky illustrates how early Jewish sources also read this narrative in terms of the fall.

Conclusion

In our discussion of this theme we have seen that each literary source has its own way of emphasizing what went wrong when Israel venerated the calf. If we follow the non-Priestly version, ignoring Exodus 25–31 and allowing chapter 32 to follow directly chapter 24, then the sin is clearly a violation of the command not to make idols (Exod. 20:4–6, 23). Jeffrey Tigay astutely observed the seriousness of the crime when he wrote: "At the very moment that God was giving Moses the Tablets of the Pact, which forbids idolatry, the people were demanding just that. In modern terms, 'the ink was not yet dry' on the covenant when the people violated it."[15] Read on its own, the act of shattering the tablets of the pact (32:19) followed by the cutting of new ones to replace them (34:1) bookend the penitential sequence.

But once the command to build the tabernacle interrupts the story, this sin brings with it an additional consequence: it threatens the promise God made to dwell among his people and lead them to the land of Canaan. I have suggested that the insertion of Exodus 40:36–38 into the close of that chapter points in two directions. On the one hand, it points back to Moses's passionate pleas that God personally accompany his people to the promised land and not send a surrogate (Exod. 33:12–16). On the other hand, the text points forward to the moment when Israel leaves the environs of Sinai and heads toward the promised land under the guidance of God himself (Num. 9:15–23). The fit is so exact that it seems hard to imagine that the redactor who added these verses did not intend it. But even if one prefers to be agnostic on that question, there can be no doubt that Exodus 40:36–38 signals the end of the penitential sequence in the present form of the book.

In the end, how we read Exodus 25–40 depends on how we view the text. For most of the twentieth century, scholars have ignored the final canonical form and read Exodus 32–34 solely in light of its non-Priestly antecedents. But beginning in the 1970s with the work of Brevard Childs in North America and Rolf Rendtorff in Europe, an interest in reading Scripture as a canonical whole emerged.[16] The reading strategies of these scholars is not a return to a

---

15. Berlin and Brettler, *Jewish Study Bible*, 183. See also Joel Baden, "What Was the Sin of the Golden Calf?," www.thetorah.com/article/what-was-the-sin-of-the-golden-calf. But Baden's point is that the sin of the golden calf violates the beginning of what is known as the "Covenant Code" (i.e., 20:23) rather than one of the Ten Commandments.

16. Brevard Childs, *Introduction to the Old Testament as Scripture* (Philadelphia: Fortress, 1979). Rolf Rendtorff's work began at roughly the same time as Childs, but the best introduction to his work in English is *Canon and Theology: Overtures to an Old Testament Theology* (Minneapolis: Fortress, 1993).

precritical stage of harmonizing all the difficult points of difference. Canonical readers respect the source differences at play but also keep a vigilant watch for those broader thematic connections that link the two narratives. Moreover, as canonical readers are quick to emphasize, this sort of "holistic" reading was intended by the final editors of the biblical story. That our redactor employed Priestly and non-Priestly vocabulary in Exodus 31:18 (tablets of the covenant, tablets of stone) shows beyond a shadow of a doubt that the disparate origins of individual narratives was not to have the final word. The whole is truly greater than the sum of its parts.

CHAPTER 8

The Binding of Isaac and Sacrifice

The full implications of [the binding of Isaac] are not spelled out in [Genesis 22]. However, the exegetical effect of the formation of the larger canon (the Pentateuch) sets up a distant resonance between Genesis and Leviticus. The God who required and yet supplied his own sacrifice to Abraham, acts in a similar way in the institutionalized worship of Leviticus. Although the two witnesses are only indirectly related, Genesis 22 points in a direction which calls for fuller theological reflection on the whole sacrificial system of Leviticus in light of God's gracious revelation of his will to Abraham.

Brevard Childs[1]

I call heaven and earth to witness against me: Whenever anyone — Gentile or Jew, man or woman, male or female slave, reads [the law for sacrifice in Leviticus 1], the Holy One (blessed be He!) remembers the binding of Isaac.

Leviticus Rabbah 2:11

In my previous chapter I considered the way the final editors of the book of Exodus stitched together the stories of the golden calf and the tabernacle. I observed that the assembling process was not thoroughgoing. In other words, the editorial team did not rewrite their source narratives such that they would become a single, unified story. Rather, the integrity of each tradition was, for the most part, respected. All that was added were key transitional verses at the seams (and occasional notes in the middle) to guide the reader. A canonical

---

1. Brevard Childs, *Biblical Theology of the Old and New Testaments: Theological Reflection on the Christian Bible* (Minneapolis: Fortress, 1992), 335.

reading, as Childs has described it, must (1) respect the independent origin of the source material and not offer "forced harmonizations," but (2) press further to see what sort of deeper meanings emerge from such juxtapositions.

In this chapter I will push the canonical mode of reading one step further. Not only must the interpreter make sense of textual linkages signaled by a redactor, but one must also make sense of the larger flow of information across biblical books. One good example of this can be found in the stories Israel told about the origins of the sacrificial cultus.

In my fourth chapter I followed the standard convention among scholars of trying to discern the meaning of the sacrificial act from the confines of the Priestly texts. This is a challenging approach, as I noted, because the Priestly texts say almost nothing about the purpose or meaning of sacrifice; their interest is on the proper rules that must be followed when making a sacrifice. For this reason scholars have turned to other parts of the biblical canon as well as cognate materials from the cultural neighbors of ancient Israel in order to get some purchase as to what biblical sacrifice might mean. One text rarely pulled into the orbit of these modern discussions is the sacrifice of Isaac. This is surprising given the foundational role it plays in the book of Genesis. As it turns out, recent research has revealed two ways in which the story of the near sacrifice of Isaac is related to Exodus 25–40.

Genesis 22 and Moses's Prayer of Intercession

As we have seen, the author of the golden calf story was unaware of the Tabernacle Narrative that came to surround it. But those responsible for assembling the Bible in its final form did not mindlessly juxtapose these independent units but added linking verses (such as Exod. 31:18) to tie them together. The connections established by these editorial additions are not limited to the immediate environment of the Tabernacle Narrative (Exod. 25–31, 35–40). Some scribes looked further afield and tried to draw lines of connection between the books of Genesis and Exodus. A good example of this can be found in Moses's intercessory prayer after the sin of the golden calf. In seeking to overturn the divine verdict to destroy Israel in punishment for this sin, Moses reminds God of the promise made to the patriarchs in Genesis.

Although my ultimate interest is in the relationship of the promises in Genesis to their deployment in Exodus, we cannot fully understand the treatment in Exodus without considering a variant tradition in Deuteronomy. The bulk of Deuteronomy (chs. 12–26) concerns the rehearsal of the Sinaitic law code prior to the entrance of Israel into the promised land. But the book opens with a brief review of the events immediately prior to that: the giving of the law, the veneration of the golden calf, and Moses's intercession on behalf of Israel.

A comparison between Moses's prayer on behalf of Israel in the two versions is instructive. The prayer in Deuteronomy is brief and generic in tone:

Remember your servants, Abraham, Isaac, and Jacob. (Deut. 9:27)

In Exodus, Moses's plea begins with those words but goes on to specify what God must call to mind,

Remember your servants Abraham, Isaac, and Israel, how you swore to them by your own self, saying to them, "I will multiply your descendants like the stars of heaven, and all this land that I have promised I will give to your descendants, and they shall inherit it forever." (Exod. 32:13)

Most scholars believe that the shorter version in Deuteronomy is older. What we see in Exodus is a scribal expansion whose purpose is to create a linkage back to the patriarchal promises found in Genesis.

To be more specific, the citation in Exodus 32 recalls the terms of the promise made to Abraham in Genesis 22 and then repeated to Isaac in Genesis 26. I have marked those portions of these two texts that have been recycled in Exodus 32:13.

[15] And the angel of the LORD called to Abraham a second time from heaven, [16] and said, "*By myself I have sworn*, says the LORD, because you have done this, and have not withheld your son, your only son, [17] I will indeed bless you, and *I will multiply your descendants as the stars of heaven* and as the sand which is on the seashore. And your descendants shall possess the gate of their enemies, [18] and by your descendants shall all the nations of the earth bless themselves, because you have obeyed my voice." (Gen. 22:15–18)

[2] The LORD appeared to Isaac and said, "Do not go down to Egypt; settle in the land that I shall show you. [3] Reside in this land as an alien, and I will be with you, and will bless you; for to you and to your descendants I will give all these lands, *and I will fulfill the oath that I swore* to your father Abraham. [4] *I will multiply your descendants as the stars of heaven*, and *will give to your descendants all these lands*; and all the nations of the earth shall

gain blessing for themselves through your offspring, [5] because Abraham obeyed my voice and kept my charge, my commandments, my statutes, and my laws."[2] (Gen. 26:2–5)

If we look back at Exodus 32:13, we will see that each of its constituent parts (swearing an oath, multiplying descendants like the stars, and granting land to those same descendants) has been anticipated in these two texts from Genesis. This explicit verbal agreement shows us that the shapers of the biblical canon were trying to coordinate these (once) independent stories so that the plea of Moses could appeal to the promise made to Abraham.

Having established that Moses's argument against God in Exodus 32 directs the reader back to the promise made to Abraham, the question becomes, What is its specific force? In a groundbreaking article, Walter Moberly argued that the repetition of the promise to Abraham (Gen. 22:15–18) is a late editorial addition to the story that functions as its earliest commentary. Though the terms of the promise in this chapter draw on expressions found earlier in the book, there is one significant innovation. "One of the most notable features about the divine promises elsewhere in Genesis," Moberly observes, "is that they always constitute a unilateral and unconditional offer on God's part. The promise precedes an initial obedient response on Abraham's part (Gen. 12:1–3, 4) and is reaffirmed (e.g. 15:5, 18:18) independently of any notable action on Abraham's part to occasion it."[3] In theological terms, these earlier texts ground the promise in grace alone, without any consideration of human worthiness. But things change dramatically in Genesis 22. The promise made to Abraham is regrounded in his obedience ("*because* you have done this . . . I will indeed bless you" [v. 16]). Moberly aptly describes the theological force of this innovation when he writes:

A promise which previously was grounded solely in the will and purpose of YHWH is transformed so that it is now grounded *both* in the will of YHWH *and* in the obedience of Abraham. It is not that the divine promise has become contingent upon Abraham's obedience, but that Abraham's obedience has been incorporated into the divine promise. Henceforth Israel owes its existence not just to YHWH but also to Abraham.[4]

2. Translation of the NRSV is slightly altered to bring out the similarity in diction between the two texts.

3. R. W. L. Moberly, "The Earliest Commentary on the Akedah," *VT* 38 (1988): 318.

4. Moberly, "Earliest Commentary," 320–21.

Because the terms of Moses's argument in Exod. 32:13 are derived from Genesis 22:15–18, it is only natural that the theology of that promise plays a role in Moses's deployment. Building on the insights of Moberly, the obedience of Abraham becomes a crucial ingredient in dissuading God from destroying Israel. To use the language of later rabbinic Judaism, it was the foundational, merit-worthy action of Abraham that Moses was able to draw upon in this period of national distress.

Genesis 22 and the Tamid Sacrifice

The sacrifice of Isaac is not related solely to the golden calf in Exodus 32–34; it can also be read as grounding the character of Israel's sacrificial service outlined in Exodus 29. In order to appreciate how this works, we must attend to the location of the ordeal that Abraham and Isaac undergo. After God calls Abraham by name he commands him: "take your son . . . and go to the land of *Moriah* and offer him there as a burnt offering on one of the mountains that I will show you" (Gen. 22:2). The only other place in the Bible where we find this location is 2 Chronicles 3:1: "Solomon began to build the house of the LORD in Jerusalem on Mount *Moriah*, where the LORD had appeared to his father David." An additional point that should not be missed is that both texts highlight the significance of God making himself visible at the location where he will be worshipped. In Genesis, Abraham names the spot where he offered a ram in place of Isaac, "the LORD will *see*" (*ra'ah*, active voice), to which the narrator adds: "as it is said to this day, "the LORD shall be *seen*" (*ra'ah*, passive voice). In Chronicles, the author observes that Solomon will build his temple on the site "where the Lord had *appeared* [*ra'ah*] to his father David." Scholars have long observed that altars or temples were often built to commemorate a theophany that took place there. Jacob, for example, erects an altar at Bethel after God appears to him in a dream (Gen. 28:10–22; cf. 35:6–7). But the connection between seeing God and the building of a sanctuary is even more explicit in Genesis 22 and 2 Chronicles 3. In both passages there is a pun on the verb *ra'ah* (to see, be seen, appear) which, as Jon Levenson has argued, "is to be associated with the name . . . Moriah on which both Gen 22:14 and 2 Chr 3:1 play" (as though Moriah could be derived from the root *ra'ah*).[5] According to Levenson, the purpose of such a linkage was to explain

---

5. Jon Levenson, *Death and Resurrection of the Beloved Son* (New Haven: Yale University Press, 1993), 115. Of course Moriah is not etymologically related to *ra'ah* in any strict

the *location* for the temple. Mount Moriah came to mean "the place where God made himself visible."

Brevard Childs comes at the question from a slightly different direction. He notices that three of the key words in Genesis 22—ram, burnt offering, and the verb "to see, appear"—play a prominent role in the foundational texts about Israel's sacrificial cult in Leviticus 8–9.

> The effect for the informed reader is that the story of Abraham's uniquely private experience is thus linked to Israel's collective public worship, and conversely Israel's sacrifice is drawn into the theological orbit of Abraham's offering: "God will provide his own sacrifice." In terms of the Old Testament canon, these two witnesses are not conflicting historical ideologies, but diverse witnesses within the cult to the same gracious ways of God with Israel. It is not surprising when the rabbis held that the sacrifices and festivals of Israel were efficacious by virtue of the "binding of Isaac" (cf. Schoeps, *Paul*, 143ff.).[6]

Childs's view has been enthusiastically endorsed by Georg Steins, Jan Gertz, and Konrad Schmid. The latter writes, "it is striking that apart from Gen 22 and Lev 8–9, there are no other instances in the Bible where a burnt offering (*'ōlāh*), a ram, and an appearance of God are combined (so, Steins). Given the probable Persian period origin of Gen 22, it is only to be expected that the sacrifice of Abraham's son is described in terms of the current theology, namely that of the Priestly texts."[7]

Schmid's position is the most robust in terms of the intertextual connection. Because he presumes that Genesis 22 was written at the very end of the biblical period, he concludes that its author must have been familiar with the Priestly writings. On this view, the Akedah would not be gesturing toward the sacrificial cult in general but would be referring directly to the eighth day rite in Leviticus 9. I do not share his certainty about the dating of Genesis 22, and with Childs I would worry about this sort of "backwards" reading that allows Leviticus 9 to determine the way we understand Genesis 22. Whenever

---

scientific sense, but the folk etymologies created by biblical authors are not governed by the principles of modern philology.

6. Childs, *Biblical Theology*, 327–28. Childs here cites H. J. Schoeps, *Paul: The Theology of the Apostle in the Light of Jewish Religious History*, trans. H. Knight (London: Lutterworth, 1961).

7. Konrad Schmid, "Abraham's Sacrifice: Gerhard von Rad's Interpretation of Genesis 22," *Interpretation* 62 (2008): 274.

possible we should let the narrative order of the biblical books govern our reading. Childs's more measured approach is preferable. Genesis 22 points forward to the beginnings of the public cult and, in so doing, sets up a framework for understanding biblical sacrifice.[8]

As we have noted, the sacrifice that marks the onset of the public cult (Exod. 29:38–42) and serves as its very foundation (cf. Num. 28–29) is the morning and evening tamid. As it was the first sacrifice offered in the morning, all subsequent sacrifices offered during the day were placed upon it. As the last sacrifice of the day offered in the evening, it assured that the (divine) fire upon the altar would never be extinguished. Genesis 22, of course, does not single out this sacrifice because the offering Abraham makes is a onetime, nonrepeatable affair; precisely what the tamid is not. But a typological reading need not be limited by such literalistic strictures. If the tamid is Israel's preeminent offering and the binding of Isaac represents the deepest form of offering that could be asked of Abraham,[9] it does not require a great deal of theological imagination to associate the two. Indeed, the modern commentator Georg Steins and the medieval thinker Rabbi Hasdai Crescas (fourteenth century) come to very similar conclusions. Steins writes that "the ram is representative of Isaac, i.e., of Abraham's descendants and thus of Israel (cf. 22:17f). In the context of the central texts on burnt offerings, there is a subtle interpretation of Israel's sacrifice: Gen 22 narratively unfolds how it became possible for Israel's (daily burnt) sacrifice to be Israel's self-sacrifice."[10] R. Hasdai Crescas asserts that "the fruits of the loins of the ram," are offered by Israel who is, in turn, "the fruit of the loins of Isaac." In this fashion "the daily offering is a substitute for the Jewish people and when they bring the ram near to the altar, they will be all brought near to the service of the Lord."[11]

8. As Brevard Childs puts the matter, attention to the canonical shape of a text does not yield a single meaning. Rather, it puts in play a number of readings (often unintended by the original authors) that informed readers can discover in the text.

9. Jon Levenson captures well the profundity of what was demanded of Abraham when he writes: "Abraham's own destiny is so entwined with that of Isaac, and the 'great nation' that is eventually to descend from him, that the demand is even harder than the demand upon any other loving father to offer up his beloved son. Psychologically, what is asked is not only an inexpressibly painful act of sacrifice; it is also an act of self-sacrifice." See *Inheriting Abraham: The Legacy of the Patriarch in Judaism, Christianity, and Islam* (Princeton: Princeton University Press, 2012), 68–69.

10. Georg Steins, *Die "Bindung Isaaks" im Kanon (Gen 22)* (Freiburg: Herder, 1999), 195.

11. Hasdai Crescas, *Light of the Lord (Or Hashem)*, trans. R. Weiss (Oxford: Oxford University Press, 2018), 162.

It is not my claim that this typological reading was intended by either the author of Genesis 22 or Exodus 29. In all likelihood these two stories were written independent of one another. Both make sense in their immediate literary environments and do not *require* the other to become intelligible. But when these texts become part of a single, extended narrative—a narrative shaped by editorial verses designed to link passages like these—reading them in light of one another becomes eminently plausible. For this reason, it cannot be accidental that the Aramaic Levi Document (hereafter, Aramaic Levi), our earliest commentary on the tamid offering, grounds the tamid in the binding of Isaac. For Childs the key to understanding the intertextual relationship of these stories is to distinguish between individual textual witnesses and the theological "substance" (*Sache* in German; *res* in Latin) shared between them. Because sacred Scripture is ultimately inspired by God, it is incumbent on the reader to pursue a strategy of reading that can lay bare what texts like these can tell us about the nature of sacrifice itself, not simply what the various textual witnesses say about it. We could find an analogy in the reading strategy demanded by the New Testament. It is not enough to articulate the various portraits of Jesus drawn by the individual witnesses of the Gospels. To profess the Christian faith means professing belief in the "one Lord Jesus Christ, the only begotten Son of God." Somehow the various portraits (i.e., witnesses) must be read in such a way as to enhance our understanding of who Jesus was and is. When we read Aramaic Levi, we encounter a very early reader of the Bible trying to explain how the sacrifice of Isaac might inform our understanding of the tamid rite.

Aramaic Levi

Aramaic Levi was written sometime between the mid-third century to the early second century BCE. And like most of our earliest biblical commentaries, it does not comment on the biblical text in a line-by-line fashion. Rather, its commentary is presented as an imaginative retelling of Israel's story taking care to connect various portions of the biblical text that might be missed by a casual reader.

Aramaic Levi takes as its point of departure the priestly role of Levi, the third son of Jacob. Though the biblical author was aware that Israel's priests descended from the loins of Levi, Genesis passes over this detail in silence. The author of Aramaic Levi senses this anomaly and retells the biblical story, adding details about the priestly office.

The point of departure is Jacob's journey to Bethel in Genesis 35. Jacob had recently returned to the land of Israel after his painful exile in Aramea. Though he had left his home with nothing to his name, he returned with two wives, twelve children (eleven sons and one daughter), and a multitude of livestock. God appears to Jacob and says, "Arise and go up to Bethel, and settle there. Make an altar there to the God who appeared to you when you fled from your brother Esau" (Gen. 35:1). Before complying with this command, Jacob asks the members of his household to set aside their alien gods and purify themselves (vv. 2–5). Jacob then goes up to Bethel, builds an altar (vv. 6–8), and (presumably) pays the tithe that he had vowed prior to his departure for Aramea (cf. Gen. 28:20–22). After all of this is accomplished, Jacob heads to Hebron to visit with his father Isaac shortly before his death.

> [27] Jacob came to his father Isaac at Mamre, or Kiriath-arba (that is, Hebron), where Abraham and Isaac had resided as aliens. [28] Now the days of Isaac were one hundred eighty years. [29] And Isaac breathed his last; he died and was gathered to his people, old and full of days; and his sons Esau and Jacob buried him. (Gen. 35:27–29)

Aramaic Levi takes this short notice as the occasion to fill in the details as to how Levi became familiar with the practice of sacrifice.

> [6] And we went from Bethel and we encamped at the residence of Abraham our father alongside Isaac our father. [7] And Isaac our father saw all of us and blessed us and rejoiced. [8] And when he learned that I was a priest of the Most High God, the Lord of heaven, he began to instruct me and to teach me the law of the priesthood. (ALD 5:6–8)[12]

The first two sentences (5:6–7) paraphrase what was said in Gen. 35:27–29, adding the detail about Isaac's blessing of his children. Sometimes in the Bible, and very frequently in postbiblical tradition, the death of a patriarch becomes the occasion for such a blessing. Jacob's long address to his sons in Genesis 49 is an excellent example of this. Aramaic Levi presumes that Isaac must have done the same thing and describes the event in 5:8. Most of the details of

---

12. Translation from Jonas C. Greenfield, Michael Stone, and Esther Eshel, *The Aramaic Levi Document: Edition, Translation, Commentary*, SVTP 19 (Leiden: Brill, 2004).

that blessing remain unrecorded, but we are told that Isaac passed on crucial sacrificial lore to Levi.

Because the centerpiece of the cult is the morning and evening tamid, Isaac turns his attention to the mechanics of that sacrifice. His instructions begin with the requirements to wash and vest before approaching the altar. If we recall the mosaic from Sepphoris (fig. 4.1), the panel devoted to the tamid places the laver for washing prominently beside the altar where Aaron, properly vested, prepares to offer the morning sacrifice.

> [1] And when you are about to enter the Sanctuary, wash in water and then put on the priestly garment. [2] And when you are robed, lave your hands and feet again before you approach the altar at all. [3] And when you are about to sacrifice anything fitting to offer up on the altar, wash your hands and feet once again. (ALD 7:1–3)

As Hillel Mali has shown, the ritual described in Aramaic Levi builds on the laws governing the use of the laver in the Tabernacle Narrative.[13]

> [20a] When they go into the Tent of Meeting, they shall wash with water, so that they might not die. [20b] And when they come near the altar to minister, to make an offering by fire to the Lord, [21] they shall wash their hands and feet, so that they might not die. (Exod. 31:20–21)[14]

This text makes it clear that one act of washing (v. 20a) is required for entry into the tent plus an additional washing (v. 20b) before approaching the altar. Aramaic Levi derives from this distinction the protocol required of the priest when he begins his sacrificial service. Before entering the sanctuary (to offer incense at the inner altar), the priest must wash his entire body and put on his priestly robes (7:1). After leaving the sanctuary, but before reaching the outer altar, he must wash his hands again (7:2). And should this priest be the one who actually sacrifices the animal, he must wash his hands and feet again prior to slaughtering the animal (7:3).

Having described the ritual precautions that are required to approach the altar, the next step is selecting the appropriate wood.

---

13. Hillel Mali, "Priestly Offering: Law and Narrative in the *Aramaic Levi Document*," forthcoming in *Harvard Theological Review*, 2023.
14. The translation reflects the Samaritan version of this text. For a discussion of its relevance to Aramaic Levi, see Mali, "Priestly Offering."

⁴ And offer split wood, and examine it first for worms and then offer it up, for thus I saw my father Abraham acting with care. ⁵ Of any of all twelve kinds of wood which are fitting, he told me to offer up on the altar, whose smoke rises up with a pleasant odor. ⁶ And there are their names—cedar and juniper, and almond and fir and pine and ash, cypress and fig and oleaster, laurel and myrtle and asphalathos. ⁷ These are those that he told me are fitting to offer up beneath the holocaust upon the altar. (ALD 7:4–7)

It is worth pausing on the deliberation required to select the proper wood for the altar. According to Leviticus 9:23–24, the inauguration of the altar was marked by the appearance of a miraculous divine fire that consumed the first public sacrifices. It is this *sacral* fire that will consume all subsequent sacrifices. As a result, the book of Leviticus commends great care be taken to assure that this fire never goes out: "The fire on the altar shall be kept burning; it shall not go out. Every morning the priest shall add wood to it, lay out the burnt offering on it, and turn into smoke the fat pieces of the offerings of well-being" (6:12). "The sacrifices offered up at the inauguration of the public cult," Jacob Milgrom observes, "were consumed by a divine fire (9:24), and it is this fire that is not allowed to die out, so that all subsequent sacrifices might claim divine acceptance (see Philo, *On the Special Laws*, 1.286)."[15] Milgrom's observation is certainly correct. But we should not put an undue emphasis on its utilitarian dimension. The attitude is not so much, "tend the fire to be assured of divine acceptance" but rather the reverse: "since the fire is holy, do whatever is necessary to honor its nature." The admonition regarding the sacrality of the altar is worth repeating: "whatever touches the altar shall become holy" (Exod. 29:37).

In the Second Temple period this worry about the sacral character of the fire led to a concern regarding what type of wood would be appropriate to ignite it. The first hints of such a concern can be found in the list of temple obligations in the book of Nehemiah.

³² We also lay on ourselves the obligation to charge ourselves yearly one-third of a shekel for the service of the house of our God: ³³ for the rows of bread, the regular grain offering, the regular burnt offering, the sabbaths, the new moons, the appointed festivals, the sacred donations, and the sin

---

15. See Milgrom's annotation to Leviticus 6:13 in *The HarperCollins Study Bible*, ed. H. Attridge (San Francisco: HarperCollins, 2006), 159.

offerings to make atonement for Israel, and for all the work of the house of our God. [34] We have also cast lots among the priests, the Levites, and the people, for the *wood offering*, to bring it into the house of our God, by ancestral houses, at appointed times, year by year, to burn on the altar of the LORD our God, *as it is written in the law [of Moses]*. (Neh. 10:32–34; emphasis added)

And lest one be tempted to think of the wood offering as a mere afterthought in this laundry list of temple obligations, it should be noted that Nehemiah concludes by singling out this obligation in particular: "And I provided for the wood offering, at appointed times, and for the first fruits. Remember me, O my God, for good" (13:31).

Strikingly, Nehemiah 10:34 grounds the obligation to bring the wood offering in the law of Moses ("as it is written in the law [of Moses]"). One thing Nehemiah does not spell out is which types of wood would qualify for use on the altar. A full-fledged exposition of this particular detail awaits the interpretive efforts of Aramaic Levi, Jubilees, and eventually rabbinic texts.

Let us return to the narrative frame of Aramaic Levi. All of this instruction about the morning sacrifice comes from the mouth of Isaac. But how does Isaac know the rules about the wood offering? According to Aramaic Levi, Isaac learned them through observation: "thus I saw my father Abraham acting with care." As Hillel Mali explains, Isaac watched closely as his father selected the wood to be used for his immolation: "So Abraham rose early in the morning, saddled his donkey, and took two of his young men with him, and his son Isaac; *he cut the wood for the burnt offering* and set out and went to the place in the distance that God had shown him" (Gen. 22:3). Although this verse does not explicitly require Abraham to pick one of the twelve acceptable types of wood (ALD 7:6), something like this could be inferred from the phrase in Genesis 22:3 of "wood of the burnt offering" (*atse olah*). The NRSV renders this phrase as a genitive of purpose, "wood *for* the burnt offering." But it could just as easily be understood as a genitive of quality, "wood *fit* for the burnt offering." Pseudo-Jonathan, an Aramaic translation (targum) of the Bible, renders the clause in precisely this fashion. Evidently, Aramaic Levi understood the verse this way as well. By carefully attending to how his father gathered the wood prior to their journey to Mount Moriah, Isaac learned the rudiments of this selection process. Now we can see why Isaac is the one who teaches Levi about his priestly duties and not his father Jacob. "Isaac is cast as an instructor," Mali concludes, "because he could teach the order of service . . . from personal experience, as the sacrifice."[16]

This striking move to link the founding of the priesthood to an act of (self-) sacrifice can be found in a different form in the book of Jubilees.

> That night he stayed at Bethel. Levi dreamed that he—he and his sons—was appointed and ordained to the priesthood of the Most High God forever. When he awakened, he blessed the Lord. Jacob got up early in the morning on the fourteenth day of this month and gave a tithe of all that had come with him—from people to animals, from money to all utensils and clothing. He gave a tithe of all. At that time Rachel was pregnant with her son Benjamin. Jacob counted his sons from him. He went up (the list), and it came down on Levi in the Lord's share. His father put priestly clothes on him and ordained him. (Jub. 32:1–3)[17]

According to this text, when Jacob is about to pay his tithe on this return to Bethel, he counts his sons backwards beginning with Benjamin. Because Levi is the tenth, he along with the rest of his belongings which he pledged is given over to God.

What we see in these examples from the lives of Isaac and Levi is the understanding that the priest is not only the one who offers the sacrifice, but the grounds for his being able to do so are established by the fact that he was once a sacrifice himself. The lesson to be learned from all of this must be underscored: The claim to the priestly office rests on being both priest and victim.

Sepphoris Mosaic

The understanding of the binding of Isaac as a foundational story for understanding temple sacrifice is beautifully exemplified in the synagogue mosaic from Sepphoris. In chapter 4, we examined the way in which the tamid sacrifice was depicted in the upper panels of that carpet mosaic. If we step back and look at the entire floor (fig. 8.1), we'll notice that the tamid sacrifice is balanced at the bottom panels by the binding of Isaac (fig. 8.2). Somehow the daily offering taps into the power of that foundational moment.

16. Mali, "Priestly Offering," 26.
17. Translation from James VanderKam, *Jubilees: A Commentary in Two Volumes*, Hermeneia (Minneapolis: Fortress, 2018), 876.

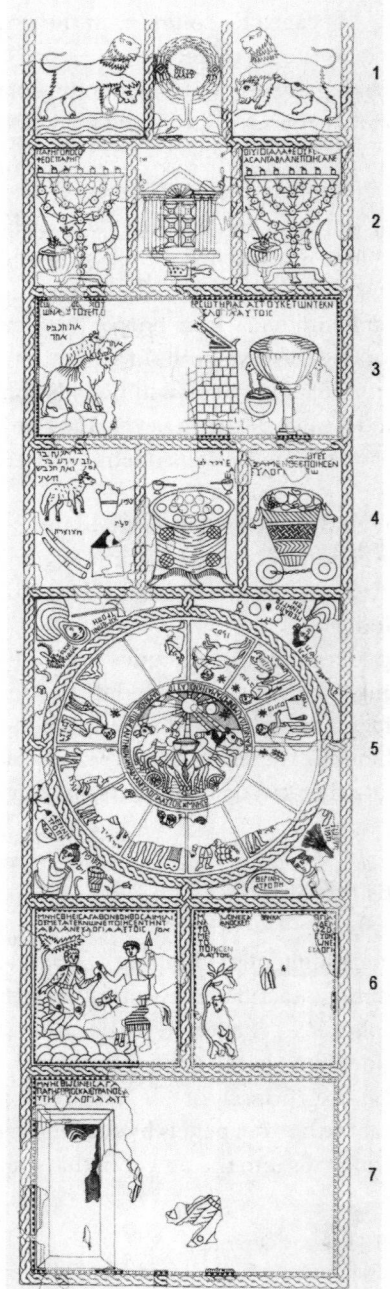

Figure 8.1 Drawing of the entire mosaic floor of the Sepphoris synagogue; drawing by Pnina Arad, courtesy of Zeev Weiss, the Sepphoris Excavations, the Hebrew University of Jerusalem

Figure 8.2 Close-up of panel 6, portraying the binding of Isaac, of the Sepphoris mosaic; drawing by Pnina Arad, courtesy of Zeev Weiss, the Sepphoris Excavations, the Hebrew University of Jerusalem

The sacral character of the location is made evident in the mosaic by the fact that Abraham and Isaac have removed their shoes before approaching the altar. As one can learn from Exodus 28, the chapter that describes the vestments of Aaron and his sons, there is no mention of any sort of covering for the feet. No doubt this is because the wearing of sandals on sacred ground was thought to be an affront to the demands of holiness. When God called Moses from the burning bush, he addressed him in an emphatic fashion: "Moses! Moses!" to which Moses replied, "Here I am." Thereupon God declared: "Come no closer. Remove the sandals from your feet, for the place on which you are standing is holy ground" (Exod. 3:5). Similarly, when God sent Abraham and Isaac to the mountains of Moriah, they would have removed their shoes before approaching the altar. Early interpreters presumed that this custom was well known and that Abraham and Isaac respected it.

Though the mosaic clearly wants to compare the tamid to the binding of Isaac, it has no way of imposing a specific interpretation of its significance. In the final publication of the excavations, Zeev Weiss points out several possibilities.[18] One example is based on a close reading of Leviticus 1, the

18. Zeev Weiss, *The Sepphoris Synagogue: Deciphering an Ancient Message through Its Archaeological and Socio-Historical Contexts* (Jerusalem: Israel Exploration Society, 2005), 239–42.

laws that govern the whole burnt offering, and exactly the type of sacrifice that takes place at the morning and evening rites. Leviticus 1 divides into three parts: the rules that govern animals from the herd (vv. 3–9), the flock (vv. 10–13), and birds (vv. 14–17). The rules for the animals are very similar:

Herd	Flock
1:3 If the offering is a burnt offering from the herd, you shall offer a male without blemish;	1:10 If your gift for a burnt offering is from the flock, from the sheep or goats, your offering shall be a male without blemish.
you shall bring it to the entrance of the tent of meeting, for acceptance in your behalf before the LORD. 4 You shall lay your hand on the head of the burnt offering, and it shall be acceptable in your behalf as atonement for you.	
5 The bull shall be slaughtered before the LORD; and Aaron's sons the priests shall offer the blood, dashing the blood against all sides of the altar that is at the entrance of the tent of meeting.	11 It shall be slaughtered on the north side of the altar before the LORD, and Aaron's sons the priests shall dash its blood against all sides of the altar.

The instructions given for the lamb repeat many of the instructions for the bull. Some of the details are omitted, such as bringing the animal to the entrance of the tent of meeting and laying a hand upon its head. Readers could presume they were to be carried out for the flock as well; no need for excessive repetition. But this explanation would be harder to employ for an addition unique to the flock:

The bull shall be slaughtered before the LORD. (v. 5)

[The lamb] shall be slaughtered *on the north side of the altar* before the LORD. (v. 11)

The significance of the geographical reference in v. 11 is not clear. Were the other animals sacrificed on a different side? By and large, modern readers have ignored this detail, but it drew the attention of rabbinic readers. To explain this curiosity they turned to Genesis 22.

When our father Abraham bound Isaac his son, the Holy One (blessed be He!) established the institution of the two lambs (tamid), one in the morning and one in the evening (Exod. 29:38–42). Why so often (i.e. every single day, morning and evening)? Because when Israel would sacrifice the daily offering on the altar and recite this verse ("on the side of the altar *ṣ-p-n-h* before the LORD"), the Holy One (blessed be He!) would remember the binding of Isaac. (Lev. Rab. 2:11)[19]

I left *ṣ-p-n-h* untranslated because this is the key to the rabbinic interpretation. The Hebrew text was originally written without vowels and rabbinic readers always felt free to explore other ways of vocalizing words they found puzzling. In the traditional view, the consonants *ṣ-p-n-h* are rendered *ṣāpōnâ*, a directional term meaning "toward the north side," as a consultation of any modern translation of the Bible will confirm. But the rabbis eschewed the obvious sense of this word in order to create a linkage to the story of Isaac. They accomplished this by playfully misreading the word as *ṣəpūnâ*, a feminine passive participle meaning "hidden." The word "hidden" would then refer to the story of the binding of Isaac.[20] We could paraphrase the end of the midrash as follows: "Why sacrifice a lamb every morning and evening? Because when Israel would sacrifice those lambs on the altar and at the same time recite this verse—'hidden [*ṣəpūnâ*] before the LORD'—the Holy One (blessed be He!) would remember the binding of Isaac." In other words, in the rabbinic mind Israel's daily sacrificial service was nothing other than a memorial to the heroic self-offering of the patriarch Isaac. Every time Israel made her sacrifice on earth, God was prompted to remember the merits of Isaac "hidden" in heaven. And perhaps even more surprising, especially to the Christian reader who often thinks of Judaism in narrow and parochial terms, are the universal consequences of this foundational action:

19. My translation. Though this text is traditionally attributed to Leviticus Rabbah it is not original to that work. It is a later insertion that has found its way into most printed editions of the book. Originally the text belonged to *Tanna de-vei Eliyahu*. See the discussion of J. Kanarek, *Biblical Narrative and the Formation of Rabbinic Law* (Cambridge: Cambridge University Press, 2014), 58.

20. It should be noted that the repointing of the word "northward" to "hidden" does not, in and of itself, provide the link back to Isaac. One could imagine many things that might be "hidden" within the altar. Rather we must assume that the author of this midrash is working from a tradition that has already associated Isaac with the tamid and that he makes that preunderstanding explicit by grounding it in the word *ṣəpūnâ*.

I call heaven and earth to witness against me: Whenever anyone—Gentile or Jew, man or woman, male or female slave, reads this verse ("on the north-side before the LORD"), the Holy One (blessed be He!) remembers the binding of Isaac, as it is written: "on the north side in the presence of the LORD." (Lev. Rab. 2:11)

The notion that a meritorious action could serve as an aide-mémoire for the deity is reflected elsewhere in the Bible. In the book of Tobit, when the angel Raphael reveals his identity and the source of Tobit's good fortune, he declares that whenever Tobit risked his life to perform an act of corporal mercy (e.g., burying the dead) he would bring the *memorial* (*mnēmosynon*) of that action before the "glory of the Lord" (Tob. 12:12). Similarly, in the book of Acts when Cornelius is confronted by an angel of God he is told: "Your prayers and alms have ascended as a *memorial* (*mnēmosynon*) before God" (Acts 10:4). What the rabbis have done in this midrash is extend this notion to the binding of Isaac.[21]

The influence of this midrashic understanding is considerable. Many Jewish prayer books include the binding of Isaac at the beginning of the morning prayer service. And shortly afterward the text turns to the rites of the tamid. After reading the Torah portions devoted to the washing of hands (Exod. 30:17–21), attending to the wood (Lev. 6:1–6 [Hebrew]), and making the sacrifice itself (Num. 28:1–8 [= Exod. 29:38–42]), the text doubles back and includes the verse about slaughtering the animal on the "north side of the altar" (Lev. 1:11), a verse that links all these Levitical rituals back to its foundation narrative in Genesis.[22] There are also a number of medieval Bibles that include a picture of the binding of Isaac at the top of the opening chapter of Leviticus (fig. 8.3). This reflects an interpretive move similar to that of the mosaic at Sepphoris, the reader is directed back to Genesis 22 as the sacrifice that grounds all subsequent sacrifices at the altar.

One of the more striking features of this midrashic understanding of Leviticus 1:11 is the way it brings together the argument Moses made on behalf of sparing Israel (Exod. 32:13) and the role the binding of Isaac played in the establishment of Israel's sacrificial cult. Although the specific philological details of the midrash (reading "hidden" in place of "northward") are fanciful

---

21. Though we should note that the virtuous actions of Tobit and Cornelius were limited to their own person or immediate family. Abraham and Isaac, however, represented all of Israel and so the merits of their actions extended to the entire nation.

22. See Jonathan Sacks, ed., *The Koren Siddur* (Jerusalem: Koren, 2009), 42–45.

Figure 8.3 The opening chapter of the book of Leviticus, which describes the whole burnt offering; it is part of a manuscript of the Pentateuch, Germany, dated to 1340; Bodleian Library at Oxford, MS Opp. 14, folio 22v

and do not respect the literal sense, the association it presumes between this founding sacrifice and the promise it generates are profoundly biblical.

Attending to the Bible's Final Canonical Shape

I have devoted so much time to Aramaic Levi and the mosaic from Sepphoris because these two examples of ancient exegesis sensitively tease out what can be learned from the Bible's larger narrative arc. What is written in the book of Genesis can shed light on what we encounter in Exodus. With the rise of historical criticism and its interest in recovering the Bible's original sources, attention to the Bible's final form has suffered an eclipse. Modern scholars exhibit great anxiety over attempts to harmonize what are believed to be un-related narrative motifs. In this book, I have also presumed that the author of the Tabernacle Narrative knew nothing of the golden calf story that now cuts it in two. But this does not mean that the scribe (perhaps a priest himself) who inserted the golden calf story did so in a mindless fashion. I find it hard to believe that the ironical contrast between Moses's receipt of instructions for true worship and Israel's simultaneous pursuit of idolatry was not intended. The juxtaposition of these two stories creates a new level of meaning that neither story has on its own.

Sometimes the simple act of juxtaposing two independent stories provides the occasion for seeking a new level of meaning. But other times, the final shapers of the canon go further and insert verses—such as Genesis 2:4 and Exodus 31:18—to connect unrelated stories. In both of these examples we have a Priestly and non-Priestly narrative that were written independently but were self-consciously welded together by redactional verses placed at their seams.

But the final editors of the Bible were not concerned solely with linkages between adjoining stories. They also attempted to create bridges across bib-lical books. An example of this is the intercessory prayer of Moses recorded in Exodus. This Exodus version of the prayer expands an earlier, very generic appeal to the promise to the patriarchs in Deuteronomy to include the spe-cific terms of that promise in the second angelic address of Genesis 22 (and repeated in Gen. 26). In this way, a meritorious act of obedience became the focal element in an appeal for mercy before the divine tribunal.

Konrad Schmid believes that a similar level of textual dependence can be presumed for the onset of public sacrifice in Leviticus 9 and Genesis 22. Arguing from the presumption that Genesis 22 is a very late composition, he finds it impossible to imagine that this author would have been ignorant of the well-known Priestly narrative. The similar vocabulary between these two chapters, he claims, is the result of conscious borrowing. I do not share Schmid's confidence in this sort of historical reconstruction. I would contend that the linkage of Abraham's sacrifice to the tamid occurs at the level of the final canonical shaping of the biblical text. I think that Childs comes to a more measured and careful conclusion when he writes:

> The full implications of this witness (sc. Genesis 22) are not spelled out in this chapter. However, the exegetical effect of the formation of the larger canon (the Pentateuch) sets up a distant resonance between Genesis and Leviticus. The God who required and yet supplied his own sacrifice to Abraham, acts in a similar way in the institutionalized worship of Leviticus. Although the two witnesses are only indirectly related, Genesis 22 points in a direction which calls for fuller theological reflection on the whole sacrificial system of Leviticus in light of God's gracious revelation of his will to Abraham.[23]

Perhaps an analogy will help clarify the difference. Imagine that a homeowner goes to the store and picks out a woven wall hanging for her living room. Once it is installed, the colors assume a new role as they interact with the upholstery of the surrounding pieces of furniture and the color of the wall itself. The way this piece of art is viewed is now governed by its new environment. The creator of the wall hanging would have had one set of intentions regarding his selection of colors, but the room in which it was placed could overrule those intentions and alter the focus of the viewer.

And so for Childs's position regarding Genesis 22. Once the sacrificial texts of Exodus and Leviticus become part of a larger collection known as the Bible, the sacrifice of Abraham is read in light of its new environment. Schmid, on the other hand, presumes that our homeowner took note of the colors of her living room and then went into her workshop and manufactured a wall hanging to fit. On his view, there can be no gap between the intentions of the person who wove the hanging and its installer.

In order to lend more precision to this analogy it might be useful to consider the distinction Childs makes between textual witnesses and the underlying subject matter of the Bible as a whole. The exegetical task, in his mind, involves at least two stages. First is the identification of what each textual

23. So the general point made by Childs in n. 6 above.

witness wishes to say. In this instance, this would mean laying out the meaning of Genesis 22 and Exodus 29 in their immediate literary contexts. But exegesis cannot stop here lest the Bible be reduced to a catalogue of unrelated and perhaps competing viewpoints. The *witnesses* of Genesis 22 and Exodus 29, Childs contends, "are only indirectly related" because they were written independently of each other, each one for its own specific ends. But because they share a common *subject matter* ("The God who . . . supplied his own sacrifice to Abraham, acts in a similar way in the institutionalized worship of Leviticus"), they call for a deeper "theological reflection" on the subject of sacrifice more generally understood.

Aramaic Levi and the mosaic at Sepphoris are helpful resources for the interpreter because they demonstrate that early readers of the Bible were sensitive to these connections and pursued their deeper theological content. The modern reader, to be sure, will find some of the details of this exegesis to be rather fanciful and going well beyond the text's simple sense. For example, the notion that Abraham took special care to select certain species of wood for sacrifice and passed on that information to his son Isaac, who in turn relayed it to Levi, strains even the most vivid imagination! Yet, the inclination to see principles in Abraham's burnt offering that can inform all subsequent sacrifices is hardly unreasonable. The idea that the noun "northward" should be read as a passive participle, "hidden," is also an overly wrought product of the rabbinic imagination. But, at the same time, given the foundational role played by the sacrifice of Isaac in Moses's dispute with God (Exod. 32), it is not unreasonable to think that the daily tamid (Exod. 29) tapped into its power as well.

The issue at stake in this sort of interpretive deliberation, as Brevard Childs saw so well, concerns the underlying subject matter of the text. If we presume that Genesis 22 wants to say something about the fundamental character of sacrifice, and Exodus 29:38–42 is the founding sacrifice, then there are prima facie grounds for seeing a connection between the two. In chapter 4 we suggested that the tamid provides the liturgical occasion for Israel to serve her God through gifts. The binding of Isaac, on the other hand, is a demonstration of just how far the virtue of gift-giving can go. Does Abraham love his God so much that he will give that which he holds most dear? "Now I know that you fear God," declares the angel, "since you have not withheld your son, your only son, from me" (Gen. 22:12). Jon Levenson brilliantly captures the theological logic of this story when he writes that Abraham's willingness to donate his son not only allows him to "retain him, but to some degree merit the extraordinary promises that rest on his only/favored son. . . . In the paradoxical, sacrificial logic of which this text is the outstanding Jewish example, it is our ungrudging willingness to give that leads to gaining and retaining that which is most precious. It is in rising above self-interest that we secure that which a calculus of self-interest can never yield—or understand."[24] The final form of Israel's Torah allows the reader to see this story as not only establishing the privilege of Jerusalem as Israel's most holy site, but this particular burnt offering as the deepest expression of her devotion to and love for God. On this view, the tamid becomes the liturgical mechanism that re-presents this primordial act before the people Israel.[25]

---

24. Levenson, *Inheriting Abraham*, 84–85.

25. That this perspective has deep Jewish roots can be seen in a variety of places: Sepphoris, Leviticus Rabbah, the Jewish prayer book (*Siddur*), the illumination found on the first page of Leviticus, and the medieval theologian Hasdai Crescas. None of this, however, proves that this was the meaning intended by the original author of Genesis 22. It is, rather, an interpretive possibility that the final canonical form of the text has made possible. See my analogy of the wall hanging above.

CHAPTER 9

Incarnation

Now worship under the Law was a figure of the mystery of Christ, and so all their actions were a figure of things having to do with Christ.

St. Thomas Aquinas, *Summa theologiae*
I-II, Q. 102, A. 6

The problem of the early church was not what to do with the Old Testament in the light of the Gospel, but rather the reverse. In light of the Jewish scriptures, how were Christians to understand Jesus Christ?

Brevard Childs[1]

In these final two chapters I want to return to the themes raised at the beginning of this book. We noted that there are two thematic centers to the Tabernacle Narrative, each marked by its own theophany: the indwelling of the tabernacle and the service of God at his altar. For a Christian reader, these two themes have a natural affinity to the concepts of incarnation and atonement. Before we turn to these important correlates in the New Testament, it would be worthwhile to pause for a moment and consider how we are to understand the relationship between the two Testaments of the Christian Bible. Just as we saw in our previous chapter that the integrity of the final canonical form of the Jewish scriptures puts some pressure on the reader to articulate how the sacrificial character of Genesis 22 is to be related to the sacrificial cult established at the tabernacle, so the unity of the Christian Bible does the same regarding the way each Testament speaks to the themes of indwelling and sacrifice.

---

1. Brevard Childs, *Biblical Theology of the Old and New Testaments: Theological Reflection on the Christian Bible* (Minneapolis: Fortress, 1992), 226.

A Two Testament Bible

The best guide to this sort of challenge would be the work of the biblical scholar Brevard Childs. Over the course of his career he returned time and again to ponder how the Old Testament was related to the New. In his magnum opus, *Biblical Theology of the Old and New Testaments: Theological Reflection on the Christian Bible*, he wrote:

> At the heart of the problem of Biblical Theology lies the issue of doing full justice to the subtle canonical relationship of the two testaments within the one Christian Bible. On the one hand, the Christian canon asserts the continuing integrity of the OT witness. It must be heard on its own terms. On the other hand, the NT makes its own witness. It tells its own story of the new redemptive intervention of God in Jesus Christ. The NT is not just an extension of the Old, nor a last chapter in an epic tale. Something totally new has entered in the gospel.[2]

A few issues are worth flagging here. First, the New Testament is not simply an extension of the Old, as one might say of the Deuterocanonical books such as Tobit, Judith, or Ben Sira. Something radically new has occurred in the person of Jesus Christ. Elsewhere Childs writes, "it is basic to emphasize that something totally new began with the resurrection, and this sharp discontinuity in Israel's tradition is rightly reflected in the formation of two separate and distinct testaments. The old came to an end; the new began."[3] This is nicely illustrated in the Prologue of John's Gospel which traces an arc from creation to the tabernacling of the divine Word in the person of Jesus. As we saw, the contours of this arc derive from the Old Testament, but the conception of a person replacing the temple is without precedent.

Yet this "newness" manifested in the incarnation does not undercut the value or authority of the Jewish scriptures. Nevertheless, some have claimed that their ongoing authority for the early church only went as far as the explicit christological extensions that one could find in the New Testament. On this view, "the Old Testament provided a depository of imagery which could be freely construed to function as a prophetic warrant for the Christ event. Often its use entailed modification and alteration of the biblical text, and even outright rejection of large portions of the Old Testament in order to sustain

---

2. Childs, *Biblical Theology*, 78.
3. Childs, *Biblical Theology*, 225.

its new role within the church." Such a judgment, Childs concludes, "is highly misleading and one-sided in the extreme."

> Although it is obviously true that the Old Testament was interpreted in the light of the gospel, it is equally important to recognize that the New Testament tradition was fundamentally shaped from the side of the Old. The Old Testament was not simply a collage of texts to be manipulated; they were held as the authoritative voice of God, exerting a major coercion on the early church's understanding of Jesus's mission. In fact, the Jewish scriptures were the church's only Scripture well into the second century. As H. von Campenhausen has forcefully stated, the problem of the early church was not what to do with the Old Testament in the light of the gospel, which was Luther's concern, but rather the reverse. In the light of the Jewish scriptures acknowledged to be the true oracles of God, how were Christians to understand the good news of Jesus Christ?[4]

The Deference of the New Testament to the Old

Perhaps the best way to illustrate the continuing authority of the plain sense of the Old Testament is by way of an example. Christopher Seitz, perhaps the best known of Childs's many students, has thought long and hard about these issues. And the test case that animates much of his writing is the book of Isaiah. This book has long been dear to Christian readers, so dear, in fact, that Ambrose was known to refer to this venerable prophet as "the First Apostle" and instructed the newly converted Augustine to read this book carefully in order to learn about the gospel. Yet for all this, in a recent essay on the usage of Isaiah in the New Testament, Seitz comes to a startling observation. "What is striking," he concludes about all of these citations, "is that none of them pick up Isaiah's royal texts for their own sake to show that Jesus is the messiah promised of old by God's prophets."[5] One might presume that this conclusion would be hard to maintain in light of Matthew's first citation of Isaiah about the coming figure of Emmanuel (Isa. 7:14). Yet even in this citation the text-

---

4. Childs, *Biblical Theology*, 225–26; H. Von Campenhausen, *The Formation of the Christian Bible* (Philadelphia: Fortress, 1972).

5. Christopher Seitz, *Word without End: The Old Testament as Abiding Theological Witness* (Grand Rapids: Eerdmans, 1998), 216.

shows more interest in the virginal birth of Jesus and his divine origins than establishing the fact that he fulfills the full array of hopes attached to Israel's messianic faith.

Though it would be impossible to enter the minds of the various New Testament writers and know exactly what concerns dictated their use of the Old Testament, this reluctance to engage the powerful royal promises in Isaiah in favor of other themes, such as God's intention to incorporate the gentiles, is striking. For Seitz there are a number of answers that could be offered. Perhaps these promises of Isaiah were not compatible with the predominant interests of the early New Testament community. In this case, the most important point to be established was rather the authorization of the mission to the gentiles. Or maybe these promises, because they were so focused on glory, were not seen as fit instruments for rendering the unique picture of Israel's suffering messiah. Seitz evinces some unease with explanations such as these because they configure the picture as though the usage of the Old Testament in the early church was governed solely by the interests of the kerygmatic needs of the first apostles. In Christ all the answers were to be found; the Old Testament was simply mined for appropriate prooftexts. But what if we consider the matter from a quite different vantage point? What if Isaiah's own voice had not been lost from view but still continued to resound within the gathering halls of early Christian assemblies? What if the eschatological royal promises found in Isaiah—promises that seem so "over the top," promises that tell of all the nations streaming to Zion to hear God's Torah, the coming reign of Israel's king that will usher in a day when the wolf shall dwell with the lamb, the leopard shall lie down with the kid and neither the Sun nor moon will be required because God's own light will shine over all—continued to function as they did in Isaiah, as promises of what Christ's coming rule will bring to fulfillment?

Though it may be impossible to make any conclusive decisions about the intentions of the writers of the New Testament themselves, there can be no doubt that the early church heard eschatological texts such as these in precisely this fashion. Origen, for example, specifically says that the promise in Zechariah 9:9 regarding Israel's messiah entering Jerusalem on an ass fulfilled in Matthew 21:5 cannot be understood in a simple historical manner as though the events of Palm Sunday constituted the complete fulfillment of this messianic vision. As Origen's Jewish interlocutors made clear, the literary context of Zechariah makes such a reading impossible.[6] For in the verse immediately

---

6. Origen's discussion of the problem can be found in book 10 of his *Commentary on*

following the prediction of the Palm Sunday entrance Zechariah writes: "And he will destroy the chariots out of Ephraim, and the horse out of Jerusalem, and the bow for war will be destroyed, and a multitude and peace from the gentiles, and he will rule the waters to the sea and the springs of the rivers of the earth."[7] Yet nothing of the sort occurred during the last week of Jesus's earthly life. A simple promise-fulfillment reading, Origen concludes, cannot make sense of the narrative sequencing of Zechariah's own voice. And in this meeting of the two Testaments, Origen will not allow the voice of the Old Testament to be eviscerated in favor of its reception in the New.

The complex manner in which the church has heard the eschatological royal promises of the Old Testament is perhaps best illustrated in the liturgical celebration of Advent. For the church's celebration of Christ's advent contains two parts: first, the proclamation that the hope of Israel's restoration had appeared, but second, that the full scope of the kingdom he wished to inaugurate is yet to come. In short, the first advent of Israel's messiah does not result in the fulfillment of the full array of Israel's messianic hopes. God's intentions for his people and the world have not been brought to completion. In this fashion the recent document issued by the Pontifical Biblical Commission strikes exactly the right note:

> What has already been accomplished in Christ must yet be accomplished in us and in the world. The definitive fulfillment will be at the end with the resurrection of the dead, a new heaven and a new earth. Jewish messianic expectation is not in vain. It can become for us Christians a powerful stimulant to keep alive the eschatological dimension of our faith. Like them, we too live in expectation. The difference is that for us the One who is to come will have the traits of the Jesus who has already come and is already present and active among us.[8]

So in Advent Christians are put in the peculiar position of celebrating one advent while awaiting another. The readings of the first few Sundays are most

---

the Gospel of John. A convenient translation and discussion of the text can be found in Joseph Trigg, *Biblical Interpretation* (Wilmington, DE: Glazier, 1988), 105–6.

7. Trigg, *Biblical Interpretation.* The citation here, following the practice of Origen, is from the Greek translation of the Hebrew Bible.

8. Pontifical Biblical Commission, "The Jewish People and their Sacred Scriptures in the Christian Bible" (Vatican City: Vatican Press, 2002), 60. The text can be found at: www.vatican.va/roman_curia/congregations/cfaith/pcb_documents/rc_con_cfaith_doc _20020212_popolo-ebraico_en.html.

explicit here, for their apocalyptic tenor clearly puts most of the emphasis on the second coming. Paradoxically, it is in the liturgical celebration of Advent that Jewish and Christian messianic hopes come together in the closest possible way. The Old Testament is not simply a pointer to the New—even in regard to the messiah—but an independent witness whose integrity must still be respected.

And what is the rub for us? It is that Isaiah's full eschatological horizon is not exhausted by the appearance of the earthly Jesus. In the church's elaboration of her eschatological hopes she *defers* to the larger scope of Isaiah's eschatological horizon. Seitz writes:

> But the larger point is that the horizon of Isaiah in respect of royal promises is not a past fulfillment in Jesus that validates Christian hopes and invalidates those of the Jews. In Advent we do not just look back nostalgically on a perfect fit between the prophet's longings and their absolute fulfillment in Christ: like arrows hitting a bull's-eye. Instead, Isaiah's horizon remains the final horizon for Jew and Christian and Gentile: Christ's coming, Christ's advent in glory and in judgment. This is absolutely consistent with the New Testament's own per se witness to Isaiah, as we have seen by tracking how Isaiah is heard *in novo receptum*, where Isaiah's promises are not explicitly referred to as fulfilled but *deferred* [emphasis mine] to as *per se* promises yet to be fulfilled.[9]

Israel's hope has not been superceded. Rather, the church's true frame for construing the role of the earthly Jesus in ushering in the kingdom has been interpreted so as to conform to the larger horizon of Old Testament expectation. The Old Testament is not simply *background* to the gospel; it is part of the very fabric of the gospel whose full meaning can only be articulated by a conversation between the two.

The Word Became Flesh and Tabernacled among Us

One of the most often cited texts from the Gospel of John is the line from the Prologue that reads, "the Word became flesh and dwelt among us." Though many Christian readers of this verse will presume instantly that they know what this is all about, it must be said that this exegetical confidence comes

9. Seitz, *Word without End*, 227.

not so much from the simple sense of John's Gospel as from the influence of the rule of faith or creed on what is at stake. One meaning, however, is ruled out, even among the most ardent supporters of Chalcedon: the flesh of Jesus is not wholly convertible with the being of God. The Logos does not become the physical body of Jesus without remainder. But, on the other hand, the flesh cannot be a purely accidental feature unrelated to the task of identifying the Second Person of the Trinity.

The German New Testament scholar Klaus Berger has provided sufficient grounds for seeing why this text has been such a controverted problem in early Christianity.[10] For Berger, following in part the lead of Käsemann, the Prologue of John is still a long way from what will become the standard christological teaching of the church. That the word becomes flesh does not imply any sort of intrinsic relation between the two. Rather, the flesh and bones of this first-century Jew are merely the accidental occasion for a momentary epiphany of the Logos or divine Word. As proof for his thesis, he refers us to a document known in Greek as the *Paraleipomena Jeremiou* (Things left out of the book of Jeremiah), also known as 4 Baruch, which probably dates to sometime after the destruction of the temple by the Romans in 70 CE. In this text we read of an eagle sent by Baruch to Jeremiah and his exilic brethren in Babylonia.[11] At precisely the moment of its arrival, Jeremiah and a coterie of exiled Judeans are making their way outside the city to bury a corpse. The eagle suddenly speaks and says, "I say to you Jeremiah, the chosen one of God, go and gather together the people and come here so that they may hear a letter which I have brought to you from Baruch and Abimelech" (4 Bar. 7:16). As the eagle begins to descend, it alights upon the corpse whereupon it miraculously revives. The narrator remarks that all "this took place so that they might believe." Then the people rise up and solemnly acclaim: "Is this not God who appeared to our fathers in the wilderness through Moses and now in the form of an eagle he has appeared to us" (7:20).[12] Berger remarks: "As in the first chapter of John, there is found here, a statement of identification (the eagle is God) and a statement as to how it came to this identity. From the manner of its coming to this identity

---

10. Klaus Berger, "Zu 'Das Wort ward Fleisch' Joh. 1 14a," *NovT* 16 (1974): 161–66.

11. See the recent bilingual edition of Robert Kraft and Ann-Elizabeth Purintun, *Paraleipomena Jeremiou* Texts and Translations 1 (Missoula: Scholars Press, 1972). The section that tells the story about the eagle can be found in 7:1–23.

12. I have slightly adjusted the translation given by Kraft and Purintun, *Paraleipomena Jeremiou*.

it is clear that we are not talking about a transformation of the eagle into a god, but of God's presence being momentarily manifest in the eagle."[13]

My point is not to say that Berger is correct in identifying this text as an apt parallel to the Christology of the Prologue. I doubt that Raymond Brown would have found this thesis compelling. But it should also be noted that Brown recognized the persuasive elements in Käsemann's position, which is closely related. Brown writes that Käsemann "insists that the scandal [of the incarnation] consists in the presence of God among men and not its becoming flesh—not the how, but the fact. For Käsemann verse 14a ["the word became flesh"] says no more than 10a, 'He was in the world.' The parallelism between 14a and 14b ["and made his dwelling among us"] gives support to Käsemann's contention."[14] The point I would like to emphasize here is that identifying Jesus as "the Word made flesh" does not inexorably point to the high Christology of Chalcedon. In brief, to repeat a line found in many handbooks on patristic theology, there were good exegetical grounds for many of the positions that the latter church would deem heretical.

What is striking, however, when one turns to patristic attempts to sort out the various exegetical options for the phrase "the Word became flesh," is that these writers operate in a manner quite different from the guild of modern New Testament studies. They do not marshal their arguments solely within the ambit of the New Testament documents and their near historical relations. Rather, the Old Testament functions as an equally powerful source for rebutting the views of those professing a low Christology. It is here that the words of Childs have real force: "The Old Testament was not simply a collage of texts

13. Berger, "Das Wort ward Fleisch," 163. Berger's essay is a response to the two-part essay of G. Richter, "Die Fleischwerdung des Logos im Johannesevangelium," *NovT* 13 (1971): 81–126, and "Die Fleischwerdung des Logos im Johannesevangelium (Forsetzung)," *NovT* 14 (1972): 257–76, who argues that John 1:14 declares that the Word truly became flesh. For Berger, the meaning of the Greek is the opposite of what Richter maintains: "Erscheinen in einer Gestalt, ohne damit diese zu 'werden.'" Strikingly, he compares this extrinsic connection of Logos to flesh to the way God inhabits a temple (164): "Das Erscheinen des Christus im Fleisch und das Wohnen unter/in der Gemeinde bedeutet also nicht, dass der Kyrios mit diesen Menschen identisch wird, sondern dass er in ihnen als in einem heiligen Tempel wohnt (so wie man es sonst vom Pneuma sagt)." This precise question, whether God appeared in the flesh or became that very flesh, was the subject of enormous disagreement in the fourth- and fifth-century christological controversies.

14. Raymond Brown, *The Gospel according to John I–XII*, AB 29 (Garden City, NY: Doubleday, 1966), 31.

to be manipulated, but the Jewish Scriptures were held as the authoritative voice of God, exerting a major coercion on the early Church's understanding of Jesus' [person]."[15]

In the case of the incarnation, one common point of reference in the Old Testament was that of God's dwelling within the temple or tabernacle of Israel. And indeed, that very symbol is explicitly alluded to in the Johannine Prologue. For John not only declares that the Word has become flesh but that it "dwelt among us, and we have seen its glory, the glory of a father's only son." The key clause in establishing that this text speaks to the matter of the temple is the phrase, "he dwelt among us." The Greek verb *skēnoō* clearly refers to the story of the tabernacle in Exodus. As Raymond Brown remarks, "we are being told that the flesh of Jesus Christ is the new localization of God's presence on earth, and that Jesus is the replacement of the ancient tabernacle."[16] And as such this idea nicely dovetails with another major feature of this Gospel, which is that Jesus is "the replacement of the temple (2:19–22)," which, Brown adds, is simply "a variation of the same theme."

Brown also notes the very important linkage between the "tenting" of the Word and its becoming visible to the naked eye. "In the OT," he observes, "the *glory* of God (Heb. *kabod*; Gr. *doxa*) implies a visible and powerful manifestation of God to men." Then, after reviewing several biblical texts that describe the appearance of God at the site of a temple, he concludes that "it is quite appropriate that, after the description of how the Word set up a tabernacle among men in the flesh of Jesus, the prologue should mention that his *glory* became visible."[17]

To borrow the terminology of Seitz, we could say that the author of the Gospel of John doesn't elaborate this point of how Jesus and the temple are similar because he presumes that his readers will bring to this text a knowledge of how God had indwelt the temple within Israel herself. (And this is precisely the value of Brown's commentary on John that I cited above; he locates those

15. Childs, *Biblical Theology*, 226.

16. Brown, *John I–XII*, 33. Three recent works have treated this theme at great length: Craig Evans, *Words and Glory: On the Exegetical Background of John's Prologue*, JSNTSup 89 (Sheffield: Sheffield Academic, 1993), 77–113; A. Kerr, *The Temple of Jesus' Body: The Temple Theme in the Gospel of John*, JSNTSup 220 (Sheffield: Sheffield Academic, 2002); and Craig Koester, *The Dwelling of God: The Tabernacle in the Old Testament, Intertestamental Jewish Literature, and the New Testament* (Washington, DC: Catholic Biblical Association, 1989), 100–115.

17. Brown, *John I–XII*, 34.

sections within the Old Testament that cast light upon the terse formulation in John.) Reading the Gospel of John in terms of its present canonical placement within a two-part Bible, one could say that this Gospel defers to the Old Testament. The very form of the Christian Bible asks the reader to look backwards to Exodus 25–40 and informs him or her that if you want to know more, you should then compare these two moments of divine indwelling. And indeed, this is exactly the hermeneutical path followed by St. Athanasius in his "Letter to Adelphius."[18]

For St. Athanasius (fourth century) there was only one answer to the question as to how the body of Jesus is related to the Godhead: the flesh of Jesus *participates* in the divinity of the indwelling *Logos.* The manner by which Athanasius arrives at this conclusion depends on a construal of the biblical temple as a structure that *physically* participates in the life of the God who inhabits it. In this document Athanasius is concerned about the readiness of his opponents "*to divide*" the person of Christ into two: his human side and his divine side. But to do so, Athanasius claims, would be idolatrous for when Christians prostrate themselves before Jesus they do so before the whole person, flesh and body. If the two are divisible, then the act of venerating the person Jesus results in the worship of a creature. "And we do not worship a creature," Athanasius declares. "And neither do we divide the body from the Word and worship it by itself; nor when we wish to worship the Word do we set Him far apart from the flesh, but knowing, as we said above, that 'the Word was made flesh' (John 1:14) we recognize Him as God also, after having come in the flesh." And how can an argument for this point be derived from scripture? By attending to the practice of the Jewish pilgrimage feasts testified to in the Jewish scriptures.

[7] But we should like your piety to ask them this. When Israel was ordered to go up to Jerusalem to worship at the temple of the Lord, where the ark was, "and above it the Cherubim of glory overshadowing the Mercy-seat" (Heb 9:5) did they do well or the opposite? If they did ill, how came it that they who despised this law were liable to punishment? For it is written that if a man make light of it and go not up, he shall perish from among the people (cf. Num 9:13). But if they did well, and in this proved well-pleasing to God are not the Arians, abominable and most shameful of any heresy, many times worthy of destruction, in that while they approve the former People for the honor paid by them to the temple,

18. Translation from *NPNF*² 4:577.

they will not worship the Lord Who is in the flesh as in a temple? And yet the former temple was constructed of stones and gold, as a shadow. But when the reality came, the type ceased from thenceforth, and there did not remain according to the Lord's utterance, one stone upon another that was not broken down (Matt 24:2). And they did not, when they saw the temple of stones, suppose that the Lord who spoke in the temple was a creature; nor did they set the temple at nought and retire far off to worship. But they came to it according to the Law, and worshipped the God who uttered His oracles from the temple. Since then this was so, how can it be other than right to worship the Body of the Lord, all-holy and all-reverend as it is, announced by the Holy Spirit, and made the Vesture of the Word? It was at any rate a bodily hand that the Word stretched out to raise her that was sick of a fever (Mk 1:31); a human voice that He uttered to raise Lazarus from the dead (John 11:43); and once again, stretching out His hands upon the Cross, He overthrew the prince of the power of the air, that now works in the sons of disobedience, and made the way clear for us into the heavens.

[8] Therefore he that dishonors the temple dishonors the Lord in the temple; and he that separates the Word from the Body sets at nought the grace given to us in Him. And let not the most impious Arian madmen suppose that, since the body is created, the Word also is a creature, nor let them, because the Word is a creature, disparage His Body. For their error is a matter for wonder, in that they at once confuse and disturb everything, and devise pretexts only in order to number the Creator among the creatures. (Athanasius, *Letter 40: To Adelphius Bishop and Confessor, Against the Arians* 7–8)

Athanasius's point is crystal clear. Just as the Jews had complete justification in prostrating themselves before a building of stone and not dividing the God from the house in which he dwelt—for though they knew God was not limited to any material structure, they did not use this fact as due cause for not going up to Jerusalem—so Christians have complete justification in prostrating themselves before Jesus and not dividing the indwelling God from the flesh that contains him. But equally clear is the hermeneutical direction of his argument. The New Testament does not cast light on the dark shadows of the Old. Rather, the somewhat hasty and quite brief description of the New finds a needed deepening and elaboration from the Old.

Toward a Theology of the Temple and Its Furnishings

But it could be objected that Athanasius has based his christological argument on thin exegetical grounds. Is it really the case that the Israelites paid honor to the temple itself on the grounds that in doing so they were honoring the God who dwelt within? Many readers of the Bible, I think, would reflexively answer: "No!" But our review of this problem in chapter three showed how mistaken such an answer would be. As Numbers 4:17–20 demonstrates so clearly, seeing the furniture of the temple is akin to seeing the very face of God and, as a result, approaching the furniture, like approaching God, is an activity subject to the most extreme sorts of spiritual and bodily preparation. The Jewish biblical scholar Jon Levenson observes that texts such as this "provide us with a different mode of spiritual experience from that [the aural forms] associated with Mount Sinai."[19] For at Sinai, the imageless nature of the deity is so deliberately and powerfully emphasized that one might conclude that the Israelite deity was one who revealed himself solely by decree. The militantly aniconic tone of these texts would seem to rule out any revelatory dimension to the visual. But in the texts we have examined, "it is the eye which [having beheld the temple] . . . communicates the nature of God and his special relationship to Israel."[20]

In rabbinic midrash the matter was taken one step further. In several biblical texts Israel is commanded to come to the temple on pilgrimage three times during the year "to see the Lord God."[21] The rabbis were certainly aware that the Bible only on the rarest of occasions describes the actual appearance of the Holy One in a theophany at the temple. The question then, was just how could this commandment be fulfilled? One rabbinic text suggests that during the days of a temple feast the curtains of the temple were pulled back so that the gathered throng of Israelites could gaze on the furniture: "R. Kattina said:

19. Jon Levenson, *Sinai and Zion: An Entry into the Jewish Bible* (San Francisco: Harper & Row, 1985), 150.

20. Levenson, *Sinai and Zion*, 150–51.

21. See Exodus 23:17 and parallels. It should be noted that the Massoretes vocalized the verb "to see" in this verse in the passive voice so that nearly all translations read: "to appear [sc. to be seen] before the Lord." It has long been recognized that the original vocalization of the verb was most likely in the active voice, "to see the Lord." This was already noted by Luzzatto, *Sefer Yeshayahu* (Padua, 1855), *ad* Isa. 1:12; cf. August Dillmann, *Die Bücher Exodus and Leviticus* (Leipzig: Hirzel, 1897), 276. It is worth noting that the rabbinic literature preserves solid evidence that the active form of the verb was read in the first few centuries of the common era as well. See S. Naeh, "Ha-im em la-Massoret?," *Tarbiz* 61 (1992): 413 (Hebrew).

Whenever Israel came up to the Festival, the curtain would be removed for them and the Cherubim were shown to them, whose bodies were intertwined with one another, and they would be thus addressed: Look! You are beloved before God as the love between man and woman" (b. Yoma 54a). Another text ascribes the defining mark of the Israelite people as the particular ability to gaze upon the being of God contained within the sacred ark:

> The Queen of Sheba brought circumcised and uncircumcised persons before Solomon. They were of similar appearance, height, and dress. She said to him, "Distinguish for me the circumcised from the uncircumcised." Immediately Solomon gestured to the high priest and he opened the Ark of the Covenant. Those who were circumcised bent over half-way but no more so that their faces might be filled with the radiance of the Shekinah. The uncircumcised promptly fell to the ground upon their faces. Solomon said to her, "The former ones are the circumcised and the latter are the uncircumcised." She said, "How do you know this?" He answered, "Is it not written about Balaam, 'he who gazes upon the sight of the Almighty, [fallen (partly over) but with eyes unveiled]?' (Num 24:4). Had he fallen completely to the ground, he would not have seen anything."[22]

Finally, there are other rabbinic texts that suggest that the furniture that was housed within the temple was brought out to the forecourt so that pilgrims could view it while they stood before the altar. Here the act of seeing would not be defined solely by the occasional theophany but by the ability to gaze and meditate on the material structure of the temple itself. Similarly, a whole variety of Second Temple Jewish texts develop at some length the tradition that the most precious vessels of the temple were sealed in a secret location so that the Babylonian invaders could not profane them when they destroyed the temple.[23] The only way to understand these materials is against the background of a very high theology of temple artifacts. So closely bound up were they with the identity of God that they could not be exposed to the ravages of war and exile. As God sits in anxious patience awaiting the day he can reenter

<hr>

22. *Midrash Mishle*, ed. B. Visotsky (New York: Jewish Theological Seminary, 1990), 6.
23. The hiding of the temple vessels was a widespread theme in the literature of the Second Temple and rabbinic eras. See P. R. Ackroyd, "The Temple Vessels—a Continuity Theme," in *Studies in the Religion of Ancient Israel*, VTSup 23 (Leiden: Brill, 1973), 166–81; George Nickelsberg, "Narrative Traditions in the Paralipomena of Jeremiah and 2 Baruch," *CBQ* 35 (1973): 60–68; Marilyn F. Collins, "The Hidden Vessels in Samaritan Traditions," *JSJ* 3 (1972): 97–116.

his shrine in Jerusalem, so his furniture stands at the ready for the advent of this momentous return.

We might note too at this point the argument of the Jewish theologian Michael Wyschogrod.[24] Though Jews have been reluctant to concede to the doctrine of the incarnation any truth whatsoever, Wyschogrod argues that there is no way that Judaism can rest content with a God who has no spatial location whatsoever. For Judaism has the audacity to claim that God has an address.

> There is a place where he dwells and that place is Jerusalem. He dwells in Number One Har Habayit Street. It is a real dwelling and for every Jew, the sanctity of the land of Israel derives from the sanctity of Jerusalem, and the sanctity of Jerusalem derives from the sanctity of the temple, and the sanctity of the temple derives from the sanctity of the holy of holies where God dwells.[25]

Of course, the hallowed nature of the Western Wall—the last remaining sign of the venerable structure of the temple—gives elegant testimony to this, as does the tradition of the hidden temple vessels. But Wyschogrod's point is deeper than this. For if God can have an earthly address, then his identity must have some spatial dimension.

> God has undertaken to enter the world and to dwell in a place. That, of course, is still a far distance from saying that God dwells in a particular human being and that as a particular human being walks by us—there is God walking! On the other hand, it is the dimension of spatiality, of the presence of God in a particular place, which would not be possible if there were not some sense in which God has entered space and therefore some sense in which incarnational thinking is justified.[26]

The Temple and Incarnation among the Antiochenes

At this point it should be obvious that texts such as John 1:14 compelled Christian thinkers to consider the singularity of the incarnation against the background of God's indwelling of the temple. Given the importance of this christological theme in the Bible and the early church, one might have expected

---

24. M. Wyschogrod, "Incarnation," *Pro Ecclesia* 2 (1993): 208–15.
25. Wyschogrod, "Incarnation," 210.
26. Wyschogrod, "Incarnation," 211.

that this "temple theology" would have had a long afterlife. But it does not go much further than Athanasius. This is because of what happens within the school of Antiochene Christianity. There, already with the figure of Theodore of Mopsuestia, it is propounded that God abandons Jesus at his passion and lets the man suffer on his own. Though the textual justification is grounded in a textually problematic verse from Hebrews, the larger thematic argument comes from the metaphor of a temple.[27] For though God can indwell a temple such that his presence infuses even the furniture and masonry, he can also depart from a temple and go into exile. Ezekiel is the best witness to this theologoumenon. For in a famous section of his book, he articulates in considerable detail how God mounted his chariot throne in the holy of holies and departed the temple, making it completely vulnerable to the assaults of the Babylonian invaders (Ezek. 8–11).

Pursuing this aspect of temple theology to its logical end, Theodore, and later most notoriously Nestorius (early fifth century), argued that the indwelling of God in Jesus's body, like a temple, is a wholly extrinsic affair. There was no intrinsic relationship between the temple and the deity who resided within. God was free to come and go at his leisure. And such was the method of reading the Gospels evidenced by Nestorius and his circle. In some parts of the Gospel story we see only the weak human body that Jesus inhabits; in other parts the deity bursts onto the scene. At the crucifixion, God literally departs from his temple and leaves the man Jesus to die on his own.

Theodore's position is well illustrated in his *Commentary on the Nicene Creed*.[28] Throughout this text Theodore distinguishes what happened to the man Jesus—here described as the material framework of the temple—in contrast to God who resided within him, here understood like the glory of the LORD that sits atop the ark and is free to come and go as it pleases. As a result, Theodore could not countenance any sort of "strong-reading" of John 1:14; the Word appears in the flesh but does not in any way become flesh.[29]

---

27. Theodore grounded this remarkable assertion in a textual variant of Hebrews 2:9. "And in order to teach us why He suffered and became 'a little lower [than the angels]' he said: 'Apart from God [in place of, 'by the grace of God'] He tasted death for every man.' In this he shows that the Divine nature willed that He should taste death for the benefit of every man, and also that the Godhead was separated from the one who was suffering in the trial of death, because it was impossible for Him to taste the trial of death if (the Godhead) were not cautiously remote from Him." From A. Mingana, ed., *Theodore of Mopsuestia on the Nicene Creed*, Woodbrook Studies 5 (Cambridge: Heffer, 1932), 86–87.

28. Mingana, *Theodore of Mopsuestia on the Nicene Creed*.

29. See the good discussion of Frances M. Young, *From Nicaea to Chalcedon* (Lon-

It is not Divine nature that received death, but it is clear that it was that man who was assumed as a temple to God the Word which was dissolved and then raised by the one who had assumed it. And after the Crucifixion it was not Divine nature that was raised but the temple which was assumed, which rose from the dead, ascended to heaven and sat at the right hand of God; nor is it to Divine nature—the cause of everything—that it was given that every one should worship it and every knee should bow, but worship was granted to the form of a servant which did not in its nature possess (the right to be worshipped). While all these things are clearly and obviously said of human nature he referred them successively to Divine nature so that his sentence might be strengthened and be acceptable to hearers. Indeed, since it is above human nature that it should be worshipped by all, it is with justice that all this has been said as of one, so that the belief in a close union between the natures might be strengthened, because he clearly showed that the one who was assumed did not receive all this great honor except from the Divine nature which assumed Him and dwelt in Him.[30]

If this text is read side by side that of Athanasius, one can see significant points of continuity. And this should occasion no surprise, for Theodore thought of himself as a vigorous defender of Nicene orthodoxy. Athanasius's opponents were his own opponents. Most important in this regard is his claim that because God indwelt Jesus as he had dwelled in Israel's temple, so one can worship and bend the knee toward Jesus. Theodore, however, goes one step further. He takes special pains to emphasize the division between the body and the God who indwelt it. The relationship between the two bespeaks, to be sure, "a close union between the natures," but a union that remains sufficiently divisible such that God can abandon this temple and three days later raise it up. Proper gospel interpretation, by extension, requires the ability to divide the human figure from the divine being who indwells him. This propensity to

---

don: SCM, 1983), 209: "The Logos could not move from place to place, nor 'become' flesh except *kata to dokein*—he meant 'metaphorically' rather than 'docetically' because he continued: 'In appearance, not in the sense that he did not take real flesh, but in the sense that he did not become flesh.' For Theodore truer expressions are to be found in the phrases 'he tabernacled among us' or 'he assumed flesh'—'flesh' being a term which he explicitly takes to mean human nature in its entirety. So the incarnation could not imply any change in the essential Godhead any more than it could undermine the autonomy of the manhood."

30. Mingana, *Theodore of Mopsuestia on the Nicene Creed*, 66.

divide the person of Christ met extreme resistance in the person of Cyril of Alexandria and the controversy that erupted between him and Nestorius.

Mary and the Temple

In the aftermath of the Nestorian controversy the temple metaphor as a means of understanding the incarnation was categorically rejected. Leo the Great's homilies on the nativity make this clear:

> For this wondrous child-bearing of the holy Virgin produced in her off-spring one person which was truly human and truly Divine, because nei-ther substance so retained their properties that there could be any divi-sion of persons in them; *nor was the creature taken into partnership with its Creator in such a way that the One was the in-dweller, and the other the dwelling,* but so that the one nature was blended with the other.[31]

In this text Leo desires to make clear that the concept of a "close union" be-tween deity and humanity that Theodore favored was not adequate for defin-ing the christological mystery. What was needed was an idiom of speech that allowed the two natures to interpenetrate one another so fully that such a separation would be very difficult. For these purposes the doctrine of *commu-nicatio idiomatum* (what can be predicated of the divine can also be said of the human and vice versa) provided far better service. In this vein, the metaphor

31. Leo the Great, *Sermon* 23.1 [3.1] (emphasis mine). The text can be found in *NPNF*[2] 12:132. For Leo it is crucial that there be no division between God and man in the person of Jesus Christ. As a result, the temple metaphor, as deployed by the Antiochene school, is allowed no place at the table. In Leo's mind, Nestorius had effectively divided the in-dweller (God the Son) from the dwelling (Jesus as man) and hence ruled out any direct comparison of Jesus to the temple. For the Latin original, see Léon le Grand, *Sermons*, ed. Dom René Dolle, 2nd ed., SC 22 (Paris: Cerf, 1964), 94–99. The note appended by Dom René Dolle, the editor of the text, is worth citing: "C'était là, en effet, une expression employée par Nestorius pour caractériser l'union du Verbe divin avec l'homme Jésus. Dans une letter à S. Cyrille, il écrivait: 'Il est exact et conforme à la tradition évangélique, d'affirmer que le corps du Christ est le temple de la divinité' (PG 77, 49), texte qui pouvait certes s'entendre dans un sens orthodoxe mais qui prenait un sens très particulier dans le contexte de pensée nestorienne; par ailleurs le XIe Anathématisme de saint Cyrille s'exprimait ainsi: 'Quiconque ne confesse pas que la chair du Seigneur donne la vie et qu'elle est la proper chair du Logos divin, mais pretend qu'elle appartient à un autre que lui, qui ne lui est uni que par la dignité et qui a servi de demeure à la divinité'" (97 n. 3).

of the temple would no longer be appropriate because Ezekiel's depiction of the exile allowed one to construe the relation of the indweller to the dwelling in a far too casual manner.

But then what became of the rich temple language of the Old Testament once it lost its natural connection to the person of Christ? It was far too central a witness to be passed over in silence. If the integrity of the character of God across the two Testaments was to be preserved, the metaphor of the temple could not be ignored. The logical place to turn was the womb of the Virgin Mary. That person who would be identified in the iconographic tradition as "the container of the uncontainable"—an unmistakable allusion to the God of Israel, whose being could not be contained even by the highest of the heavens (1 Kings 8:27) yet nevertheless deigned to dwell in Jerusalem—proved a fit dwelling wherein the Creator of the universe could find habitation. Leo writes:

> For the uncorrupt nature of Him that was born had to guard the primal virginity of the Mother, and the infused power of the *Divine Spirit had to preserve intact the chamber of chastity and the dwelling place of holiness that it had chosen for itself*: that Spirit (I say) who had determined to raise the fallen, to restore the broken, and by overcoming the allurements of the flesh to bestow on us in abundant measure the power of chastity: in order that the virginity which in others cannot be retained in child-bearing, might be attained by them at their second birth.[32]

Mary does not become God, of course, but she does "house" God in the most intimate way imaginable. The extrinsic manner of relating God to temple is put to good use: Mary both receives the divine son and gives birth to him. But in the logic of the incarnation this moment transforms her forever. Her body remains holy forever thereafter as a result of housing the Holy One of Israel. And as the temple could be revered and praised on its own terms without any worry of committing some form of idolatrous apostasy, so Mary could be revered and adored, not as a god(dess), but as the one who housed God. If one could turn to the temple and say, "how lovely is thy dwelling place" and attend to its every architectural detail, why would one not do the same with the Theotokos?

---

32. Sermon 22, in *NPNF*² 12:130 (emphasis mine). For the Latin, see SC 22:80–81. I have slightly altered the English translation. My thanks to Brian Daley for assisting me with the Latin.

In late Byzantine hymns to Mary, the temple imagery reaches new heights. Indeed a brief scansion of the patristic homilies that Brian Daley has collected and edited in his fine volume on the Assumption of the Blessed Virgin reveals how important the Old Testament stories about the tabernacle and temple were for the construction of her character.[33] Almost anything that was said about this Old Testament precursor became fair game for depicting the life of the Virgin Mary that the New Testament authors in their great modesty "neglected" to tell us. Consider this sample from John of Damascus:

> And so your holy, spotless body is committed to a reverent burial, as angels go before you and stand around you and follow after, doing all the things by which it is fitting to serve the mother of their Lord. The Apostles, too, are there, and all the full membership of the Church, crying out divine hymns to the music of the harp of the Spirit: "holy is your temple, wonderful because of God's salvation" (Ps 64:5) and again, "the most High has made his tabernacle holy" (Ps 45:5), and "God's mountain is a mountain of plenty, the mountain where God is pleased to dwell" (Ps 67:16). The company of the Apostles lift you up on their shoulders, the true ark of the Lord God, as once the priests lifted up the typological ark that pointed the way to you. Your immaculate, completely spotless body was not left on earth, but you have been transported to the royal dwelling-place of heaven as queen, as lady, as mistress, as Mother of God, as the one who truly gave birth to God.[34]

Or in turn, consider the description of the procession of Mary's bier from Mount Zion to Gethsemane found in Theoteknos of Livias. It is created, in large part, from stories about the procession of the ark in the Old Testament.

> [6] The all-blessed body, then, of the holy one was being carried towards the place I have mentioned, accompanied by angels' songs of praise; and the unbelieving Jews, who had killed the Lord, looking down the valley, saw her remains lying on the bier and went towards it, intending to do violence in that very spot to the body which God had honored; his temple, his lampstand, his vessel containing the pure oil, his altar of holocausts, appearing in splendor within the Holy of Holies.

33. Brian E. Daley, *On the Dormition of Mary: Early Patristic Homilies* (Crestwood, NY: St. Vladimir's Seminary Press, 1998).

34. Daley, *On the Dormition*, 197–98.

All those who meant to attack her and to burn her body were struck with blindness; and one of them, who touched her bier with his own hands, was deprived of them—they were cut off! (cf. II Sam 6). So that immaculate flesh was glorified; all of them came to believe and confessed her Mother of God, and the one whom they had vilified as a seductress they now praised in song as God's own mother. And those who had lost their sight saw the wonders worked by God toward his mother. . . . For a wonderful thing happened: the hands of the one who had lost them [were restored to him.] And all believed in Christ, who was before her and from her and with her, "the Son of David according to the flesh" (Rom 1:3).

Let no one think that the miracle worked by the all-holy body of the Mother of God was something impossible—for she had remained a virgin incorrupt. It was, after all, fitting for the spiritual ark, which contained the vessel of manna and the blooming rod of Aaron (Num 17:8), for she blossomed and bore the fruit that can never be consumed. The former ark defeated the hostile foreigners, who wanted to do it violence; how much more, then should the spiritual ark defeat those who from the beginning have fought against God and against the beautiful name "that is invoked over us" (Jer 14:9).

[7] For she is ark and vase and throne and heaven. She was judged worthy to be entrusted with ineffable mysteries; she was judged worthy to reveal things hidden and sealed in the Book of Daniel, and through her "all of us, with faces unveiled, will gaze on the glory of the Lord (2 Cor 3:18). Through her, the veil on Moses' face has been lifted.[35]

The cult of Mary in the medieval period is greatly indebted to this development. But I would commit a grave error if I left my story in this simple developmental sequence. To be sure, temple images for Jesus become difficult to sustain after Chalcedon and their logical referent becomes that of the Virgin Mary. But it is not accurate to say that Mary's character is developed in a whole new direction. One thinks, for example, of the Protevangelium of James, an ancient apocryphal Gospel that dates to sometime within the second century.[36] The central purpose of this text is to tell the story of the birth of Jesus

---

35. Daley, *On the Dormition*, 75–76.

36. On the importance of this text and a good account of how the figure of Mary is ordered to a specific christological end, see M. Bockmuehl, *Ancient Apocryphal Gospels* (Louisville: Westminster John Knox, 2017), 66–67: "Th[is] *Infancy Gospel* [Bockmuehl's term for the work] is an early example of Marian theology in the service of Christology. . . . The *Infancy Gospel of James* thus sets a highly influential precedent for Christian doctrine

through the lens of Mary, beginning with the account of her miraculous birth to her parents, Anna and Joachim, who previously appeared unable to have children. Like Hannah in the book of Samuel, Anna and Joachim turn their child over to the priests at the temple, where she resided from her third year forward. When she had reached the age of twelve, she was appointed to spin the fabrics that would be used for the temple veil. It was during her time in this profession that the angel Gabriel appeared to her and announced that she would conceive the Christ child. And so the theology of John 1:14 was ampli-fied in a Marian direction: she who was to bear the Word of God was also the one who fashioned the fabrics of the temple in which the Word had formerly dwelt. In this way Mary was imagined as a living, breathing temple into which the Creator of the universe has taken up residence. What we witness in the developments after Chalcedon is a marked amplification of a theological motif already fully formed a century after the life and death of Christ.

Mary in the Old Testament: A Methodological Reprise

The development of the temple metaphor in relationship to the incarnation sheds considerable light on how the early church conceived the relationship between the two Testaments. The relationship between the two is not primar-ily predictive but figural.[37] It is this sort of figural relationship that defines the

---

when it draws so heavily on Mariology in support of its Christology. While Christology is at the heart of the fifth-century Nestorian controversy about Mary as 'mother of God' (*theotokos*), the *Infancy Gospel*'s appeal to Mary in relation to Christology is not without parallel in the second century."

37. Figural readings are already attested in the Old Testament itself; it is a category native to the biblical tradition. A classic example of this can be found in Genesis 12 when Abraham, facing a famine in the land of Canaan, descends to the land of Egypt. As the story unfolds, Abraham fears that the Egyptians will murder him in order to acquire his wife. So he advises her to identify herself as his sister. When Pharaoh learns of her beauty, he takes her into his household and Abraham is compensated with great wealth. But all is not well. God takes umbrage at Pharaoh's actions and sends mighty plagues upon his house. Pharaoh calls Abraham into his court, releases Sarah and allows them to return to Canaan with all the wealth they have acquired. As numerous interpreters have noted, this whole sequence anticipates the story of the exodus where Israel, facing famine, will descend into Egypt and be faced with the imminent death of all her males. God will send plagues on that nation and eventually Israel will be released and leave Egypt with great wealth (Exod. 12:35). It is important to note that this story about Abraham is not a predic-tion of the events of the exodus. Rather, Abraham preenacts the national epic within his own life. The events of his own life become a figure or type of what is to come. Of course

Old Testament as something that can do more than simply anticipate the New; it can take a necessary role in filling out what the New has not fully disclosed. Such a move is perhaps best illustrated in Augustine's reading of the book of Psalms. Since Jesus adopts Israel's persona on the cross by expressing his grief through the opening words of Psalm 22 ("My God, my God, why hast thou forsaken me"), Augustine reasoned that the rest of the Psalter could be understood in a similar fashion. This opened up a dramatic new vista into the person of Jesus Christ that forever altered how the book of Psalms would be read. One could learn as much about the person of Jesus from the Psalter as one could from the Gospels. A similar hermeneutical move is made with the temple and eventually the figure of Mary. Once the figural link is established, the character of Mary grows well beyond what little the New Testament had revealed.

It should be emphasized that I am not saying that the Old Testament texts about the tabernacle and the temple predict in a univocal way the coming of Mary. Here the interpretation of the Psalter is of considerable value. All the Psalms, even in the Augustinian register, retain their—historically primary—Israelite voice. Indeed they *must* retain their original voice because it is that specific voice that Jesus wishes to assume. Jesus cannot speak *in persona Israel* if there is no *vox Israel* to assume! When Ezekiel, for example, spoke of Israel's eager hope for the rebuilding of the temple (Ezek. 40–43) and the return of God's presence to dwell within it (43:1–4), Christian homilists almost uniformly assumed that the ultimate referent was the person of Mary. Indeed, in the icons used during the Marian feasts in the Eastern Church, Ezekiel is almost always shown holding his temple, a figure for the person of Mary.[38]

---

it is crucial to observe that the story of Abraham is fully intelligible on its own. But once we see its connection to the exodus, we get a deeper picture of the character of Abraham and his relationship to the people who will descend from him. As the medieval Jewish commentator Nachmanides said: "none of the events that happened to the father failed to happen to the descendants."

38. The evangelical scholar Timothy George in "The Blessed Virgin Mary in Evangelical Perspective," in *Mary, Mother of God*, ed. Carl Braaten and Robert Jenson (Grand Rapids: Eerdmans, 2004), 109, notes that Luther, Calvin, and Zwingli were all in agreement about the perpetual virginity of Mary even though scripture makes no explicit judgment on this matter. "Strangely enough," George concludes: "Zwingli attempted to argue for this teaching on the basis of scripture alone, against the idea that it could only be held on the basis of the teaching authority of the church. His key proof text is Ezekiel 44:2: 'This gate is to remain shut. It must not be opened: no one may enter through it. It is to remain shut because the Lord, the God of Israel, has entered through it.' But this is hardly as strange as it appears. Zwingli is simply working from a typological identification that goes back to the Patristic period" (109).

But this does not obliterate the primary historical reference the text has in the prophet's own self-consciousness and within the subsequent living Jewish tradition. To illustrate this, consider the rendering of Ezekiel in Michelangelo's Sistine Chapel. The prophet Ezekiel stands just below the fifth and central panel of the Genesis cycle (see fig. 1.1) that adorns the ceiling. In this panel Eve comes forth from Adam's rib, a painting that can also be read as the church (i.e., Mary) issuing forth from the rib of Christ.[39] Loren Partridge catches the drama well:

> Ezekiel has just spun around from one genius—his scarf and scroll still rippling from the sudden movement—to carry on an intense polemic with the other angelically beautiful genius who points heavenward with both hands while Ezekiel's open-palm gesture equivocates between accepting and questioning. His extraordinary physical and rhetorical energy [...] is heightened by the parallel diagonals of bull neck, thick torso, titanic limbs and broad lavender drapery falling across his orange tunic and between his splayed knees.[40]

Why such excitement and surprise? I would suggest that Michelangelo knows that what the prophet is made to say within the Christian tradition is not what the prophet himself had in mind. His scroll in his left hand points in one direction—to *terra firma*—while the angelic figure to his right points upward. As Eric Auerbach had argued so well, the Christian figural tradition attempted to retain an integral voice to the Jewish scriptures while, at the same time, reconfigure its various compass points to point beyond themselves.[41]

39. On the relationship of Eve to Mary on the Sistine Ceiling see the extended discussion in Gary Anderson, *The Genesis of Perfection* (Louisville: Westminster John Knox, 2002), 1–20 and esp. 4–7. For a brief review of the pertinent data consider these comments of Loren Partridge, *Michelangelo: The Sistine Ceiling, Rome* (New York: Braziller, 1996), 50. He argues that this panel's "pivotal role was both deliberate and appropriate, for it was a common symbol of the founding of the Church, embodied by the Virgin, the second Eve, just as the Virgin's Assumption, to which the chapel was dedicated, symbolized the Church's triumph. Eve's importance is underlined by the mighty figure of God, cramped within the pictorial field, who appears for the first time standing on the earth. Born from the side of Adam, Eve also alludes to the Church's principal sacraments of baptism and Eucharist, for both water and blood flowed from the side of Christ, the second Adam. And indeed, Adam is intended to suggest the sacrificial Christ by his crumpled sleeping figure leaning awkwardly against a dead, cross-like stump."
40. Partridge, *Michelangelo*, 80.
41. As is well known, Auerbach exerted a strong influence on the work of Hans Frei

But this process of development should not be left solely within the plane of hermeneutics, as if all we are talking about are rules of literary growth. What allows the church fathers to proceed in the direction they do is a profound appreciation of what Childs called the underlying subject matter or *res* of the various biblical witnesses.[42] Both the Old and New Testaments are chock-full of references to how God takes up residence amid his people. And these texts are not simply symbolic, for to paraphrase and domesticate the fiery tongue of Flannery O'Connor, if they were merely literary devices then their relationship is endlessly fungible. And could one confidently declare that God was present in any of them?

The challenge to the reader, following the path laid down by Brevard Childs, is to see how these references to God's real presence—both in Israel and within the church—relate to one another. On the one hand, scripture witnesses to the deeply transformational quality of these moments of indwelling. As the biblical author makes very clear, God wants the tabernacle built not simply as a place for him to dwell, but so that he can dwell among his chosen people, Israel (Exod. 25:8). As a result of this indwelling, Israel is obligated to live a life that befits such holiness (e.g., Lev. 11:44–45). All of the moral and sacral legislation of Leviticus and Numbers depends on this crucial point. But on the other hand, the object of this incarnation—be it tabernacle, temple or womb—becomes worthy of veneration in its own right. This is not a vestige of paganism or a form of idolatry; it is the reverent admission that any part

---

and many of the "narrative theologians" who came to make up the Yale school. In this instance, Michelangelo's understanding of Ezekiel allows the prophet to retain his historical voice within the community of ancient Israel. Ezekiel thought that Israel's restoration would require the rebuilding of the actual temple in Jerusalem. The angel, however, alerts the prophet that God's providential ordering of his words will result in a very different interpretation from what he had intended.

42. For Childs it is crucial to distinguish between the voice of a specific scriptural *witness* and its underlying *subject matter*, which it shares with other parts of the Bible. Different biblical authors have their own ideas as to how they conceive of the "dwelling of God." For the book of Exodus, it is the tabernacle in the desert; for the book of Kings, it is the temple that Solomon builds; for Ezekiel is the eschatological hope of a restored Israel; and for the Gospel of John is the person of Jesus Christ. Though the individual witnesses vary considerably in their specific architectural/physical details, there are broad areas of agreement about the subject matter and how the deity inhabits physical space. In this chapter we have seen how this underlying subject matter informs how Athanasius understands the character of the incarnation and how Mary's person is expanded once she is conceived as a temple-in-miniature, or as one who "contains the uncontainable."

of creation brought that close to the presence of God is overwhelmed by his power and sanctity.[43]

The liturgy of the Angelus allows one to recall and *adore* this event afresh. Here, the witness of the Old Testament is absolutely crucial in order to counter the charges brought against the Catholic Church in the wake of the Reformation. The Holy One of Israel cannot indwell a space and leave it unchanged. Venerating Mary as Mother of God (*Ave Maria, gratia plena* . . .), does not detract from the doctrine of the incarnation; it safeguards it. (On this point, consider the acts of veneration that Jews bestow on sacred texts which hold the veritable name of God.)

My own approach to the development of Mary's person has gone in a somewhat different direction from that of the Lutheran–Roman Catholic commission that produced the influential and stimulating volume *Mary in the New Testament*.[44] In this volume the interests were necessarily quite different than mine. A vigorous scholarly attempt was made to read each New Testament author on his own and not to allow later church doctrines anachronistically to be read back into the original voices of the text. The results of this study were clear, sober, and unassailable. But the end result of the volume was unsatisfying for me because the implication was that the growth of Marian doctrine was conceived to be a slow and careful outgrowth of what the New Testament had only hinted at. One would not have gathered from this volume that the

---

43. For these reasons we should not accept the proof of the perpetual virginity put forward by Zwingli (see n. 39). Though his figural understanding of the temple imagery is logical, it represents an overspecification of what such figuration can reveal. Reading Ezekiel in this fashion turns the words of his prophecy into an arcane code that the prophet himself would not have recognized. The notion of figuration that I am proposing makes a broad identification at the level of basic subject matter between an eschatological temple and the coming of Jesus Christ, but this does not authorize the reader to turn each and every verse into a specific feature of the person of Jesus or his mother. Childs puts the matter well when he writes: "If the first level of exegesis focusses on the relation of text to history (i.e. Ezekiel in his 6th century context), the second . . . seeks to analyse the relationship between the two witnesses (Ezekiel and John 1:14). . . . Specifically in terms of an understanding of God, what features do the two testaments hold in common respecting the mode, intention, and goal of God's self-manifestation? A comparison is being made, *but neither witness is absorbed by the other, nor [are] their contexts fused*." See Childs, *Biblical Theology*, 379–83 (emphasis mine). Zwingli's comparison, in my view, has fused the contexts.

44. Raymond Brown, Karl Donfried, Joseph Fitzmyer, and John Reuman, eds., *Mary in the New Testament: A Collaborative Assessment by Protestant and Roman Catholic Scholars* (Philadelphia: Fortress, 1978).

elaboration of Mary in the church was just as much an attempt to understand her in light of the church's two-part Bible.

But I should concede that the two-Testament witness of the Christian Bible is not the whole story. In addition, one must reckon with the influence of the vicissitudes of history. Had Theodore of Mopsuestia not brought to light that the deity seems free to enter and leave the temple as witnessed in Ezekiel 8–11 the wholesale transfer of the temple form to Mary might not have happened. Though texts like the Protevangelium of James were already moving far in that direction, most patristic writers up to Chalcedon seem most comfortable using the image of the temple as a metaphor for the indwelling of the Godhead within the person of Jesus. In addition, the rising importance of the Marian feasts within the liturgical life of the church in the wake of Chalcedon should not be underemphasized. These feasts quickened the need for and the development of icons and innumerable homilies. And both the icons and the homilies provided the fertile soil from which the growth of Mary's temple-like being could flourish. Given the paucity of material about Mary in the New Testament, it can hardly be surprising that the homilies on the Dormition that Brian Daley has collected devote such an extraordinary amount of space to the metaphor of Mary as temple.

In sum, one can see that the doctrine of the incarnation was not understood in patristic tradition as solely an affair of the New Testament. In some very important ways, the New Testament was thought to defer to the Old. The task of the reader of the Old Testament is perhaps best illustrated by Michelangelo. In keeping with the historical sense, it is absolutely crucial that we allow this Old Testament prophet his own voice. Otherwise, whence will come his surprise? The Old Testament, with complete theological integrity, imagines that all world history points toward God rebuilding Zion. We cannot compromise this perspective. In the New Testament, on the other hand, that hope takes a radical and unexpected turn, but not one that renders null and void the subject matter of Ezekiel's hopes. As Michelangelo indicates, God has indwelt a virgin and the task of the Christian reader is to explore how Ezekiel's words and imagery take new shape in light of the mystery of Christ. The prayer known as the Angelus is one such means the tradition has offered for adoring the moment of incarnation. For when Mary responds "*fiat mihi*," her body becomes a fit vessel (*gratia plena*) to contain the uncontainable. Like the Israelites of old who fell on their faces in adoration when they witnessed the descent of God to earth to inhabit his tabernacle, so for the church (*ave maria . . . dominus tecum*). In this fashion a high doctrine of Mary both ensures and safeguards the doctrine of the incarnation.

CHAPTER 10

Atonement

> When our father Abraham bound Isaac his son, the Holy One (blessed be He!) established the institution of the two lambs, one in the morning and one in the evening. And for what reason? Because when Israel would sacrifice the daily offering on the altar and recite Leviticus 1:11, the Holy One (blessed be He!) would remember the binding of Isaac.
>
> Leviticus Rabbah 2:11

> We may identify the central focus of Christian worship as the celebration of the Eucharist, the constantly renewed participation in the priestly mystery of Jesus Christ, at the same time the full scope of that worship must always be kept in mind: it is always a matter of drawing every individual person, indeed, the whole of the world, into Christ's love in such a way that everyone together with him becomes an offering that is "acceptable, sanctified by the Holy Spirit" (Rom 15:16).
>
> Benedict XVI[1]

The atonement has become a problematic category in contemporary theology because it seems to presume that the forgiveness of sins requires the suffering of the sinner or someone who represents him or her. In its most severe expression, God the Father sends his Son to his death on the cross in order to satisfy the infinite punishment that his justice demands. Expressed in this bald, unnuanced fashion, it is obvious why many theologians have recoiled at the proposition. Benedict XVI is altogether typical when he writes: "Again and again people say: It must be a cruel God who demands infinite atonement. Is this not a notion unworthy of God? Must we not give up the idea of

---

1. Benedict XVI, *Jesus of Nazareth: Holy Week* (San Francisco: Ignatius, 2010), 2:238.

atonement in order to maintain the purity of our image of God?"[2] For some feminist scholars, the conception of God the Father executing the Son for the sins of others represents a form of divine child abuse.[3] There is an enormous body of literature in both North America and Europe that justly condemns this particular expression of the Christian faith.[4]

Happily for us, the story of the passion in the Gospels makes no mention of Jesus "paying God back" for the cost of our sins. As David Yeago has observed, "There is no invisible transaction going on behind the scenes of the narrative we rehearse each Passiontide. Jesus is doing just what appears in the story: he is being faithful to his Father even to death, and in this way realizing in himself, in his own person, the covenant partnership that is Israel's vocation and God's ultimate purpose for the whole human race."[5] But the question still remains: how do we understand the redemptive character of Christ's life?

Deification

Some have proposed that we turn to the orthodox concept of deification, that is, the notion that salvation entails being conformed to the divine pattern of life that is revealed in Jesus of Nazareth. The advantage of this construal is that it releases us from the problematic notion of sacrificial suffering. To illustrate this, I would like to turn to the Orthodox theologian Andrew Louth. He is a leading authority in Orthodox theology and, on those grounds alone, his views merit serious consideration.

2. Benedict XVI, *Jesus of Nazareth*, 2:232.

3. The classic article on this subject in the English-speaking world is that of J. Brown and R. Parker, "For God So Loved the World?," in *Christianity, Patriarchy, and Abuse: A Feminist Critique*, ed. J. Brown and C. Bohn (New York: Pilgrim, 1989), 1–30. For a brief survey of similar literature in Germany, see Bernd Janowski, "'Hingabe' oder 'Opfer'? Zur gegenwärtigen Kontroverse um die Deutung des Todes Jesu," in *Das Kreuz Jesu: Gewalt-Opfer-Sühne*, ed. R. Weth (Neukirchen-Vluyn: Neukirchener, 2001), 23–26.

4. Though one should add that the doctrine of "penal substitution" as it is known, need not be expressed in the violent and distasteful manner that has become common over the past generation or so. For a judicious summary of the theological issues at stake and why some aspects of this mode of thinking still warrant serious attention, see the chapter-length treatment of Oliver Crisp in his *Approaching the Atonement: The Reconciling Work of Christ* (Downers Grove, IL: InterVarsity, 2020), 96–113.

5. David Yeago, "Crucified for Us under Pontius Pilate," in *Nicene Christianity: The Future for a New Ecumenism*, ed. C. Seitz (Grand Rapids: Brazos, 2001), 87–105, here 100–101.

Louth begins his discussion of deification with the classic definition of St. Athanasius: "[The Word of God] became human that we might become God; and he revealed himself through a body that we might receive an idea of the invisible Father; and he endured insults from humans that we might inherit incorruption." The purpose of the incarnation, according to Athanasius, is not simply God's sharing our human nature, but our coming to share in his divinity. As Irenaeus puts it, "in his immense love he became what we are, that he might make us what he is."

It is striking that Athanasius believes a key feature of the incarnation was to make the Godhead perceptible to humanity at large. If the goal of salvation is "a face-to-face encounter with God" then God has to become visible to make that possible. As the Prologue of John puts it, God's "tabernacling among us" was ordered to our being able "to see his glory." From this verse, Louth concludes that "deification is the fulfillment of creation, not just the rectification of the Fall. One way of putting this is to think in terms of an arch stretching from creation to deification, representing what is and remains God's intention: the creation of the cosmos that, through humankind, is destined to share in the divine life, to be deified."[6]

In Accordance with the Scriptures

One question that we must pose is whether Louth's understanding of the incarnation can be squared with what we have seen in the Old Testament. The Nicene Creed famously declares that the pattern of Christ's life ("For us men and for our salvation he came down from heaven, and by the Holy Spirit was incarnate of the Virgin Mary, and became man") was "in accordance with the scriptures." Louth's initial description of deification follows from the Prologue of John's Gospel, which, in turn, is clearly patterned on the Old Testament. The Prologue begins with a paraphrase of Genesis 1:1. Instead of "In the beginning, God created the heavens and the earth," John writes, "In the beginning was the Word." But the point of the opening verses in both of these books was not to describe the creation of the physical order alone. The ultimate intention of both verses was to point forward to that moment in time in which God would assume residency among the human beings he fashioned and so deeply loved.

6. Andrew Louth, "The Place of *Theosis* in Orthodox Theology," in *Partakers of the Divine Nature*, ed. Michael Christiansen and Jeffrey Wittung (Grand Rapids: Baker Academic, 2007), 34–35.

In the Old Testament, this meant the point at which God assumed residency in the tabernacle and made his glory visible to Israel. For John, the goal was God's "tabernacling" in the person of Jesus so that same glory could be seen anew. The arch of the New Testament maps directly to the arch laid down in the Old, as depicted in figure 10.1 below. Perhaps better stated, the arch of the incarnate Logos was a figural extension of its Old Testament prototype.

But Louth's exposition does not stop here. He recognizes that the sacrificial redemption of Christ is also part of the scriptural story. The question is how to relate the sacrificial component of Christ's life to the incarnation. Louth notes that the sin of Adam has frustrated the destiny for the human race that God had intended. There was need then for a "lesser arch," whose purpose was "to restore the function of the greater arch from creation to deification." The problem for Western Christians, as Louth describes it, is that our attention has been so focused on this "lesser arch," that we have lost sight of the more important dimension of Christ's life:

> The loss of the notion of deification leads to lack of awareness of the greater arch from creation to deification, and thereby to concentration on the lower arch, from Fall to redemption; it is, I think, not unfair to suggest that such a concentration on the lesser arch at the expense of the greater arch has been characteristic of much Western theology. The consequences are evident: a loss of the sense of the cosmic dimension of theology, a tendency to see the created order as little more than a background for the great drama of redemption, with the result that the Incarnation is seen simply as a means of redemption, the putting right of the Fall of Adam.[7]

There is much to commend about the picture that Louth has drawn. But the biblical story cannot be summarized by a simple correlation of creation and indwelling. As we have noted, the climax of the Tabernacle Narrative has two interlocking focal points: the building of the tabernacle in the book of Exodus and the onset of sacrificial service in Leviticus. The theophany that marks the completion of the building and its indwelling by the deity (Exod. 40:34–35) has been closely coordinated with the theophany that attended the first public offerings (Lev. 9:23–24). Although there can be no sacrifice without a tabernacle, the tabernacle itself remains unfinished until the altar is put into operation. If we want to fill out John's portrait on the basis of its Old Testament model, we must allow the complete Old Testament picture to fill in

7. Louth, "Place of *Theosis*," 35.

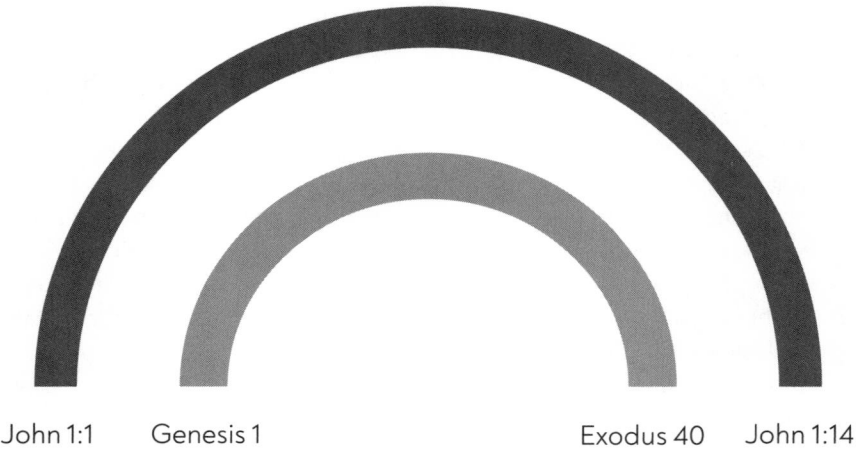

John 1:1   Genesis 1   Exodus 40   John 1:14

Figure 10.1 The arch of the New Testament trajectory as extension of the arch of the Old Testament trajectory as conceived by Andrew Louth, from creation to incarnation

a narrative detail that fell outside the immediate purview of John 1:14. Figure 10.2 represents a more accurate depiction of the Old Testament witness, and if the story of Christ's life is to be told "in accordance with the scriptures," then the role of his sacrificial death cannot be reduced to a "lesser arch." Indwelling (Exod. 40) and sacrifice (Lev. 8–9) cannot be pulled apart.

The Tamid Is *Not* a Rite of Atonement

Now on the face of it, the linkage of sacrifice to indwelling would seem to refute Louth's proposal. But somewhat ironically, what looks like a problem could also contribute to the solution. In order to unpack this claim we must return to the problem of the tamid sacrifice.

As we noted in our earlier chapter, the pinnacle of the tabernacle sequence is the onset of the tamid sacrifice. The significance of this rite can be measured in several ways. First of all, as the calendar of Israel's festivals in Numbers 28–29 shows, the tamid is the baseline sacrifice to which all the additional festival sacrifices are added. The same thing could be said about the quotidian sacrifices that were offered every day. Since the tamid

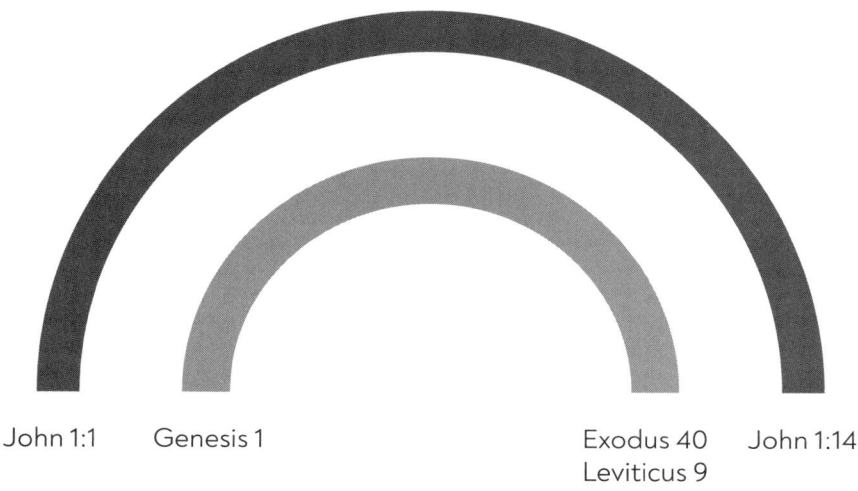

John 1:1   Genesis 1   Exodus 40   John 1:14
                                                   Leviticus 9

Figure 10.2 The arches properly drawn to reflect the trajectory from creation to incarnation and sacrifice

is offered first thing in the morning, all subsequent sacrifices are placed on top of it. And at the end of the day, the second tamid is offered to assure that the sacrificial pyre burns throughout the evening. The book of Daniel, we should recall, summarized the cessation of sacrifice with reference to the tamid alone. As Joseph Blenkinsopp noted, mention of this sacrifice is a metonymy for the rest.[8]

For our purposes, the key feature to observe is that the tamid sacrifice is not an atonement rite. There is a tendency among Christian readers to presume the centrality of atonement in Israel's cultic life. Because Christ's sacrificial death is an atoning act, and since it brings the sacrificial system of the Old Testament to closure, it is easy to understand why theologians have inferred that Israel's cult was one large atonement mechanism. But as biblical scholars have repeatedly argued, this understanding grossly misrepresents the character of the tamid sacrifice. Jonathan Klawans is right on target when he writes: "The typical understanding of the way daily sacrifice [= tamid] and grave sin are related is, I believe, backward. It is not that the daily sacrifice undoes the

8. See Daniel 8:11–13; 11:31; and 12:11; and J. Blenkinsopp, *Ezra-Nehemiah: A Commentary*, OTL (Louisville: Westminster John Knox, 1988), 98.

damage done by grave transgression. Quite the contrary: grave transgression undoes what the daily sacrifice produces."[9]

Klawans goes on to observe that the difference between these two formulations is of fundamental importance. "What it boils down to," he argues, "is whether a sacrifice is considered, in and of itself, a productive act. Those who argue that expiation is at the core of all or most sacrificial rituals ultimately view sacrifice not as something productive in its own right but as a correction or a reversal of something else that was wrong." The question then becomes in what way is the tamid a productive act? That is, in what way is it an action that does not simply remove an error, but possesses a good internal to itself; an act that one would wish to undertake even if there was no sin to remove? The answer to this question, as we noted earlier in chapter 4, lies in the immediate literary context of the tamid rite (Exod. 25–40): the installation of the deity into his new home. As Jeffrey Tigay has shown, the running of the temple is modeled on a royal palace.[10] Service of the human king becomes an analogy for service to the King of kings. Like any king, God needs a house suited to his majesty. On this understanding, sacrifice can be construed as the provisioning of the deity's banquet table. It is simply one among a number of ritual acts that symbolize the miraculous availability of God within the temple and provide a liturgical means of displaying one's service and devotion to God.

Within the biblical narratives, the tamid sacrifice is the single most important feature of the liturgical life of the temple. The tremendous importance of this sacrifice is certainly related to the fact that it—unlike the other dimensions of temple life—required daily maintenance and upkeep by the community of worshippers. In other words, this mode of affording honor and reverence toward the deity is unique, insofar as it requires constant human attention. And it should cause no surprise that the word for "service" in the Bible becomes the standard rabbinic term for divine worship. In the act of providing a sacrifice, Israelites were not only providing a service to the deity, but also setting themselves in a position of subservience to their God.

9. Jonathan Klawans, *Purity, Sacrifice and the Temple: Symbolism and Supersessionism in the Study of Ancient Judaism* (Oxford: Oxford University Press, 2006), 71.

10. Jeffrey Tigay, "Some Aspects of Prayer in the Bible," *AJSR* 1 (1976): 363–79, esp. 364–65. Though it should be noted that Tigay sees the sacrifices as analogous to the tribute that subjects pay a king. But the analogy that he points to could easily be extended to refer to provisioning the table of earthly and divine kings.

The Tamid and the Akedah

So far our discussion has focused on the role played by the tamid sacrifice within the framework of the Tabernacle Narrative alone. But as we have seen, the story of the binding of Isaac has been linked to these narratives, and if we wish to attend to the Bible's final canonical form we must push forward and ask what sort of impact this larger literary context will have on our reading of the Bible. As Childs notes, the formation of the canon sets up a "resonance between [the books of] Genesis and Leviticus." The story of Abraham's near sacrifice of Isaac calls for "fuller theological reflection on the whole sacrificial system of Leviticus." To invoke the terminology of Childs, though the textual *witnesses* of Genesis 22 and Exodus 29 were written independently of one another, they share a common *subject matter*—the fundamental meaning and purpose of the sacrificial act.[11] It is the obligation of the theological reader to move beyond simply a description of what each witness wants to say (i.e., the authors of Genesis 22 and Exodus 29) and to describe the underlying subject matter of the canonical whole.

But if we grant that the Akedah is to be correlated with the onset of sacrificial service, the question then becomes: what is the meaning of the Akedah? Or, perhaps, better stated: what are we to learn from its expression of a sacrificial ideal that could be applied to the tamid? Before proceeding any further, we should note that the tamid sacrifice is an offering incumbent upon all of Israel. Though the sons of Aaron will be the ones directly responsible for its oversight, the obligation rests on Israel as whole (*"Command the Israelites*, and say to them . . . 'This is the offering by fire that you shall offer to the Lord: two male lambs a year old without blemish, daily as a tamid offering'" [Num. 28:2–3]). This fact is fundamental to the figural reading proposed by Hasdai Crescas:

It appears that the intention of the two daily offerings, the morning offering and the evening offering . . . is to indicate that this is an atonement for all Israel. It is as if these daily offerings are in exchange for all Israel and in offering them, the entirety of the people are drawn nearer to the worship of God. Therefore the daily offerings were lambs, which come from the ram, just as the nation as a whole is a descendant of Isaac.[12]

11. Brevard Childs, *Biblical Theology of the Old and New Testaments: Theological Reflection on the Christian Bible* (Minneapolis: Fortress, 1992), 80–90.
12. Hasdai Crescas, *Light of the Lord (Or Hashem)*, trans. R. Weiss (Oxford: Oxford University Press, 2018), 162.

Because all of Israel descends from the loins of Isaac, his near-death at the altar on Mount Moriah represents the near-death of all Israel. And because each of the lambs offered during the tamid service are related to the ram that Abraham offered in Genesis 22, then every time the lamb of the tamid is offered, the sparing of Isaac is recalled.

Before addressing the Akedah directly, we need to make sure we have understood its larger literary setting. We will do this by describing how Genesis 22 is related to chapter 12, and how the latter, in turn, is related to chapter 11.

Genesis 12:1–3 and 22:2

As recognized already by the rabbis, the story opens in a way that recalls the story of Abraham's initial call:

> [1] Now the LORD said to Abram, "*Betake yourself* [*lekh-lekha*] from (1) your country and (2) your kindred and (3) your father's house *to the land that I will show you*. [2] I will make of you a great nation, and I will bless you, and make your name great, so that you will be a blessing. [3] I will bless those who bless you, and the one who curses you I will curse; and in you all the families of the earth shall be blessed." (Gen. 12:1–3)

> [God] said [to Abraham], "Take (1) your son, (2) your only son, (3) whom you love, (4) Isaac and *betake yourself* [*lekh-lekha*] to the land of Moriah, and offer him there as a burnt offering *on one of the mountains that I shall show you*." (Gen. 22:2)[13]

These two commands have a lot in common. First, the command "betake yourself" is a rare expression; it is used only here in the entire Hebrew Bible. Second, the location of each destination is left undisclosed. Abraham is to "betake himself" to the land or mountain that God will show (or tell) him. Third, the cost of what Abraham must give up is graded from the least to the most dear. Just as it is more difficult to leave the warmth of one's father's house than one's more distant kindred or even country, so the difficulty of offering one's beloved son is more painful than any other son.

It is one thing to see the formal similarities but another to assess their significance. Levenson suggests that the parallels show that in the story of the

13. I have slightly altered the translation of the NRSV.

Akedah, God has returned Abraham to his starting point, "alone with God, attentive to an unexpected and mysterious divine command, and prepared to leave home even for a destination that is as yet unspecified. . . . The man who gave up his father's house must now give up the son on whom he has staked his life."[14] I should add that both commands are associated with wildly improbable outcomes. In the first instance, Abraham's consent to become an alien in a foreign land is described as a stepping stone to wealth and fame. This, of course, happens in short order (see Gen. 12:16, 20). But we should not lose sight of the fact that "migrant workers" in antiquity had far less chance of succeeding in their new homes than they do today. We should also take a proper measure of the sacrifice that is being demanded of him. Once Abraham departs for the land of Canaan, he would never see his family again. Finally, we should observe that God was good for his word, even in this most improbable of circumstances. This must be factored into our assessment of Abraham's obedience in Genesis 22. Abraham had good reason to believe that God would be true to his promises no matter what the peril.[15]

Genesis 11:4 and 12:2

Genesis 12, however, is not the only text we need to factor into our equation. Genesis 12 is also related to the tower of Babel story in Genesis 11:

> [1] Now the whole earth had one language and the same words. [2] And as they migrated from the east, they came upon a plain in the land of Shinar and settled there. [3] And they said to one another, "Come, let us make bricks, and burn them thoroughly." And they had brick for stone, and bitumen for mortar. [4] Then they said, "Come, let us build ourselves a city, and a tower with its top in the heavens, *and let us make a name for ourselves*; otherwise we shall be scattered abroad upon the face of the whole earth." [5] The LORD came down to see the city and the tower, which mortals had built. [6] And the LORD said, "Look, they are one people, and they have all one language; and this is only the beginning of what they will do; nothing

14. Jon Levenson, *Inheriting Abraham: The Legacy of the Patriarch in Judaism, Christianity, and Islam* (Princeton: Princeton University Press, 2012), 69.

15. In his conclusion to his treatment of the Akedah, Levenson says that the focus of the story is on "Abraham's absolute commitment to God—his obedience to God, his faith in God, his love of God. These, the traditions maintain, are priceless spiritual habits whose relevance, like that of the Aqedah, has not faded." See *Inheriting Abraham*, 112.

that they propose to do will now be impossible for them. ⁷ Come, let us go down, and confuse their language there, so that they will not understand one another's speech." ⁸ So the LORD scattered them abroad from there over the face of all the earth, and they left off building the city. ⁹ Therefore it was called Babel, because there the LORD confused the language of all the earth; and from there the LORD scattered them abroad over the face of all the earth. (Gen. 11:1–9)

The key element for our purposes is the motivation of the builders of the tower: achieving for themselves a great name (v. 4). This motivation stands in striking contrast to the deployment of this motif in the promise made to Abraham. After commanding Abraham to leave his fatherland, God says, "I will make your name great." Though the reward is exactly that of the tower builders, the mode of acquisition could not be more different. The builders of the tower wish to acquire a great name by their own hard efforts. Abraham, on the other hand, is granted a great name as a divine gift.

It should also be noted that these two stories illustrate the two major ways of acquiring a great name in the ancient Near East: through monumental building projects or progeny. Ben Sira captures this well when he writes: "children and the building of a city establish one's name" (40:19). As Ronald Hendel observes,

> In Israel and the ancient Near East, kings established a lasting name by their great building projects. The fame of Solomon rests, in part, on his construction of the Jerusalem temple (1 Kgs 6–8), as does that of Gilgamesh on his construction of the great walls of Uruk (Gilg. I.11–21). . . . These are human forms of immortality. The building project in Babel is a way to establish a name that transcends the lifespans of its builders, establishing a kind of immortality.[16]

Genesis 11:30

For Abraham in Genesis 12, the acquisition of a great name is not about monuments but offspring. But several verses prior to the declaration of the promise, almost as an afterthought, the narrator introduces a detail which will constitute a considerable impediment to the realization of the promise:

16. Ronald S. Hendel, *Genesis 1–11*, Anchor Bible (forthcoming 2024).

²⁷ Now these are the descendants of Terah. Terah was the father of Abram, Nahor, and Haran; and Haran was the father of Lot. ²⁸ Haran died before his father Terah in the land of his birth, in Ur of the Chaldeans. ²⁹ Abram and Nahor took wives; the name of Abram's wife was Sarai, and the name of Nahor's wife was Milcah. She was the daughter of Haran the father of Milcah and Iscah. ³⁰ *Now Sarai was barren; she had no child.* (Gen. 11:27–30)

But this barrenness is not simple "bad luck." This tragic condition serves to underscore what the promise is all about. If Abraham and Sarah are to have children, it will occur only by way of direct divine intervention. They cannot make their own names great; only God can.

Abraham's Self-Sacrifice

When Abraham hears the command to sacrifice the son whom God had given, the risks involved can be calculated at several levels. First of all, with the dispatching of Ishmael a chapter earlier (Gen. 21:8–21), Isaac becomes Abraham's last remaining child. The odds of securing additional heirs through Sarah, barring another divine miracle, are zero. And children, we should recall, have an additional value for biblical figures that modern persons often fail to recognize. One of the chief obligations of a child was to sustain their parents in their old age and to remember their names once they had passed. This is brought out vividly in the book of Ruth when the women of Bethlehem comment on Naomi's great fortune to have a pregnant daughter-in-law. True, biblical law commanded Israelites to care for the widow and the poor, but it does not take much imagination to realize that such support is going to be far more substantive and reliable if it comes from a family member. The death of Isaac would potentially leave Sarah and Abraham with no one to support them in the infirmity of old age. The immediate danger to Abraham and Sarah's livelihood is captured well by Jon Levenson:

> Everything has now come down to Isaac. . . . The great name, the great nation, the blessing, the land of Canaan—all that Abraham has been promised from his call and commission in Genesis 12—now rests upon Isaac. But it is Isaac he must offer up. Abraham's own destiny is so entwined with that of Isaac, and the "great nation" that is eventually to descend from him, that the demand is even harder than the demand upon any

other loving father to offer up his beloved son. Psychologically, what is asked is not only an inexpressibly painful act of sacrifice; it is also an act of *self*-sacrifice.[17]

It is worth pausing a moment on the theme of self-sacrifice. Interpreters often presume that Genesis 22 could only be read that way when we invest the figure of Isaac with true agency. And, truth be told, a number of early interpreters do just this, as we saw in our discussion of the Aramaic Levi Document in chapter 8. But the simple sense of Genesis 22 makes this sort of reading implausible. Isaac is a passive participant in this story, as he is in most of the book of Genesis. But, as Levenson has shown, we do not require a willing Isaac. By complying with the command, Abraham has put his own (and God's!) future at grave risk.

Paradoxically, the end result of Abraham's obedience is the exact opposite of what he must have feared. Rather than losing his only son, Abraham receives him back and, in the process, the divine promise is regrounded in his obedience. And Isaac, as we learn at the end of the story, becomes a man destined for marriage and able to continue the family line.[18] Levenson aptly summarizes the surprising end to the story:

> By preferring the fear of God to Isaac and all that his beloved son signi-
> fies for his relationship with God (and otherwise), Abraham retains the
> son he did not withhold and receives anew all the promises that have so
> long stood at the heart of his relationship with God. In the paradoxical,
> sacrificial logic of which this text is the outstanding Jewish example, it is
> our ungrudging willingness to give that leads to gaining and retaining that
> which is most precious. It is in rising above self-interest that we secure
> that which a calculus of self-interest can never yield—or understand.[19]

The Akedah as a Figure of Christ's Sacrifice

The key to reading this story as part of the larger Christian Bible is to see how the mystery of Christ's person is figurally represented in the "paradoxical, sac-

17. Levenson, *Inheriting Abraham*, 68–69.
18. H. C. White ("The Initiation Legend of Isaac," *ZAW* 91 [1979]: 1–30) traced a number of parallels to "coming of age" stories in other cultures where the young adolescent
boy must face a great trial on the way to adulthood.
19. Levenson, *Inheriting Abraham*, 84–85.

rificial logic of Genesis 22." An obvious parallel can be found in the hymn that the apostle Paul cites in his letter to the Philippians (2:6–11). Christ is exalted by his divine Father and given "the name that is above every name" (v. 9) because he "humbled himself," becoming "obedient to the point of death—even death on a cross" (v. 8). The parallels to the life of Abraham could not be closer. Like Abraham, Christ acquires his great name by sacrificing what appeared to be the logical means to attaining it.

Another spot to look would be the story of the rich young man as told in the Gospel of Mark (10:17–31). As I have argued elsewhere, this story is something of a play within a play within Mark's travel narrative (8:22–10:52).[20] The key theme in this portion of the Gospel is the threefold repetition of the prophecy of the passion (8:31; 9:31; 10:33–34). In each instance, the disciples fail to understand what Jesus is trying to teach them because they believe that his messianic office is defined by the political power he will eventually wield and how they, as his closest companions, will share in that glory. What Christ, however, wishes to teach is that he must die first in order to enter into the promised glory. A similar misunderstanding attends the story of the rich man. He approaches Jesus desiring to know how to attain eternal life. Jesus answers that he must first give away all his wealth and that then he will possess a true and secure treasury through which he can merit the reward he so deeply desires. True wealth, Jesus wishes to say, can only be acquired by giving up earthly riches. Not only does the young man leave despondent, for he was incapable of such a sacrifice, but the disciples are aghast at what Jesus had asked of him. If this is what is required for salvation, who could ever be saved (v. 26)? Yet the logic of what Jesus proposes aligns perfectly with his understanding of his own messianic office. Losing your life turns out to be the way of gaining it. The story of the rich young man ends in a similar fashion. Giving is the road to receiving:

> Truly I tell you, there is no one who has left house or brothers or sisters or mother or father or children or fields, for my sake and for the sake of the good news, who will not receive a hundred-fold now in this age— houses, brothers and sisters, mothers and children, and fields, with persecutions—and in the age to come eternal life. (Mark 10:29–30)

What we see in this exchange between Jesus and the disciples is an articulation of what Levenson described as the lesson to be drawn from the Akedah:

20. G. Anderson, "Metaphysics and Money," *America*, April 13–20, 2015, 15–18.

"it is our ungrudging willingness to give that leads to gaining and retaining that which is most precious."[21] Origen certainly recognized this in his homily on Genesis 22. He cites the story of the rich young man as a key New Testament parallel to what was demanded of Abraham. He also compares the offering of Abraham to that of God the Father: "behold God contending with men in magnificent liberality: Abraham offered God a mortal son who was not put to death; God delivered to death an immortal son for men."[22]

The Redemptive Character of the Cross

As I have told the story so far, one might conclude that the redemptive character of the cross has completely disappeared. In order to correct this impression we should recall our discussion of Moses's intercession on behalf of Israel after the sin of the golden calf. As we noted in the book of Deuteronomy, Moses made a general appeal to God's promise to the patriarchs in order to lift the penalty of death from the nation ("Remember your servants Abraham, Isaac, and Israel" [Deut. 9:27]). But in the book of Exodus, the generic character of this appeal was rendered in far more detailed terms ("Remember your servants Abraham, Isaac, and Israel, how you swore to them by your own self, saying to them, 'I will multiply your descendants like the stars of heaven, and all this land that I have promised I will give to your descendants, and they shall inherit it forever'" [Exod. 32:13]). In that version, Moses cited the terms of the promise that were specific to the so-called "second angelic address" (Gen. 22:15–18). In other words, the dire penalty was lifted as a result of the merits that had accrued to Abraham's stupendous act of obedience. And it was this meritorious action that became the centerpiece of the text from Leviticus Rabbah, which declared that every time the tamid offering was made, God would recall the merits of Abraham's obedience and apply its benefits to the nation of Israel (and even the world).

If we understand the tamid sacrifice through the lens of the Akedah, a striking figural relationship is established between the sacrifice of Christ on the cross and its memorial celebration in the Eucharist. The *Catechism of the Catholic Church* puts it thus:

---

21. Levenson, *Inheriting Abraham*, 85.

22. Origen, *Homilies on Genesis*, trans. R. Heine (Washington, DC: Catholic University Press, 1981), 136–47, here 144.

The Eucharist is thus a sacrifice because it *re-presents* (makes present) the sacrifice of the cross, because it is its *memorial* and because it *applies* its fruit:

> [Christ], our Lord and God, was once and for all to offer himself to God the Father by his death on the altar of the cross, to accomplish there an everlasting redemption. But because his priesthood was not to end with his death, at the Last Supper "on the night when he was betrayed," [he wanted] to leave to his beloved spouse the Church a visible sacrifice (as the nature of man demands) by which the bloody sacrifice which he was to accomplish once for all on the cross would be re-presented, its memory perpetuated until the end of the world, and its salutary power be applied to the forgiveness of the sins we daily commit.[23]

As we saw in Childs's description of the Akedah, the onetime act of obedience on the part of Abraham was not a "private experience" but pointed forward to "Israel's collective public worship." And conversely, "Israel's sacrifice [was] drawn into the theological orbit of Abraham's offering." Just as Moses could appeal to the merits of that founding sacrifice in order to redeem Israel from the penalty of idolatry, so the memorial of Christ's passion was conceived of as an act which could "apply the fruits" of the passion for the benefit of all Christ's church.

Louth's Two Arches: A Reprise

We began this chapter with a discussion of the theological challenge Christ's atoning sacrifice has had for contemporary theology. That God the Father would demand the suffering of his Son to deal with human sin is, as Benedict XVI put it, a "notion unworthy of God." In order to circumvent this problem, many have suggested abandoning the emphasis of the West on Christ's sacrificial action and put the incarnational dimension of his life on center stage. Louth suggested that the "greater" arch of deification should not be overshadowed by the "lesser" arch of sacrifice. We noted, however, that this sort of ranking was not "in accordance with the scriptures." The outline of the

---

23. *Catechism of the Catholic Church: Revised in Accordance with the Official Latin Text Promulgated by Pope John Paul II* (Washington, DC: United States Catholic Conference, 2000), §1366.

Tabernacle Narrative makes it clear that the theme of indwelling and sacrificial service cannot be prioritized in this fashion.

But, perhaps surprisingly to many readers, this does not return the notion of penal suffering to center stage. The Old Testament sacrificial system, as we have seen, does not have the atonement for sins as its central concern. In the broader canonical scope of the Pentateuch, the daily sacrifice was tied to the foundational sacrifice of Abraham, the surrendering of what appeared to be his only chance of securing a "great name" (i.e., a sizeable family). Yet it was the willingness to offer his only remaining son that led to the promise being regrounded on his stupendous obedience. And it was that act of obedience that Moses drew upon to save Israel from the tragic consequences of her egregious act of apostasy. Abraham's willingness to offer back to God what he held most dear turned out to be the most fitting antidote to the problem of human sin. The Old Testament, in the end, provides a path to understand the atonement that frees us from the cruel dimension that Benedict XVI so rightly worried about.

Having said this, however, I should add that I do believe that there is a "redemptive" dimension to Christ's sacrifice. One can and must speak of the suffering that Christ endured as a consequence of our sins.[24] A number of New Testament texts make this point but perhaps none so clearly as 1 Peter 2:24: "[Jesus] himself bore our sins in his body on the cross, so that free from sins, we might live for righteousness; by his wounds you have been healed." But the exposition of that dimension of the problem would require an exegetical detour that would depart from the central concerns of this book. What my discussion in this chapter has tried to argue is that the Old Testament sacrificial system can be deployed in a meaningful way to illumine Christ's sacrifice in a nonpunitive modality. In his treatment of the subject of sacrifice, Thomas Aquinas articulated three reasons for why human beings must offer sacrifice to God. First would be for the remission of sins, second for the preservation of the state of grace, and third to be perfectly united to God. With respect to the last reason, Joseph Wawrykow has written: "Even those whose sins are

---

24. Khaled Anatolios has recently argued that "Christ saves us by vicariously repenting for humanity's sinful rejection of humanity's doxological vocation and its violation and distortion of divine glory." See Khaled Anatolios, *Deification through the Cross: An Eastern Christian Theology of Salvation* (Grand Rapids: Eerdmans, 2020), 32. In his book he labels this form of suffering "doxological contrition." In a forthcoming essay, I will explain how this notion can be grounded in the Old Testament.

forgiven and so are in correct relationship to God, will sacrifice to God."[25] Sacrifice, on this view, is not paying a price for sin but an act of radical self-emptying (cf. Phil. 2:5–9). And it is precisely this dimension of sacrifice that St. Augustine alludes to when he describes how we can participate in the offering Christ made:

> it obviously follows that the whole redeemed city, that is, the congregation and fellowship of the saints, is offered to God as a universal sacrifice through the great priest who, in his passion, offered himself for us in the form of a servant, to the end that we might be the body of such a great head. For it was this servant form that he offered, and it was in this form that he was offered, because it is according to this form that he is the mediator, in this form that he is the priest, and in this form that he is the sacrifice. . . . The Church celebrates this mystery in the sacrament of the altar, well-known to the faithful, where the Church offers herself through what is being offered. (*City of God* 10.6)[26]

Conclusion

The goal of this chapter was to articulate how the Old Testament sacrificial system might shed light on the problem of Christ's sacrifice. Following the logic of St. Augustine (which in turn is grounded in the thought of St. Paul and cited by St. Thomas!), we have presumed that worship offered to God by the people of Israel was a figure of the Christ who was to come. We accept the Old Testament as canonical Scripture, Augustine argues, in order to understand the promises contained in the New Testament. One dimension of the New Testament that has come under heavy scrutiny over the past several generations has been the supposition that it teaches that Christ had to pay the price owed by human sins to appease the anger of his divine father. Sacrifice, on this view, is the means by which that price is paid and God's anger is assuaged. Numerous theologians have sought means to rectify this unhappy picture. One such strategy has involved invoking what is thought to be the distinctive way in which Christ's saving work has been described in the Eastern church. As an example

25. J. Wawrykow, "The Holy Spirit in the Eucharistic Teaching of Thomas Aquinas," unpublished manuscript.

26. Augustine, *City of God: Books 1–10*, trans. William Babcock (Hyde Park: New City Press, 2012), 311.

of this, we turned to Andrew Louth's proposal that we ground the purpose of Christ's life under the arch of the incarnation. This does not mean denying the role of the cross, but it does entail subordinating the sacrifice of Christ to God's primary providential end—the divinization of humanity by dint of the incarnation. If we follow Augustine's reading of St. Paul, however, we should be suspicious of this sort of subordination. The Old Testament does link the indwelling of God to creation as we have seen, but it also creates an unbreakable bond between the act of indwelling the tabernacle and the sacrificial service that will be conducted there. These arches, to return to Louth's striking image, are in parallel to one another; there is no subordination. But Louth was correct to indicate that incarnation can be thought of apart from the demand to rectify human sin. It is not the case that the incarnation has been made contingent on an act of rebellion against God. And we could say a similar thing about the sacrificial cult. The purpose of sacrifice in the Tabernacle Narrative is not first and foremost that of effecting atonement. It is rather to enable the enactment by Israel of a radical self-emptying before her God. Paradoxically, as it turns out, that sort of total self-giving becomes the defining way of reconciling humanity to God. This is enacted in the prayer of Moses when he asks God to recall the sacrifice of Abraham in order to avert the destruction that has been threatened toward the people Israel. Though the sacrifice of Isaac can be an effective means of dealing with human sin, its essential nature is not limited to an atoning role. In this way the Old Testament can be a powerful witness to a means of understanding the incarnation and atoning work of Christ that avoids the cruel picture of God that emerges from theories of sacrifice built upon the model of penal suffering alone.[27]

27. One should note the painting titled *The Presentation in the Temple* in the National Gallery of London by the Master of the Life of the Virgin (ca. 1460–1475; go to national gallery.org.uk to see the image). The priest Simeon receives the Christ child from the hands of Mary (Luke 2:22–40). But instead of standing before the altar in front of the temple, he stands in front of a church altar. Behind him is an altarpiece, but the expected image of the crucifixion has been replaced by the sacrifice of Isaac in keeping with the "Old Testament" setting of the event.

Bibliography

Achenbach, Reinhard. "Das Versagen der Aaroniden: Erwägungen zum literar-historischen Ort von Leviticus 10." Pages 55–70 in *"Basel und Bibel": Collected Communications to the XVIIth Congress of the International Organization for the Study of the Old Testament, Basel, 2001.* Edited by Matthias Augustin and H. M. Niemann. Frankfurt am Main: Lang, 2004.

———. *Die Vollendung der Torah: Studien zur Redaktiongeschichte des Numeribuches im Kontext von Hexateuch und Pentateuch.* Wiesbaden: Harrassowitz, 2003.

Ackroyd, P. R. "The Temple Vessels—a Continuity Theme." Pages 166–81 in *Studies in the Religion of Ancient Israel.* Vetus Testamentum Supplements 23. Leiden: Brill, 1973.

Aejmelaeus, Anneli. "Septuagintal Translation Techniques: A Solution to the Problem of the Tabernacle Account." Pages 381–402 in *Septuagint, Scrolls, and Cognate Writings.* Edited by George Brooke and Barnabas Linders. Atlanta: Scholars Press, 1992.

Albertz, Rainer, "Beobachtungen zur Komposition der priesterlichen Texte Ex 25–40." Pages 277–95 in *Pentateuchstudien.* Edited by Jakob Wöhrle. Forschungen zum Alten Testament 117. Tübingen: Mohr Siebeck, 2018.

———. *Exodus 19–40.* Zurich: Theologischer Verlag, 2015.

Anatolios, Khaled. *Athanasius.* New York: Routledge, 2004.

———. *Deification through the Cross: An Eastern Christian Theology of Salvation.* Grand Rapids: Eerdmans, 2020.

Anderson, Gary. "The Akedah in Canonical and Artistic Perspective." Pages 43–61 in *Genesis and Christian Theology.* Edited by Nathan MacDonald, Mark Elliott, and Grant Macaskill. Grand Rapids: Eerdmans, 2012.

———. "'As We Have Heard So We Have Seen': The Iconography of Zion." *Conservative Judaism* 54 (2002): 50–59.

———. "The Date of the Tabernacle's Completion and Consecration." https://

www.thetorah.com/article/the-date-of-the-tabernacles-completion-and
-consecration.

——. *The Genesis of Perfection*. Louisville: Westminster John Knox, 2002.

——. "The Inauguration of the Tabernacle Service at Sinai." Pages 1–15 in *The Temple of Jerusalem: From Moses to the Messiah*. Edited by Steven Fine. Leiden: Brill, 2010.

——. "Leviticus." Pages 101–22 in *The Paulist Biblical Commentary*. Edited by Richard Clifford et al. Mahwah, NJ: Paulist Press, 2018.

——. "Literary Artistry and Divine Presence." Pages 85–102 in *Contextualizing Jewish Temples*. Edited by Tova Ganzel and Shalom Holtz. Boston: Brill, 2020.

——. "Mary in the Old Testament." *Pro Ecclesia* 16 (2007): 33–55.

——. "Sacrifice and Offerings." Pages 870–86 in vol. 5 of *Anchor Bible Dictionary*. New York: Doubleday, 1992.

——. "The Tabernacle Narrative as Christian Scripture." Pages 81–95 in *The Character of Israel's God*. Edited by Donald Collett, Mark Elliott, Mark Gignilliat, and Ephraim Radner. Atlanta: Scholars Press, 2021.

——. "'Through Those Who are Near to Me, I Will Show Myself Holy': Nadab and Abihu and Apophatic Theology." *Catholic Biblical Quarterly* 77 (2015): 1–19.

——. "To See Where God Dwells: The Tabernacle, the Temple, and the Origins of the Christian Mystical Tradition." *Letter & Spirit* 4 (2008): 13–45.

——. "Towards a Theology of the Tabernacle and Its Furniture." Pages 161–94 in *Text, Thought, and Practice in Qumran and Early Christianity*. Edited by Ruth A. Clements and Daniel R. Schwartz. Leiden: Brill, 2009.

Baden, Joel. "What Was the Sin of the Golden Calf?" www.thetorah.com/article/what-was-the-sin-of-the-golden-calf.

Baentsch, Bruno. *Exodus, Leviticus, Numeri*. Göttingen: Vandenhoeck & Ruprecht, 1903.

Barag, Dan. "The Table of the Bread of Presence and the Façade of the Temple upon the Coins of the Bar Kokhba War." *Qadmoniot* 20 (1987): 22–25. (Hebrew)

Bar-On, Shimon. "The Development of the Tamid Offering and Its Place in the Priestly Calendar of Sacrifices." *Proceedings of the Twelfth World Congress of Jewish Studies A* (1997): 143–53. (Hebrew)

Benedict XVI. *Jesus of Nazareth: Holy Week*. San Francisco: Ignatius, 2010.

Benedict XVI and Robert Cardinal Sarah. *From the Depths of Our Hearts: Priesthood, Celibacy, and the Crisis of the Catholic Church*. San Francisco: Ignatius, 2019.

Berger, Klaus. "Zu 'Das Wort ward Fleisch' Joh. 1 14a." *Novum Testamentum* 16 (1974): 161–66.

Bibb, Bryan. "Nadab and Abihu Attempt to Fill a Gap: Law and Narrative in Leviticus 10:1–7." *Journal for the Study of the Old Testament* 96 (2001): 83–99.

Blenkinsopp, Joseph. *Ezra–Nehemiah*. Louisville: Westminster John Knox, 1988.

———. "The Structure of P." *Catholic Biblical Quarterly* 38 (1976): 275–92.

Blum, Erhard. *Studien zur Komposition des Pentateuch*. Berlin: de Gruyter, 1990.

Bockmuehl, Markus. *Ancient Apocryphal Gospels*. Louisville: Westminster John Knox, 2017.

Bodner, Keith. "Ark-Eology: Shifting Emphases in 'Ark Narrative' Scholarship." *Currents in Biblical Research* 4 (2006): 169–97.

Boorer, Suzanne. *The Vision of the Priestly Narrative: Its Genre and Hermeneutics of Time*. Atlanta: Society of Biblical Literature, 2016.

Bovon, François. "Fragment Oxyrhynchus 840, Fragment of a Lost Gospel, Witness of an Early Christianity Controversy over Purity." *Journal of Biblical Literature* 119 (2000): 705–28.

———. "The Suspension of Time in Chapter 18 of Protevangelium Jacobi." Pages 393–405 in *The Future of Early Christianity*. Edited by Birger Pearson. Minneapolis: Fortress, 1991.

Brown, Joanne, and Rebecca Parker, "For God So Loved the World?" Pages 1–30 in *Christianity, Patriarchy, and Abuse: A Feminist Critique*. Edited by Joanne Brown and Carolyn Bohn. New York: Pilgrim Press, 1989.

Brown, Raymond. *The Gospel according to John I–XII*. Anchor Bible 29. Garden City, NY: Doubleday, 1966.

Brown, Raymond, Karl Donfried, Joseph Fitzmyer, and John Reuman, eds. *Mary in the New Testament: A Collaborative Assessment by Protestant and Roman Catholic Scholars*. Philadelphia: Fortress; New York: Paulist, 1978.

Buchinger, Harald, and Elizabeth Hernitscheck. "P. Oxy. 840 and the Rites of Christian Initiation: Dating a Piece of Alleged Anti-sacramentalistic Polemics." *Early Christianity* 5 (2014): 117–24.

Caquot, André, and Philippe de Robert. *Les livres de Samuel*. Commentaire de l'Ancien Testament. Geneva: Labor et Fides, 1994.

Carasik, Michael. *The Commentator's Bible: The JPS Miqra'ot Gedolot*. Philadelphia: Jewish Publication Society, 2005.

Cassuto, Umberto. *A Commentary on the Book of Genesis*. Jerusalem: Magnes, 1961.

Chapman, Stephen. *1 Samuel as Christian Scripture*. Grand Rapids: Eerdmans, 2016.

Chavel, Simeon. "The Face of God and the Etiquette of Eye-Contact: Visitation,

Pilgrimage, and Prophetic Vision in Ancient Israelite and Early Jewish Imagination." *Jewish Studies Quarterly* 19 (2012): 1–55.

Childs, Brevard. *Biblical Theology of the Old and New Testaments: Theological Reflection on the Christian Bible*. Minneapolis: Fortress, 1992.

———. *The Book of Exodus*. Old Testament Library. Philadelphia: Westminster, 1974.

———. *Introduction to the Old Testament as Scripture*. Philadelphia: Fortress, 1979.

Chisholm, Robert. *1 and 2 Samuel*. Grand Rapids: Baker Books, 2013.

Collins, Marilyn F. "The Hidden Vessels in Samaritan Traditions." *Journal for the Study of Judaism* 3 (1972): 97–116.

Constas, Nicholas. "Symeon of Thessalonike and the Theology of the Icon Screen." Pages 163–83 in *Thresholds of the Sacred*. Edited by Sharon E. J. Gerstel. Washington, DC: Dumbarton Oaks, 2006.

Crisp, Oliver. *Approaching the Atonement: The Reconciling Work of Christ*. Downers Grove, IL: InterVarsity, 2020.

Cross, Frank M. *Canaanite Myth and Hebrew Epic*. Cambridge: Harvard University Press, 1973.

Daley, Brian E. *On the Dormition of Mary: Early Patristic Homilies*. Crestwood, NY: St. Vladimir's Seminary Press, 1998.

Damrosch, David. *The Narrative Covenant: Transformations of Genre in the Growth of Biblical Literature*. Ithaca, NY: Cornell University Press, 1991.

Dillmann, August. *Die Bücher Exodus und Leviticus*. Leipzig: Hirzel, 1880.

Dohmen, Christoph. *Exodus 19–40*. Herders Theologischer Kommentar zum Alten Testament. Freiburg im Breisgau: Herder, 2004.

Douglas, Mary. *Natural Symbols: Explorations in Cosmology*. New York: Pantheon Books, 1970.

Driver, S. R. *The Book of Exodus*. Cambridge: Cambridge University Press, 1911.

Eichler, Raanan, *The Ark and the Cherubim*. Forschungen zum Alten Testament 146. Tübingen: Mohr Siebeck, 2021.

Eliade, Mircea. *The Sacred and the Profane*. New York: Harcourt, Brace & World, 1959.

Elliger, Karl. *Leviticus*. Handbuch zum Alten Testament. Tübingen: Mohr Siebeck, 1966.

Elliott, Mark W. *Engaging Leviticus: Reading Leviticus Theologically with Its Past Interpreters*. Eugene, OR: Cascade, 2012.

Elsner, Jaś. "The Genres of Ekphrasis." *Ramus* 31 (2002): 1–18.

Enemali, Mark. "The Danger of Transgression against Divine Presence." PhD dissertation. University of Notre Dame, 2014.

Evans, Craig. *Words and Glory: On the Exegetical Background of John's Prologue.* Sheffield: Sheffield Academic, 1993.

Fearghail, Fearghas O. "Sir 50,5–21: Yom Kippur or the Daily Whole-Offering?" *Biblica* 59 (1978): 301–16.

Feldman, Liane. *The Story of Sacrifice: Ritual and Narrative in the Priestly Source.* Forschungen zum Alten Testament 141. Tübingen: Mohr Siebeck, 2020.

Fishbane, Michael. *Haftarot: The Traditional Hebrew Text with the New JPS Translation.* Philadelphia: Jewish Publication Society, 2002.

Fraade, Steven. "Facing the Holy Ark, in Words and in Images." *Near Eastern Archaeology* 82 (2019): 156–63.

Frevel, Christian, "Und Mose hörte (es), und es war gut in seinen Augen (Lev 10,20) Zum Verhältnis von Literargeschichte, Theologiegeschichte und innerbiblischer Auslegung am Beispiel von Lev 10." Pages 104–36 in *Gottes Name(n): Zum Gedenken an Erich Zenger.* Edited by Ilse Müllner. Freiburg: Herder, 2012.

Frey, Jörg. *The Glory of the Crucified One.* Waco, TX: Baylor University Press, 2018.

George, Mark K. *Israel's Tabernacle as Social Space.* Atlanta: Society of Biblical Literature, 2009.

George, Timothy. "The Blessed Virgin Mary in Evangelical Perspective." In *Mary, Mother of God.* Edited by Carl Braaten and Robert Jenson. Grand Rapids: Eerdmans, 2004.

Gerstenberger, Erhard. *Leviticus: A Commentary.* Old Testament Library. Philadelphia: Westminster John Knox, 1996.

Gertz, Jan. "Beobachtungen zu Komposition und Redaktion in Exod 32–34." Pages 88–106 in *Gottes Volk am Sinai: Untersuchungen zu Ex 32–34 und Dtn 9–10.* Edited by Matthias Köckert and Erhard Blum. Gütersloh: Gütersloher Verlagshaus, 2001.

———. "The Formation of the Primeval History." Pages 107–35 in T*he Book of Genesis: Composition, Reception, and Interpretation.* Edited by Craig Evans, Joel Lohr, and David Petersen. Supplements to Vetus Testamentum 152. Leiden: Brill, 2012.

Gorman, Frank H. *The Ideology of Ritual: Space, Time and Status in the Priestly Theology.* Sheffield: JSOT, 1990.

Gradwohl, Roland. "Das 'fremde Feur' von Nadab und Abihu." *Zeitschrift für die Alttestamentliche Wissenschaft* 75 (1963): 288–96.

Greenstein, Edward. "Deconstruction and Biblical Narrative." *Prooftexts* 9 (1989): 43–71.

———. "An Inner-biblical Midrash of the Nadab and Abihu Episode." In *Pro-*

ceedings of the Eleventh World Congress of Jewish Studies, Jerusalem, June 22–29, 1993. Jerusalem: World Union of Jewish Studies, 1994. (Hebrew)

Haran, Menahem. "Book-Size and Thematic Cycles in the Pentateuch." Pages 165–76 in *Die Hebräische Bibel und ihre zweifache Nachgeschichte*. Edited by E. Blum, C. Macholz, and E. Stegemann. Neukirchen-Vluyn: Neukirchener, 1990.

———. *Temples and Temple Service in Ancient Israel*. Winona Lake, IN: Eisenbrauns, 1985.

Hayward, C. T. R. *The Jewish Temple: A Non-Biblical Sourcebook*. New York: Routledge, 1996.

Hendel, Ronald S. *Genesis 1–11*. Anchor Bible. Forthcoming, 2024.

———. "Sacrifice as a Cultural System: The Ritual Symbolism of Exodus 24:3–8." *Zeitschrift für die alttestamentliche Wissenschaft* 101 (1989): 366–90.

Hieke, Thomas. *Levitikus 1–15*. Herders theologischer Kommentar zum Alten Testament. Freiburg: Herder, 2014.

Hoffman, David. *Das Buch Leviticus*. 2 vols. Berlin: M. Poppelauer, 1905–1906.

Houtman, Cornelius. *Exodus*. 4 vols. Kampen: Kok Pharos, 1993–2002.

Hubert, Henri, and Marcel Mauss. *Sacrifice: Its Nature and Function*. Chicago: University of Chicago Press, 1964.

Hundley, Michael B. *Gods in Dwellings: Temples and Divine Presence in the Ancient Near East*. Atlanta: Society of Biblical Literature, 2013.

Hurowitz, Avigdor. *I Have Built You an Exalted House: Temple Building in the Bible in the Light of Mesopotamian and North-West Semitic Writings*. Sheffield: JSOT, 1992.

———. "The Priestly Account of Building the Tabernacle." *Journal of American Oriental Society* 105 (1985): 21–30.

———. "The Vessels of YHWH and the Debate over Divine Presence in the Second Temple—a Divine Symbol." Unpublished essay.

Janowski, Bernd. "'Hingabe oder 'Opfer'? Zur gegenwärtigen Kontroverse um die Deutung des Todes Jesu." Pages 23–26 in *Das Kreuz Jesu: Gewalt-Opfer-Sühne*. Edited by Rudolf Weth. Neukirchen-Vluyn: Neukirchener Verlag, 2001.

———. *Sühne als Heilsgeschehen*. Neukirchen-Vluyn: Neukirchener Verlag, 1982.

———. "Tempel und Schöpfung: Schöpfungstheologische Aspekte der Priesterschriftlichen Heiligtumskonzeption." Pages 214–46 in *Gottes Gegenwärt in Israel: Beiträge zur Theologie des Alten Testaments*. Edited by Bernd Janowski. Neukirchen-Vluyn: Neukirchener, 1993.

Japhet, Sara. *I and II Chronicles*. Old Testament Library. Louisville: Westminster John Knox, 1993.

Jenson, Philip Peter. *Graded Holiness: A Key to the Priestly Conception of the World*. Sheffield: JSOT, 1992.

Jenson, Robert. *The Triune God*. Vol. 1 of *Systematic Theology*. Oxford: Oxford University Press, 1997.

Jürgens, Benedikt. *Heiligkeit und Versöhnung: Levitikus 16 in seinem literarischen Kontext*. Freiburg: Herder, 2001.

Kaminsky, Joel. "Paradise Regained: Rabbinic Reflections on Israel at Sinai." Pages 15–43 in *Jews, Christians, and the Theology of the Hebrew Scriptures*. Edited by Alice O. Bellis and Joel Kaminsky. Atlanta: Scholars Press, 2000.

Kanarek, Jane. *Biblical Narrative and the Formation of Rabbinic Law*. Cambridge: Cambridge University Press, 2014.

Katz, Baruch. "Make Me a Sanctuary That I Might Dwell among You." *Megadim* 6 (1998): 17–21. (Hebrew)

Kearney, Peter. "Creation and Liturgy: The P Redaction of Exodus 25–40." *Zeitschrift für die Alttestamentliche Wissenschaft* 89 (1977): 375–87.

Kerr, Alan. *The Temple of Jesus' Body: The Temple Theme in the Gospel of John*. London: Sheffield Academic, 2002.

Kirschner, Robert. "The Rabbinic and Philonic Exegeses of the Nadab and Abihu Incident (Lev 10:1–6)." *Jewish Quarterly Review* 73 (1983): 375–93.

Klawans, Jonathan. *Purity, Sacrifice and the Temple: Symbolism and Supersessionism in the Study of Ancient Judaism*. New York: Oxford University Press, 2006.

Knohl, Israel. "Postbiblical Sectarianism and the Priestly Schools." *Tarbiz* 60 (1991): 139–46. (Hebrew)

Koester, Craig. *The Dwelling of God: The Tabernacle in the Old Testament, Intertestamental Jewish Literature, and the New Testament*. Washington, DC: Catholic Biblical Association, 1989.

Kugel, James. "Topics in the History of the Spirituality of the Psalms." Pages 113–44 in *Jewish Spirituality: From the Bible through the Middle Ages*. Edited by Arthur Green. New York: Crossroads, 1986.

Lambert, W. G. "Ancient Mesopotamian Gods: Superstition, Philosophy, Theology." *Revue de l'Histoire des Religions* 207 (1990): 115–30.

Laughlin, John C. H. "The 'Strange Fire' of Nadab and Avihu." *Journal of Biblical Literature* 95 (1976): 559–65.

Levenson, Jon. *Creation and the Persistence of Evil*. Princeton: Princeton University Press, 1994.

———. *Death and Resurrection of the Beloved Son*. New Haven: Yale University Press, 1993.

————. *Inheriting Abraham: The Legacy of the Patriarch in Judaism, Christianity, and Islam.* Princeton: Princeton University Press, 2012.

————. *Sinai and Zion: An Entry into the Jewish Bible.* San Francisco: Harper & Row, 1985.

Levine, Baruch. *Leviticus.* Philadelphia: Jewish Publication Society, 1989.

Liss, Hanna. "The Imaginary Sanctuary: The Priestly Code as an Example of Fictional Literature in the Hebrew Bible." Pages 663–89 in *Judah and the Judeans in the Persian Period.* Edited by Oded Lipschits and Manfred Oeming. Winona Lake, IN: Eisenbrauns, 2006.

Lo Sardo, Domenico. *Post-Priestly Additions and Rewritings in Exodus 35–40.* Forschungen zum Alten Testament II/119. Tübingen: Mohr Siebeck, 2020.

Louth, Andrew. "The Place of Theosis in Orthodox Theology." Pages 32–44 in *Partakers of the Divine Nature.* Edited by Michael Christiansen and Jeffrey Wittung. Grand Rapids: Baker Academic, 2007.

MacDonald, Nathan. "Aaron's Failure and the Fall of the Hebrew Kingdoms." Pages 197–209 in *The Fall of Jerusalem and the Rise of the Torah.* Peter Dubrovski, Dominik Markl, and Jean-Pierre Sonnet. Forschungen zum Alten Testament 107. Tübingen: Mohr Siebeck, 2016.

————. "Recasting the Golden Calf: The Imaginative Potential of the Old Testament's Portrayal of Idolatry." Pages 22–39 in *Idolatry: False Worship in the Bible, Early Judaism, and Christianity.* Edited by Stephen C. Barton. London: T&T Clark, 2007.

Mali, Hillel. "Priestly Offering: Law and Narrative in the Aramaic Levi Document." *Harvard Theological Review,* forthcoming.

Mandell, Alice. "Aaron's Body as a Ritual Vessel in the Exodus Tabernacle Building Narrative." Pages 159–81 in *New Perspectives on Ritual in the Biblical World.* Edited by Laura Quick and Melissa Ramos. London: Bloomsbury, 2022.

Markl, Dominik. "Zur literarischen und theologischen Funktion der Heiligtumstexte im Buch Exodus." Pages 57–87 in *Heiliger Raum. Exegese und Rezeption der Heiligtumstexte in Ex 24–40.* Edited by Matthias Hopf, Wolfgang Oswald, and Stefan Seiler. Stuttgart: Kohlhammer, 2016.

McCarter, P. K. *I Samuel.* Anchor Bible 8. Garden City, NY: Doubleday, 1980.

McGinn, Bernard. *The Foundations of Mysticism: Origins to the Fifth Century.* New York: Crossroads, 1994.

McVey, Kathleen. *Ephrem the Syrian: Hymns.* Classics of Western Spirituality. Mahwah, NJ: Paulist, 1989.

Milgrom, Jacob. *JPS Commentary on the Book of Numbers.* Philadelphia: Jewish Publication Society, 1989.

————. *Leviticus 1–16*. Anchor Bible 3. New York: Doubleday, 1991.

Miller, Patrick. *Interpreting the Psalms*. Philadelphia: Fortress, 1986.

Miller, Patrick D., and J. J. M. Roberts. *The Hand of the Lord: A Reassessment of the "Ark Narrative" in 1 Samuel*. Baltimore: Johns Hopkins University Press, 1977.

Moberly, R. W. L. "The Earliest Commentary on the Akedah." *Vetus Testamentum* 38 (1988): 302–23.

Morgenstern, Julian. "The Calendar of the Book of Jubilees." *Vetus Testamentum* 5 (1955): 34–76.

Muffs, Yohanan. "Who Will Stand in the Breach? A Study of Prophetic Intercession." Pages 9–48 in *Love and Joy: Law, Language, and Religion in Ancient Israel*. New York: Jewish Theological Seminary, 1992.

Naeh, Shlomo. "Did the Tannaim Interpret the Script of the Torah Differently from the Authorized Reading?" *Tarbiz* 61 (1992): 401–48. (Hebrew)

Newsom, Carol. *Daniel*. Old Testament Library. Louisville: Westminster John Knox, 2014.

————. *Songs of the Sabbath Sacrifice: A Critical Edition*. Atlanta: Scholars Press, 1985.

Nickelsberg, George. "Narrative Traditions in the Paralipomena of Jeremiah and 2 Baruch." *Catholic Biblical Quarterly* 35 (1973): 60–68.

Nihan, Christophe. "Cult Centralization and the Torah Traditions in Chronicles." Pages 253–88 in *The Fall of Jerusalem and the Rise of the Torah*. Edited by Peter Dubovsky, Dominic Markl, and Jean-Pierre Sonnet. Forschungen zum Alten Testament 107. Tübingen: Mohr Siebeck, 2015.

————. *From Priestly Torah to Pentateuch*. Forschungen zum Alten Testament 25. Tübingen: Mohr Siebeck, 2007.

Noordtzij, Arie. *Leviticus*. Grand Rapids: Zondervan, 1982.

Noth, Martin. *Leviticus: A Commentary*. Old Testament Library. Philadelphia: Westminster, 1977.

Oppenheim, A. Leo. *Ancient Mesopotamia*. Chicago: University of Chicago Press, 1964.

Owczarek, Susanne. *Die Vorstellung vom Wohnen Gottes inmitten seines Volkes in der Priesterschrift: Zur Heiligtumstheologie der priesterschriftlichen Grundschrift, Europäische Hochschulschriften*. Frankfurt am Main: Lang, 1998.

Partridge, Loren. *Michelangelo: The Sistine Ceiling, Rome*. New York: George Braziller, 1996.

Pearce, Laurie. "Cuneiform Cryptography: Numeric Substitutions for Syllabic and Logographic Signs." PhD dissertation. Yale University, 1982.

Pelikan, Jaroslav. *The Melody of Theology: A Philosophical Dictionary*. Cambridge: Harvard University Press, 1988.

Pola, Thomas. *Ursprüngliche Priesterschrift: Beobachtungen zur Literarkritik und Traditionsgeschichte von P^g*. Neukirchen-Vluyn: Neukirchener Verlag, 1995.

Price, Martin, and Bluma Trell. *Coins and Their Cities: Architecture on the Ancient Coins of Greece, Rome, and Palestine*. Detroit: Wayne State University Press, 1977.

Propp, William. *Exodus 19–40*. Anchor Bible 2A. New York: Doubleday, 2006.

Rendtorff, Rolf. *Canon and Theology: Overtures to an Old Testament Theology*. Minneapolis: Fortress, 1993.

———. *Leviticus 1,1–10,20*. Biblischer Kommentar Altes Testament 3/1. Neukirchen-Vluyn: Neukirchener Verlag, 2004.

Richter, Georg. "Die Fleischwerdung des Logos im Johannesevangelium." *Novum Testamentum* 13 (1971): 81–126 and 14 (1972): 257–76.

Römer, Thomas. "Redaction Criticism: 1 Kings 8 and the Deuteronomists." Pages 63–76 in *Method Matters: Essays on the Interpretation of the Hebrew Bible in Honor of David L. Peterson*. Edited by Joel LeMon and Kent Richards. Atlanta: Society of Biblical Literature, 2009.

Rost, Leonhard. *The Succession to the Throne of David*. Translated by Michael D. Rutter and David M. Gunn. Sheffield: Almond, 1982.

Rowe, C. Kavin. "Biblical Pressure and Trinitarian Hermeneutics." *Pro Ecclesia* 9 (2002): 295–312.

Ruwe, Andreas. "Das Reden und Verstummen Aarons vor Mose: Levitikus 9–10 im Buch Leviticus." Pages 169–96 in *Behutsames Lesen: Alttestamentliche Exegese im interdisziplinären Methodendiskurs. Christof Hardmeier zum 65. Geburtstag*. Edited by Sylke Lubs, Louis Jonker, Andreas Ruwe, and Uwe Weise. Leipzig: Evangelische Verlagsanstalt, 2007.

———. "The Structure of the Book of Leviticus in the Narrative Outline of the Priestly Sinai Story (Exod 19:1–Num 10:10*)." Pages 55–78 in *The Book of Leviticus: Composition and Reception*. Edited by Rolf Rendtorff and Robert A. Kugler. Vetus Testamentum Supplement 93. Leiden: Brill, 2002.

Schafer, B. E. "Sabbath." Page 760 in *The Interpreter's Dictionary of the Bible, Supplementary Volume*. Nashville: Abingdon, 1976.

Schäfer, Peter. "Tempel und Schöpfung." *Kairos* 16 (1974): 122–33.

Schiffman, L. "The Furnishings of the Temple according to the Temple Scroll." Pages 621–34 in *The Madrid Qumran Congress: Proceedings of the International Congress on the Dead Sea Scrolls*. Edited by Luis Vegas Montaner and Julio Trebolle Barrera. Leiden: Brill, 1992.

Schmid, Konrad. "Abraham's Sacrifice: Gerhard von Rad's Interpretation of Genesis 22." *Interpretation* 62 (2008): 268–76.

Schwartz, Daniel. "Viewing the Holy Utensils (P. Ox V,840)." *New Testament Studies* 32 (1986): 153–59.

Seitz, Christopher. *The Elder Testament: Canon, Theology, Trinity*. Waco, TX: Baylor University Press, 2018.

———. *Word without End: The Old Testament as Abiding Theological Witness*. Grand Rapids: Eerdmans, 1998.

Selz, Gebhard. "The Holy Drum, the Spear, and the Harp: Towards an Understanding of the Problems of Deification in the Third Millennium Mesopotamia." Pages 167–213 in *Sumerian Gods and Their Representations*. Edited by Irving L. Finkel and Markham J. Geller. Gröningen: Styx, 1997.

Shama, Avraham. "Two Thematic Tendencies in the Dedication of the Tabernacle and Their Reflection in the Laws of Sacrifice." *Megadim* 2 (1997): 32–44. (Hebrew)

Shinan, Avigdor. "The Sin of Nadab and Abihu in Rabbinic Literature." *Tarbiz* 48 (1978–1979): 201–14. (Hebrew)

Skehan, Patrick, and Alexander di Lella, *The Wisdom of ben Sira*. Anchor Bible, 39. New York: Doubleday, 1987.

Sommer, Benjamin. *The Bodies of God and the World of Ancient Israel*. Cambridge: Cambridge University Press, 2009.

Steins, Georg. *Die "Bindung Isaaks" im Kanon (Gen 22)*. Freiburg: Herder, 1999.

———. "'Sie sollen mir ein Heiligtum machen': Zur Struktur und Entstehung von Ex 24,12–31,18." Pages 145–67 in *Vom Sinai zum Horeb: Stationen alttestamentlicher Glaubensgeschichte*. Edited by Frank-Lothar Hossfeld. Würzburg: Echter, 1989.

Tigay, Jeffrey. "Some Aspects of Prayer in the Bible." *Association of Jewish Studies Review* 1 (1976): 363–79.

Toeg, Aryeh. "Genesis 1 and the Sabbath." *Beit Miqra* 50 (1972): 288–96. (Hebrew)

———. *The Giving of the Torah at Sinai*. Jerusalem: Magnes, 1977. (Hebrew)

Toorn, Karel van der. "Worshipping Stones: On the Deification of Cult Symbols." *Journal of Northwest Semitic Languages* 23 (1997): 1–14.

Turner, Denys. *The Darkness of God: Negativity in Christian Mysticism*. Cambridge: Cambridge University Press, 1995.

Utzschneider, Helmut. *Das Heiligtum und das Gesetz: Studien zur Bedeutung der sinaitischen Heiligtumstexte (Ex 25–40; Lev 8–9)*. Freiburg im Üchtland: Universitätsverlag, 1988.

———. "Tabernacle." Pages 267–301 in *The Book of Exodus: Composition, Reception, and Interpretation*. Edited by Thomas B. Dozeman, Craig A. Evans, and Joel N. Lohr. Leiden: Brill, 2014.

Valeri, Valerio. *Kingship and Sacrifice*. Chicago: University of Chicago Press, 1985.

VanderKam, James. *Jubilees: A Commentary in Two Volumes*. Minneapolis: Fortress, 2018.

Watts, J. W. *Leviticus 1–10*. Historical Commentary on the Old Testament. Leuven: Peeters, 2013.

———. *Ritual and Rhetoric in Leviticus: From Sacrifice to Scripture*. Cambridge: Cambridge University Press, 2007.

Wawrykow, Joseph. "The Holy Spirit in the Eucharistic Teaching of Thomas Aquinas." Unpublished manuscript.

Weimar, Peter. *Studien zur Priesterschrift*. Forschungen zum Alten Testament 56. Tübingen: Mohr Siebeck, 2008.

Weinfeld, Moshe. "Sabbath, Temple and the Enthronement of the Lord." Pages 501–12 in *Mélanges bibliques et orientaux en l'honneur de M. H. Cazelles*. Edited by André Caquot and Henri Cazelles. Neukirchen-Vluyn: Neukirchener Verlag, 1981.

Weiss, Zeev. *The Sepphoris Synagogue: Deciphering an Ancient Message through Its Archaeological and Socio-Historical Contexts*. Jerusalem: Israel Exploration Society, 2005.

Wenham, Gordon. *The Book of Leviticus*. New International Commentary on the Old Testament. Grand Rapids: Eerdmans, 1979.

Wilken, Robert. *The First Thousand Years: A Global History of Christianity*. New Haven: Yale University Press, 2012.

Williamson, H. G. *1 and 2 Chronicles*. New Century Bible Commentary. Grand Rapids: Eerdmans, 1982.

———. "1 Esdras." In *Eerdmans Commentary on the Bible*. Edited by James D. G. Dunn and John Rogerson. Grand Rapids: Eerdmans, 2003.

Winter, Irene. "The Eyes Have It: Votive Statuary, Gilgamesh's Axe, and Cathected Viewing in the Ancient Near East." Pages 22–44 in *Visuality before and beyond the Renaissance: Seeing as Others Saw*. Edited by Robert Nelson. Cambridge: Cambridge University Press, 2000.

Wright, Benjamin G. *No Small Difference: Sirach's Relationship to Its Hebrew Parent Text*. Atlanta: Scholars Press, 1989.

Wyschogrod, Michael. "Incarnation." *Pro Ecclesia* 2 (1993): 208–15.

Yeago, David. "Crucified for Us under Pontius Pilate." Pages 87–105 in *Nicene Christianity: The Future for a New Ecumenism*. Edited by Christopher Seitz. Grand Rapids: Brazos, 2001.

Young, Frances M. *From Nicaea to Chalcedon*. London: SCM, 1983.

Zeitlin, Froma. "The Artful Eye: Vision, Ecphrasis and Spectacle in Euripidean Theatre." Pages 138–96 in *Art and Text in Ancient Greek Culture*. Edited by Simon Goldhill and Robin Osborne. Cambridge: Cambridge University Press, 1994.

Index of Authors

Index of Subjects

Advent, 188–89

altar, of the Jerusalem temple: altar fire, 21, 100, 171; dedication of, 10, 43n26; holiness of, 81, 171; wood for fire, 172–73

Antiochenes, 197–200

apophaticism, 134–40

Aqedah ("binding of Isaac"): as Abraham's self-sacrifice, 167n9, 220–22; and the calling of Abraham, 218–20; depiction of, in Sepphoris mosaic, 174–76; as foundation of temple sacrifice, 166–67, 182–83; and intercessory prayer of Moses, 162–65, 228; as meritorious, 164–65, 182, 224–25; repetition of promises by angel after, 163–65, 180, 224; and the tamid, 165–80

Arians/Arianism, 6–7, 193–94

ark of the covenant: Ark Narrative (Samuel), 121–22, 138–39; and being of God, 56–61, 63; capture of, by Philistines, 56–57; danger of seeing, 57–58; improper treatment of, 122–24

Artaxerxes, 40

Athanasius, 6–8, 193–94, 198, 212

atonement: inadequate representations of, in apparent tension with goodness of God, 210–11; as not the only purpose of sacrifice, 12, 89–91; through radical self-emptying of Christ, 226–28

Augustine, 205, 227–28

Babylon, 2, 4, 22, 40

Bar Kokhba revolt, 47, 65–66, 78

Cain and Abel, 138

canonical criticism: final form of text, 11, 108, 143–44, 159–60, 161, 217; importance of Old Testament for early church, 186–89, 191–94; relationship between Old and New Testaments, 1, 3–8, 21, 184–89, 204–9, 227–28; respecting independence of sources, 161–62

Chalcedon, Council of, 9, 190–91, 203–4, 209

Christ. *See* Jesus Christ

communicatio idiomatum, 200

Cyrus, 40

Darius, 40, 41

David, 56, 76, 98, 165, 203; and the ark of the covenant, 123–24

Day of Atonement, 101

deconstruction, 134–40

Mary, mother of Jesus: as the eschatological temple, 205–6; and the Jerusalem temple, 200–209; perpetual virginity of, 205n38, 208n43; and relationship between Old and New Testaments, 204–5; transformation by indwelling of God in her, 201; use of temple language to describe, 202–4; veneration of, 207–9

materials, physical: close connection to identity of God, 59–61, 74–75, 196–97; quality of, as indication of degree of sanctity, 12–16, 54; repeated lists of, as *ekphrasis*, 70–75. *See also* incarnation, of Jesus

Mekhilta de Rabbi Ishamel, 96

memorial (representation): Eucharist as memorial of Jesus's sacrifice, 224–25; tamid as memorial of Aqedah, 177–78, 183, 218; in Tobit and Acts, 178. *See also* Eucharist; tamid

Mesopotamia, ancient: acquiring a great name in, 220; architecture, 73; beatitude after dedication of temples in, 103–5; creation myths of, 22; and the number seven, 25, 28; sacred furniture, 59–60

Michelangelo, 5, 206, 209

Mishnah, 84, 86–87, 100

Nestorius, 198–200, 204

Nicea, Council of, 6, 9, 199, 212

Nisan (month), first of, 20–21, 36, 39–43, 46nn33–34, 48

Noah, 69

Origen, 187–88, 224

Pompey, 64–65

Pontifical Biblical Commission, 188

Priestly author/source, 103, 143–47; transitional verses added between sources, 145–47, 162–63, 180

Protevangelium of James, 44–45, 203–4

Pseudo-Philo, 39

Qumran, 61–62

rabbis, 21, 102, 128, 165–67, 177–78

Rashbam, 105, 128

Rashi, 139

sacred furniture: danger of seeing, 57–58, 195–96; danger of touching, 55–56; public display of, in liturgy, 63–66, 75; tradition of hiding before Babylonian destruction, 58n9, 196. *See also* ark of the covenant; materials, physical

"sacred time," 10, 19, 43–48

sacrifice/sacrifices: consumption of, by divine fire, 20, 36; as divine-human reciprocity, 97–98; as "feeding" of deity, 91–92; inauguration of, 77–78; more than means of atonement, 12, 89–91, 214–16; paradoxical outcome of, 182–83, 222–23; as self-sacrifice, 95, 167, 173; as thanksgiving, 76, 98; violation of laws governing, 106, 116, 118. *See also* Eucharist; memorial (representation); tamid

Samaritan Pentateuch, 62–63

Seforno, 128

Septuagint, 62–63

seven, number, as symbol of completion, 25–33, 37–38, 156

Index of Scripture and Other Ancient Texts